# Mastering Change

## Introduction to Organizational Therapy
A Universal Applied Theory on
How to Lead Change for Exceptional Results
with Collaborative Leadership

Expanded and Revised Edition, 2015

Ichak Kalderon Adizes, Ph.D.
Founder and President, Adizes Institute
Santa Barbara County, California

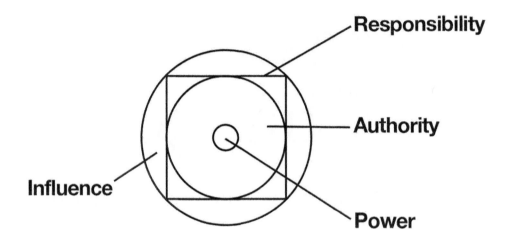

# ADDITIONAL BOOKS BY THE AUTHOR

1. Adizes, I. *Industrial Democracy: Yugoslav Style*. New York Free Press, 1971. Reprinted by Adizes Institute.
2. Adizes, I. and E. Mann-Borgese, eds. *Self-Management: New Dimensions to Democracy*. Santa Barbara, CA: ABC-CLIO, 1975. Reprinted by Adizes Institute.
3. Adizes, I. *How to Solve the Mismanagement Crisis*. Homewood, IL: Dow Jones/ Irwin, 1979. Reprinted by Adizes Institute.
4. Adizes, I. *Mastering Change: The Power of Mutual Trust and Respect in Personal Life, Family Life, Business & Society* (First Edition). Santa Barbara, CA: Adizes Institute, 1991.
5. Adizes, I. *Managing Corporate Lifecycles: An updated and expanded look at the Corporate Lifecycles* (First Edition). First printing, Paramus, NJ: Prentice Hall Press, 1999. Additional printings by the Adizes Institute Publications in two volumes: *Managing Corporate Lifecycles – How Organizations Grow, Age and Die*, Volume I. Santa Barbara, CA: The Adizes Institute Publications, in conjunction with Embassy Book Distributors, 2012. *Managing Corporate Lifecycles – Analyzing Organizational Behavior and Raising Healthy Organizations*, Volume 2. Santa Barbara, CA: The Adizes Institute Publications, 2015.
6. Adizes, I. *Pursuit of Prime*. First printing Santa Monica, CA: Knowledge Exchange, 1996. Additional printings by the Adizes Institute Publications.
7. Adizes, I. *The Ideal Executive: Why You Cannot Be One and What to Do About It*. Santa Barbara, CA: The Adizes Institute Publications, 2004.
8. Adizes, I. *Management/Mismanagement Styles: How to Identify a Style and What to Do About It*. Santa Barbara, CA: The Adizes Institute Publications, 2004.
9. Adizes, I. *Leading the Leaders: How to Enrich Your Style of Management and Handle People Whose Style Is Different from Yours*. Santa Barbara, CA: The Adizes Institute Publications, 2004.
10. Adizes, I. *How to Manage in Times of Crisis (And How to Avoid a Crisis in the First Place)*. Santa Barbara, CA: The Adizes Institute Publications, 2009.
11. Adizes, I. *Insights on Management*. Santa Barbara, CA: The Adizes Institute Publications, 2011.
12. Adizes, I. *Insights on Policy*. Santa Barbara, CA: The Adizes Institute Publications, 2011.
13. Adizes, I. *Insights on Personal Growth*. Santa Barbara, CA: The Adizes Institute Publications, 2011.
14. Adizes, I. *Food for Thought: On Management*. Santa Barbara, CA: The Adizes Institute Publications, 2013.
15. Adizes, I. *Food for Thought: On Change and Leadership*. Santa Barbara, CA: The Adizes Institute Publications, 2013.
16. Adizes, I. *Food for Thought: On What Counts in Life*. Santa Barbara, CA: The Adizes Institute Publications, 2013.
17. Adizes, I. *Insights on Management – II*. Santa Barbara, CA: The Adizes Institute Publications, 2014.
18. Adizes, I. *Insights on Policy – II*. Santa Barbara, CA: The Adizes Institute Publications, 2014.
19. Adizes, I. *Insights on Personal Growth – II*. Santa Barbara, CA: The Adizes Institute Publications, 2014.
20. Adizes, I. *Conversations with CEOs*. Santa Barbara, CA: The Adizes Institute Publications, 2015.

Dedicated to the
Certified Adizes Practitioners worldwide,
without whom the contents of this book
could not be a reality.

# CONTENTS

Acknowledgments ........................................................... vii
About the Author ........................................................... viii
Introduction to the New Edition ....................................... ix
Preface: Management, Executives, Leadership ................... xi

Conversations:

1. Change and Its Repercussions ....................................... 1
2. On Parenting, Management, or Leadership ................. 13
3. Predicting the Quality of Decisions ............................. 27
4. Efficiency and Effectiveness ......................................... 43
5. The Incompatibility of Roles ........................................ 75
6. Management, Leadership, and Mismanagement Styles ............... 99
7. What to Do About Change ......................................... 115
8. Responsibility, Authority, Power, and Influence ........ 135
9. Predicting the Efficiency of Implementing Decisions ................ 159
10. What Makes the Wheels Turn ................................... 185
11. How to Communicate with People
    Whose Style Is Different ........................................... 201
12. Perceiving Reality ..................................................... 223
13. Quality of People ..................................................... 233
14. How to Convert Committee Work into Teamwork ................. 253
15. The Adizes Program for Organizational Transformation ........ 269

About the Adizes Institute ............................................... 277

Adizes Institute Publications

MASTERING CHANGE: Copyright © 1992,
New edition 2015 by Ichak Kalderon Adizes

All rights reserved. No part of this book may be reproduced, in whole or in part, in any form or by any means, without the prior written permission of the publisher. All inquiries should be addressed to
The Adizes Institute, 1212 Mark Avenue, Carpinteria, California 93013
Printed in the United States of America  JO  9 8 7 6 5 4 3 2

Library of Congress Catalog Card Number: 91-76029
ISBN 978-0-937120-32-3

Adizes Institute Publications
Book design by Silverander Communications

# ACKNOWLEDGMENTS

The list of people who contributed to this book is quite long. I have been lecturing about this material for over forty years. It started as a small, simple model and it grew over time as people came forward and made remarks. Some disagreed and enriched me with their disagreements. Some reinforced my presentation and contributed anecdotes, jokes, case histories, even cartoons. Over time I realized that what was applicable to the organizations I was lecturing about applies to personal life too. When I was invited to speak to heads of state and their cabinets, the applicability of the material on the social-political plane became evident as well.

So, whom do I thank? Where do I start? Certain people stand out. First, my parents, who through their Sephardic Jewish wisdom taught me much about life. Outside my family, Mr. Vukadinovic, my first-grade teacher in Belgrade, Yugoslavia, stands out for a lesson I will not forget. I was an eight-year-old child saved from the Holocaust, in which most of my family perished. I was scared and timid. Another child in the class harassed me publicly with anti-Semitic insults. Mr. Vukadinovic put us both in front of the class and lectured us about brotherhood, how we look the same, yet still can enjoy the beauty of being different. He spoke about trust and respect. He had us sit at the same desk for the rest of the year, and my enemy became one of my best friends. (He perished during the NATO attack on Belgrade in 1999.)

Next I want to thank Yehuda Erel, my youth leader in the Israeli Noar La Noar youth movement. I came to Israel after World War II, looking for a home, full of fears of being rejected. He gave me roots and a sense of belonging by teaching me to serve others who were less fortunate than myself.

Then came my years of study in the United States. Professor William H. Newman of Columbia University taught me management theory, but more important than that, he taught me with

his open-mindedness and practical outlook on the management process, an approach to intellectual life which I try to emulate.

Not to be overlooked are Rosemary Sostarich, Adrienne Denny, the late Charles Mark (early edition) and Gene Lichtenstein who reedited this book, Emily See who did the copy editing, and Maya Korling and Carolyn Healey who "mother hen-ed" the new edition of this book. To all, thank you.


**Ichak Kalderon Adizes**
Santa Barbara, California, USA, 2015

# ABOUT THE AUTHOR
# ICHAK KALDERON ADIZES, PH.D.

Over the course of more than forty years, Dr. Ichak Kalderon Adizes has developed and refined a proprietary methodology that bears his name that enables corporations, governments, and complex organizations to accomplish exceptional results and manage accelerated change without destructive conflicts. *Leadership Excellence Journal* named him one of the Top 30 Thought Leaders in the United States, and *Executive Excellence Journal* put him on their list of the Top 30 Consultants in America.

In recognition of his contributions to management theory and practice, Dr. Adizes has received twenty honorary doctorates from universities in ten countries; is honorary Chancellor of the University of Fredricton, Canada; received the 2010 Ellis Island Medal of Honor and an honorary rank of lieutenant colonel from the military; and has been made an honorary citizen of two Eastern European countries.

Dr. Adizes is a Fellow of the International Academy of Management; has served as a tenured faculty member at UCLA and a visiting professor at Stanford, Tel Aviv, and Hebrew Universities; and taught at the Columbia University Executive Program. He also is the founder of the Adizes Graduate School for the Study of Collaborative Leadership and Constructive Change, and is currently an academic advisor to the Graduate School of Management of the Academy of National Economy of the Russian Federation.

Dr. Adizes is founder and president of the Adizes Institute, based in Santa Barbara, California, an international consulting company that applies the Adizes Methodology for clients in the public and private sectors. The Adizes Institute was ranked as one of the top ten consulting organizations in the United States by *Leadership Excellence Journal*.

In addition to consulting to prime ministers and cabinet-level officials throughout the world, Dr. Adizes has worked with a wide variety of companies ranging from startups to members of the Fortune 50. He lectures in four languages, and has appeared before well over 100,000 executives in more than fifty countries.

Dr. Adizes has authored more than 20 books, which have been published in 26 languages. His book *Corporate Lifecycles: How Organizations Grow and Die and What to Do About It* (subsequently revised, expanded, and republished as *Managing Corporate Lifecycles*) was named one of the Ten Best Business Books by *Library Journal*.

Dr. Adizes lives in Santa Barbara County, California, with his wife, Nurit Manne Adizes. They have six grown-up children. In his leisure time he enjoys playing the accordion and practicing meditation.

# INTRODUCTION TO THE NEW EDITION

This book was first written in 1992, more than twenty years ago. Since then I have lectured to more than 100,000 executives, consulted to leaders of countries, and published twenty more books. In other words, I have gained more experience.

In every country I lectured I learned something new. I have lectured or consulted in over fifty countries. I made it a point to respond to any invitation from a new country no matter how far, how developed or underdeveloped, so I could test my methodology and philosophy of life. And I learned a lot. I started to realize that I was not teaching only about business; that my philosophy applies to how a country needs to be led, and to family as well as personal life. A universal theory of how to manage change evolved and made the first edition of this book in need of updating.

There was another development that called for a rewrite of the first edition. Universities started teaching Adizes, so it was time to also make this book a textbook. A manual for instructors was developed and is available to those who seek it.

Over forty-plus years, I have developed a theory—a philosophy—about how to lead change, but it did not remain just a well-developed concept. I have personally applied what I teach and when I succeeded in producing the desired results, I have documented the theory in manuals, taught others, and monitored whether they had the same success in producing exceptional economic and behavioral results. When they did, with over hundreds of companies of all sizes, there was the proof that the methodology is not an accumulation of well-meaning concepts, but a science: The same method can be repeated to achieve the same results. To be sure it is universal, I have opened Adizes offices in more than ten countries and compared results. This methodology is independent of cultural and industry bias, and it applies to business as well as to non-profit organizations.

I also opened a Graduate School licensed by the State of California to grant master's and doctoral degrees in this methodology for leading change, which is akin to organizational transformation. I consider it therapy, because the aim of the transformation is to make the organization healthy. What it means to be organizationally healthy and how the transformation is conducted will be discussed in the following pages. However, I consider this book just an introduction to organizational therapy. For a more complete treatment of the subject, one should read the rest of my books, especially *Managing Corporate Lifecycles*, which discusses which problems are normal and which abnormal.

In this book I use the Socratic method of conversation to convey the material because it gave me maximum flexibility to communicate. I hope you find this book easy to read and entertaining, and its teachings worth applying.

— Ichak Kalderon Adizes, Ph.D.
Santa Barbara, California. 2015

# PREFACE
# Management, Executives, Leadership...

Over the years I have observed how the concept of solving problems for organizations has changed its name. First it was called administration. The first journal in the field was *Administrative Science Quarterly* and schools that trained corporate and organizational leaders were called Graduate Schools of Business *Administration*. The degree granted, MBA, still stands for Master in Business *Administration*.

When business administration programs did not produce the desired results, the concept of administration was relegated to a lower rank within the organization. Administrators just coordinated and supervised, and a new concept emerged: management. Gradually at first, and then rapidly, schools changed their name to Graduate School of Management.

Apparently that did not work well either, and management was relegated to the middle level of organizations. It lost its appeal and a new word was needed: executive. Graduate programs for executives and the concept of Chief Executive Officer were born.

That shift did not produce the desired results either, so recently a new theory appeared: leadership. Books are now published describing how leadership is different from management.

I believe "leadership" is just another fad. Soon, we will have another buzzword.

Why? Because we are searching for an all-encompassing concept that will cover the skills necessary for running an organization. We are all looking for a model that will describe and identify the specific kind of person who can provide the functions an organization needs so that it is effective and efficient in both the short and the long term, and that person simply does not exist.

The mistake in this way of thinking lies in the expectation: All the roles are expected to be performed by a single individual, whether he is called the administrator, the manager, the executive, or, now, the leader. In reality, one person, even someone extraordinary, can perform only one or, at most, two of the roles required to manage/lead an organization.

In this book, "leadership," "executive action," and "management process" are one and the same for me, because they follow the same wrong paradigm. The paradigm assumes that a single individual can make any organization function effectively and efficiently in both the short and long term, whether that person is called leader or manager or chief administrator or just chief.

Let me make the point clearly: An individual who can make decisions that will cause an organization to be effective and efficient in the short and long term does not and cannot exist. The roles that produce those results are internally incompatible. The ideal executive does not exist.

We are still trying to develop and train and create this elusive perfect executive/manager/leader. It cannot happen. It will not happen. It has never happened. Our management education needs revamping, and our managerial culture needs redirecting.

A single leader, no matter how functional, will eventually become dysfunctional. Over time, as the organization changes its location on the lifecycle, proceeding from early success to a booming position within the corporate field, that single executive will falter. The qualities that made her successful in the past can be the reason for failing in the future.

Building a company requires a complementary team. It needs collaborative leadership, a team of leaders who differ in their styles yet complement one another.

But here is the problem: A complementary team, since it is, by definition, composed of different styles, generates conflict. So, although conflict is good, although it is necessary and indispensable, it can be destructive and dysfunctional.

What is needed to avoid this potential dysfunctional and destructive conflict is collaborative leadership based on Mutual Trust and Respect.

This book provides a paradigm shift in how to successfully manage for exceptional, sustainable, results. Hundreds of testimonials are available, some on www.adizes.com, of companies that use the methodology described in this book. Or one can read my book *Conversations with CEOs: Adizes Methodology in Practice*.

Let us begin.

# XVIII – MASTERING CHANGE

*One afternoon I was talking with an executive of one of the companies for which I was consulting. He wanted to know the theoretical framework that I had developed that enabled me to teach and lecture worldwide, and to help CEOs of major companies implement strategic changes in their organizations rapidly and successfully, and without destructive conflict. He asked if I would take the time to talk about my field of expertise. As we talked, exchanging questions and answers, this book took shape in my mind.*

# CONVERSATION 1
# Change and Its Repercussions

*Hello.*

Hi.

*I understand that you have been studying the process of management and leadership for more than fifty years. What is it? What does it mean to you?*

We first need to define what the word manage means. Later we will define leadership and discuss the differences.

## The Traditional Theory of Management

I've found that in various languages, such as Swedish, the Slavic languages, and Spanish too, the concept "to manage" does not have a literal translation. In those languages, words like *direct*, *lead*, or *administer* are often used instead. In Spanish, for example, the word *manejar*, the literal translation for manage, means "to handle" and is used only when referring to horses or cars.

When other languages want to say "manage" in the American sense of the word, they use *direct* or *administer*, or they use the American word *management*.

Take the French language: They insist on using only French words but when it comes to "management" they use the English word. They have no literal translation. And Russians, although they try to distance themselves from the USA, nevertheless use the English word *management* too.

# 2 – MASTERING CHANGE

I suggest to you that if there is no translation, the concept is not that clear. Moreover, the process is not universally applied; different countries manage differently.

In the Yugoslav self-management system of the 1960s, the managerial process, as it is practiced in the United States and taught in American business schools, was prohibited by law. If a manager made a unilateral decision for a company, he could be prosecuted. It would be considered a negation of the industrial democratic process that was required by law. A manager had to suggest, while the workers decided. In this system they applied the principles of democracy at the enterprise level. The same is true in Israeli kibbutzim, communal self-managed organizations. The secretary of a kibbutz, who holds a managerial position, is periodically elected so that no one can claim permanence in governing others.

> *You mean the kibbutz secretaries manage for a while and then go back to milking the cows?*

Or back to serving in the dining room or washing dishes. Management is not a long-term, permanent appointment there, just as no democratically elected leadership is permanent. That would negate democracy. In a democracy, leadership—management—is not a profession. It is a calling.

> *What, then, is management, if some languages don't have a direct translation and some sociopolitical systems negate it, or practically forbid it? Would the synonyms in the dictionary provide a sufficient definition?*

Well, what synonyms would you suggest?

> *Decide, operate, plan, control, organize, rule, achieve goals, lead, motivate, accomplish...*

In several dictionaries the synonyms for manage are the ones you have mentioned. There are other intriguing synonyms, like dominate and govern, from the American Collegiate Dictionary. The Oxford Dictionary adds manipulate and connive.

> *I do not feel comfortable with the synonyms manipulate and connive.*

I do not blame you, but there is a reason why those synonyms exist. Let's analyze the common denominator shared by all the synonyms you have mentioned, excluding, for a moment, manipulate and connive. Imagine the process described by each of these synonyms; animate their meaning. Can you identify the common denominator? Operate...plan...control...organize...rule...achieve...accomplish.

*They are all a one-way process. The managing person is telling the managed person what to do. The manager determines what should be done and the managed person is expected to carry it out. Abide.*

That's why we call a manager the "head" of the department, and a valued subordinate is called the "right hand." The right hand does exactly what the head tells it to do, while the left hand behaves as if it had a will of its own. It is not fully controllable.

*But managers are also called supervisors.*

> The managerial process, or leadership, is not a value-free process. It is not only a science and an art, but also an expression of sociopolitical values.

Because a supervisor is supposed to have superior vision. Look at the insignia for military officers. You can compare the progressive ranks represented by United States military insignia to climbing a tree and then ascending to the sky. The lieutenants have bars representing the branches of a tree. The captain has more bars; he is going up the tree. The major has a leaf representing the top of the tree. Then the colonel soars like an eagle, and the general has a star. The higher they go up the organizational hierarchy, the better their vision should be.

*So?*

The problem with such a frame of mind is the lowliness of the subordinates. The lower they are on the tree, the less they can see and can be expected to know. Listen to the word: subordinates. They are sub-ordinary.

*You mean to say that the words connote that the manager is superior and the subordinates are inferior?*

In Hebrew, subordinates are literally called "bent," *kfufeem*, as if the managers had bent them to the desired mold.

*I never paid attention to this connotation. What is the cause of this?*

The managerial process, or leadership, as it is taught and practiced, is not a value-free process. It is not only a science and an art, but also an expression of sociopolitical values. It is a value-loaded political process, and it originates with the patriarchic family, I believe.

# 4 – MASTERING CHANGE

*But what about the word motivate? Does not this synonym redeem the process of management from what appears to be its hierarchical, one-way-street connotation?*

In the context of management as superior and those reporting to him or her as subordinates, where the manager decides and then has to motivate sub-ordinary people to execute his or her wishes, what would you say is the meaning of *motivate*?

*As a manager or leader, I know what I want the subordinates to do. My challenge is finding the way to motivate them to do what I have already unilaterally decided. If I can't control them, maybe I can motivate them to do what I want them to do; they have no say, they should just execute my decisions willingly.*

What does that sound like?

*Manipulation.*

Right! I remember a cartoon in the *New Yorker* magazine. A mother who is a psychologist is trying to convince her son to take out the trash. Wearily, the boy says, "Okay, okay! I'll take out the trash, but pleeeease, Mom, don't try to motivate me." Even the child sees motivation as a manipulation. What he must do has already been decided. It's only a matter of how to make him do it.

*I can see now why some labor unions often oppose programs such as job enrichment or enlargement, which management uses to "motivate" workers. Unions view these programs as ploys to increase productivity and profitability for the good of management and stockholders. The only benefit to the workers is that they may keep their jobs.*

The same connotation of manipulation comes up in the synonym *to lead*. Some theories of leadership, if you read them carefully, present the leadership function as the way to make the followers follow enthusiastically a decision that was already made. Note this quote from Dwight Eisenhower as an example: "Leadership is the art of getting someone else to do something that you want done, because he wants to do it." Notice that the decision has been made. The followers should be happy to implement the decision as if it was theirs to make. That can be seen as a manipulation, no?

In some industries, management is a dirty word. In the fine arts, in the United States, it is often synonymous with exploitation. Soon, I believe, if the paradigm does not change the same will happen with the concept of leadership.

*So, what do you suggest?*

# The Nature of Change

We have to understand the role of management, or the leadership role, by the function it performs: why do we need it? The function should be value-free, without any sociopolitical or cultural biases and applicable to any organization, in any industry, of any size, on any level—micro, mezzo, or macro—and with whatever goals the organization might have, for profit or not for profit.

> The more change, the more problems we will have.

It should be the same, whether we are managing ourselves, our family, a business, a non-profit organization, or leading a nation. Whether we speak of managing, leading, parenting, or governing, it should be one and the same process conceptually. It should be a universal theory of management, of leadership.

*This sounds very ambitious. Where do we start?*

Do you agree with one thing, that change is constant? The process has been going on since the beginning of time and will continue forever. The world is changing physically, socially, and economically. Even you are changing this very minute. Change is here to stay.

*Yes?*

Change creates problems. Because what is change? Something new has emerged. Now we have to decide what to do about it and then we have to implement that decision.

Since it is a new phenomenon or event, we cannot have all the information we might want to have. Thus, to decide about something new means that there is uncertainty. If we implement the decision there is risk: It might not work as well as we wanted.

Making decisions under uncertainty and implementing them, which entails risk, is a problem. We scratch our head: What should we do (uncertainty) and should we do it (risk)? Thus we consider a new phenomenon that impacts us as "a problem."

The more change, the more problems we will have.

Now let us assume we did decide, and implemented our decision. What happens now? We had a solution and implemented it. Right?

# 6 – MASTERING CHANGE

Notice that our solution created change, too. We can diagram the sequence like this:

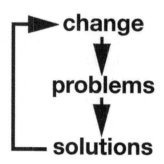

Now, looking at the diagram, if change is here to stay, what else is here to stay?

*Problems.*

And the greater the quantity and velocity of the changes, the greater the quantity and complexity of the problems we will have.

> The greater the quantity and velocity of the changes, the greater the quantity and complexity of the problems we will have.

*Right. Email and computer systems were supposed to increase our effectiveness and efficiency of work. But instead of having less work to do I have more work, more problems that face me even faster than before.*

I have the same experience. Change is accelerating, and the environment is becoming increasingly overlapping, and interdependent. A technological change can have an almost instantaneous impact on the economic or social or even political environment. Take the internet, which was a technological innovation. It impacted how retail works so it had economic repercussions. But it was also used to mobilize people to demonstrate. It had political repercussions. It also has social repercussions: how people find another person to date. . . . The environment we operate in is becoming more and more complex. Simple solutions do not work anymore. For complex problems we need complex solutions.

Furthermore change is accelerating. If our grandparents made one strategic decision in a lifetime, and our parents, let's say, every ten or fifteen years, we are making strategic decisions every five years, and our children will have to make them annually. Life is becoming increasingly stressful.

> The higher the standard of living, the lower the quality of life.

> Every problem can be an opportunity in disguise and every opportunity can be a problem in disguise.

*In my travels, I hear more laughter in one day in a developing country than in a whole year in a developed country. The more developed, the more so-called advanced, a country, it seems the less time is there for people to just laugh and enjoy life. They are all stressed.*

Yes, it seems that the higher the standard of living, the lower the quality of life. It all has to do with the velocity of change.

*But not all events caused by change are "problems." Some are opportunities.*

Absolutely so. Interesting that in the Chinese language the word *problem* or *threat* and the word *opportunity* are one and the same word: *wēijī*, 危机. This means every problem can be an opportunity in disguise and every opportunity can be a problem in disguise.

Have you ever had a problem that, by the time you solved it, you learned a lot and became much stronger because of it? That problem was really an opportunity to learn. And I am sure there were times when you saw an opportunity and tried to capitalize on it, and this opportunity turned out to be a major problem for you.

All opportunities are a response to a problem. There would not have been opportunities if there were no problems. The problems your competition has are your opportunity. And the problems you have in your company are an opportunity for your competition. But if you are smart and understand this, then why should your problems be opportunities for your competition. Why not see them as your opportunity to improve your company, to learn from your problems?

Every problem is an opportunity to learn and improve. Problems and opportunities are one and the same thing. It depends how we look at them. As we will discuss later, it has much to do with personality. For some people a problem is an opportunity; for others an opportunity is a problem.

It is all up to you whether the new event caused by change is an opportunity or a problem. It all depends on your frame of mind and on how you handle the event. Since problems are the same as opportunities, I translate the Chinese word *wēijī* to English, literarily, as oppor-threat.

## 8 – MASTERING CHANGE

*This reminds me of a joke I read in a book by Osho, the Indian philosopher:*

*A man goes to a mental hospital, and walking down the corridor sees a man in a room tearing his hair and crying: "Natasha, Natasha."*

*So he asked, "What happened to him?"*

*"He fell in love with Natasha. She left him and he lost his mind."*

*Our man continues walking down that corridor, and a few rooms later there is another guy, now even more distraught: "Natasha, Natasha." Banging his head against the wall.*

*"What about this guy?" asks our visitor.*

*"Ah, he married Natasha…"*

> We will stop encountering problems only when there is no more change.

Notice the following: Whenever we decide and implement our decision to solve a problem, we are causing more change. We are the source of change too. The change can come from the outside or the inside, caused by our own decisions. And that has repercussions.

If change is here to stay—it has been here forever and will stay here a bit longer—what else is here to stay forever?

*Problems and opportunities.*

Yes. The point is that people should not expect to permanently solve all problems. As long as there is change, it will not happen. It cannot happen. When one set of problems is solved, a new generation of problems will emerge. We will stop encountering problems only when there is no more change, and that will happen only when we are…

*Dead.*

Right! Living means solving problems, and growing up means being able to solve bigger problems. "Big" people deal with big problems. "Small" people (in spirit) deal with small problems. The more change, the more problems the system will have, whether we are talking about a human being, a marriage, a company, or a country.

> The purpose of management, leadership, parenting, or governing is exactly that: to manage change.

Having fewer problems is not a sign of growing but of dying. A young child has a lot of problems. A very old person who is dying has only one problem: how to stay alive.

*And the more change, the more stress.*

Yes. There is a psychological test for stress. You are supposed to fill out a form and for every event you note how many points of stress it gives you. For example, being fired: so many points; death in the family: so many points...going on vacation: so many points. What is the common denominator to all those events?

*Change!*

The purpose of management, leadership, parenting, or governing is exactly that: to manage change. To solve today's problems that were generated in the past and get ready to deal with future problems we create with our decisions today. No management is needed when there are no problems, and there are no problems only when we are...

*Dead.*

To manage is to be alive, and to be alive means to experience change with the accompanying problems it brings.

*To lead, manage, parent, govern a nation...means to solve problems caused by change.*

If you are not managing change—that is, solving problems caused by change—you are not managing. You are not leading. That is the essence of management, of leadership, of parenting, and of governing.

*So the anarchist political theory that tries to eliminate government and management is utopian.*

# 10 – MASTERING CHANGE

I think so.

Change can be your friend or your foe. Here is a story you might want to remember: My friend Peter Shutz, when he was appointed president of the Porsche car company, he visited all the departments of the company. When he was at the engineering department he asked those there if Porsche competes at Le Mans, which is a premier car-racing event where Porsche, a sports car company, should compete.

"We don't," they said.

"We should and next year we should win, and I rely on you to make that happen," he said.

The engineering department worked around the clock, designed and tested a racing car. The company went to the races and won. Big celebration.

The next day they found that the racing committee had changed the rules for next year's competition and they had to go back to the drawing board all over again. The engineers were depressed.

> If there is no change the mediocre eventually catch up.

Peter responded with a sentence, which I believe should be a mantra repeated by all executives: "If there is no change the mediocre eventually catch up."

Change is the best thing that can happen for a well-managed company. Change enables the well-managed company to distance itself from the poorly managed competition because it deals with change better.

Change is an opportunity for the well-managed and a problem, sometimes even a fatal problem, for the poorly managed organization.

*Change fast or die slowly.*

I repeat: Whether you are managing your own life or a company or a department, leading, governing, parenting, whatever…you have to decide and implement your decisions to deal with change, and since change is constant, this role we call management or leadership is constant too and cannot be eliminated.

How well you manage depends on how effective your decisions are and how efficiently you implement them.

# The Origin of Problems (Opportunities)

*Is there an underlying reason why problems or opportunities emerge with change?*

Everything you see around you is a system. By *system* I mean that there is interdependency in and in between everything in this world. Even the stars are interdependent.

Now, every system is composed of subsystems, which are composed again of their own subsystems, down to the nano level, and even there I believe there are yet more subsystems we will discover in time.

> Problems are manifestations of disintegration.

*So?*

When there is change, the subsystems do not advance, change, in synchronicity. Some change faster than others.

Take yourself as an example, or any other human being. You are a system composed of subsystems: You have the physical subsystem, the intellectual subsystem, the emotional subsystem, and the spiritual subsystem. They do not necessarily change in synchronicity. You might be physically 40 years old, intellectually much older because of life experiences and education, but emotionally you are still a teenager, and spiritually not born yet.

You see what might happen? There will be cracks in the system. You are "not together." Those cracks are manifested by what we call problems.

Problems are manifestations of...

*Disintegration.*

That is why when someone has too many problems we say he is falling apart, he is coming unglued. And when we are impressed with someone or a system we say this person has it all together, or this family has it all together, or this country has it all together.

Integration is the sign of health, disintegration of a malady. All problems are caused by disintegration caused by change. Show me a high rate of change and I will show you significant signs of disintegration. A house on the beach needs more maintenance than a house in the mountains. Why? The beach house is subject to more changing weather.

Any problem we might have—I repeat, any problem, whether it is a medical problem or a problem in our marriage, or that our car does not start, or there is a crime in our neighborhood—is caused by disintegration: Something has fallen apart because of change.

## 12 – MASTERING CHANGE

You go to the doctor to complain about some pain you have. What does the doctor ask you? "When did it start?" What is he looking for? What has changed? What has fallen apart?

Your car does not start? The mechanic will try to find out what has broken apart, disintegrated.

> To diagnose a problem ask yourself what has changed. What has fallen apart?

You have a problem with your spouse? Your marriage is "falling apart." The disintegration, most probably, is caused by something that has changed. Maybe the change is a new child, a new job, or new needs that were dormant until now. Who knows? But one thing is for sure: Something has fallen apart. Something has changed.

To diagnose a problem ask yourself what has changed. What has fallen apart?

*The ongoing problem the Western world has with Muslim terrorists then is a manifestation of disintegration caused by change.*

I think so. Modern society has advanced technologically, politically, and socially, and some parts of the world do not accept those changes. Like the changing role of women in society, for example. But notice it is not only a reaction of fanatic Muslims; all religions have fanatics who resist change.

*But is there a system, a process for how to manage change that works? Change without destructive forces? I notice people hate change, or they support change as long as nothing changes. I think that they want the benefits of change without the pain of change.*

That is what I have spent over fifty years studying and testing in over fifty-two countries with companies of every size, including the largest on earth, and with governments as well. That is what this conversation, as an introduction to the subject, aims to do.

*I can't wait.*

# CONVERSATION 2
# On Parenting, Management, or Leadership

*Previously we discussed that management theory, as taught in the USA and propagated around the world, is not value-free. Quite the opposite, it is a manifestation of the American culture of individualism and elitism, management being a class of people different from workers, subordinates.*

Yes.

> Not to decide is to decide not to decide.

*Furthermore, you claim that management is needed because there is change. If there were no change there would be no need for management. But then we would be dead, because change is life.*

*You also said that change produces problems and opportunities, and whether they are problems or opportunities it is up to us, and you will tell us how to convert problems into opportunities.*

I suggest that managing change involves two processes. First, you must decide what to do, and then you have to implement your decisions. Would you agree that to decide and not to implement is useless?

*But some people cannot decide. They feel they do not have enough information or they are scared of the risks involved.*

Notice: Not to decide is to decide not to decide. You are actually deciding by default. Assume you are in front of an intersection. That is a change, a new phenomenon on the road. You have to decide what to do: left, right, or go back. Assume you cannot decide for the reasons you spelled out before. What happens now? By default you have decided to stay in place. You decided not to decide.

*That could be the worst decision of them all.*

You are right. Will Rogers said it best, and I am paraphrasing: Even if you are on the right road, if you do not move, a truck can run you over.

When there is change, there is no way to avoid deciding and then implementing that decision.

For managing well, both processes are necessary, and together they are sufficient. So our diagram of the leadership process looks like this:

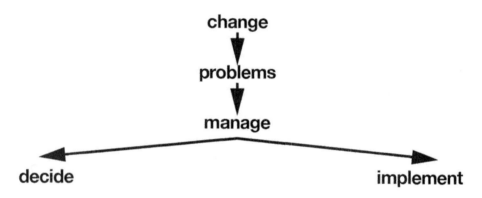

These processes—deciding and implementing—are value-free. You can apply them to manage anything from a criminal underworld to a community of saints. Whenever there is change, you must make decisions and you must carry out those decisions.

*But are both factors really necessary?*

As I have said, not deciding, or procrastinating, is a decision. You cannot escape the fact that whenever there is change, you must make a decision, or the change itself will de facto make the decision for you. And while making a decision is necessary, it is not sufficient. You also need to implement the decision.

> It is interesting that business schools, or schools of management, do not teach much, if anything, about implementation. All the courses are about how to make good decisions whether in marketing, finance, or economics. As if assuming that if the decision is a good one, it will be implemented.

As you will see soon, that explains to me why, in my experience, newly minted MBAs are a pain in the neck. Without experience they complain all day long about why their wonderful ideas do not get implemented. They need some scars on their knees to realize that good decisions, although they are very good, often do not get implemented and bad decisions do, and for a reason.

*Why?*

To manage well, you need both to make effective decisions (decisions that produce the desired results) and to implement them efficiently (with minimum energy possible).

$$\text{Quality of management} = f \begin{Bmatrix} \text{1. effectiveness of decisions} \\ \text{2. efficiency of implementation} \end{Bmatrix}$$

*You are right. Even a billion times zero is still zero. But I have a doubt: A decision is not a good one unless it includes a plan of implementation. Thus, all that is needed for managing is to make a complete decision, which should include the detailed plan of implementation, then implementation is nothing more than to do it.*

It's not so simple. Look at your personal life: How many decisions have you made that you never implemented? Even though you sat down and made a list of exactly what you would do—you even planned all the details of implementation—yet you still did not implement the decision.

Do you smoke? Maybe you overeat? Since you know these activities are bad for you, you've probably decided to change those habits. Yet you probably still go on behaving the same way despite having a detailed plan to implement change.

*You mean I'm not in control of my life?*

Are you? Have you implemented all the decisions you've made to change?

*No, I have not. For example, I'm still struggling with losing some weight. I've made the decision to change my diet many times, but have not succeeded in doing it so far. It's embarrassing.*

The same holds true for almost any organization. Management might decide to change direction, markets, product lines, or the culture of the organization. Often it will have great difficulty implementing the decisions, implementing the changes. The same phenomenon occurs in the governing of countries. Many leaders, even dictators, complain that their decisions involving change do not get implemented. For instance, Hitler could not force the implementation of his decision to burn Germany in front of the advancing Allied forces. His decision was never carried out, although he had total power to execute anyone who didn't follow his orders.

> *His order to destroy Paris was also ignored, although he could have executed those who disobeyed him. Even though he held power over their lives, people still did not follow his orders.*

> **The quality of the decision can neither predict nor assure the probability of implementation.**

Levi Eshkol, the Prime Minister of Israel, was criticized for not carrying out a certain decision. His response was, "I have committed to decide. I did not commit to implement."

I repeat again, the quality of the decision can neither predict nor assure the probability of implementation. Some decisions that require change, even if they are outstanding, do not get implemented; and some bad decisions get implemented swiftly.

*Why is that?*

Because the two processes—what makes for good decision making and what makes for good implementation—are incompatible. It's as if you are holding two books: One book tells you how to make good decisions, the other tells you how to implement decisions. For implementation, if you follow the instructions in the book on how to make good decisions, those instructions will undermine your efforts to implement the decisions efficiently. And in making decisions, if you follow the instructions in the book on how to implement efficiently, they will undermine your capability to make good decisions.

*I'd understand that better if you gave me an example.*

Look at political systems. Which system is designed to increase the probability of making good decisions? For that purpose, the system fosters open discussion and vehemently protects the freedom of information, speech, and the press so that good decisions can be made?

*Democracy.*

That's right. And have you noticed how difficult it is in a democracy to implement public policy decisions that require change? The system may make good decisions, but the legitimate political dissension necessary to make a good decision becomes a stumbling block in implementation. My experience with leaders of democratic systems is that they complain their policies don't get implemented as swiftly as they would like, or don't get implemented at all.

Now, which political system fosters quick implementation of decisions by not allowing discussion, dissension, or questions?

*A totalitarian system.*

Yes. And totalitarian regimes usually make bad decisions. Why? Because efficient implementation is carried out by forbidding freedom of the press, dissension, and discussion. It's "do it or else." This inhibits the exchange of information necessary to form educated judgments. Instead of quality decisions, such regimes eventually produce biased decisions based on the prejudices of the dictator, with horrible outcomes.

Study history: Dictators eventually harm the country they lead. Eventually. Because by not allowing dissension, information does not flow well, and the decisions are based on biased judgments of the dictator. There is no discussion, no validation of the decision, and eventually bad decisions will be made, destroying the country.

*Are you saying that good management is democracy in decision making and dictatorship in implementation?*

> Good management is democracy in decision making and dictatorship in implementation.

Correct! This does not apply just to management of companies. In personal life it means that in order to make a good decision, you must be open-minded. You must operate "democratically" within your own mind and with other people. Listen to your own voices of dissension in your head. Ask for the opinion of others who do not necessarily agree with you and understand why they disagree or dissent. Can you learn anything from their dissension? That is democratic decision making. But once a decision is made, you must become "dictatorial," which means you must commit to the decision, be strong willed, and carry it through. No more debating back and forth.

*That's easier said than done.*

Absolutely. Democracy in decision making and dictatorship in implementation is what I call "democratship." It is a difficult process. Many people mismanage by having the sequence upside down: They're dictatorial in decision making and democratic in implementation.

*That's me, I think. I'm dictatorial in deciding to lose weight: I have made up my mind absolutely and I have made a list of what I can eat and what I cannot eat and how much. There will be no more discussion. This is final, I say. And I remain resolute until the sandwiches arrive. I then conveniently turn democratic and heed the voices of dissension.*

You've got the idea, my friend. You must have democracy and dictatorship in the right sequence. You must be capable of being democratic and then dictatorial. The difficulty is in the word *then*. When do you stop being democratic and start becoming dictatorial? When do you quiet the voices of dissension?

> Democracy is an effective system but not an efficient system, while dictatorship is efficient but not effective as a system.

Some people are democratic in decision making and continue being so during implementation. They're inefficient because they keep changing their decision based on who was the last person to talk to them. These are the people you might beg to decide and stick to a decision, and stop changing their mind all the time. On the other hand, some people carry out efficient implementation too early on in the decision making process. They close their mind too quickly. They're difficult to reason with because they don't listen well. They end up making decisions in a hurry: shoot first and ask questions later. These are the people you beg to stop running forward with implementation because the decision was made in such a hurry you have not discussed the matter sufficiently.

*It looks like what you are saying is that democracy is an effective system but not an efficient system, while dictatorship is efficient but not effective as a system.*

Right. If you try to make democracy an efficient political process, it will lose its effectiveness. To be efficient it will cut down on dissension, freedom of speech, and transparency of information. There will be less democracy and the result will be faster implementation of solutions to problems, but some decisions might have bad repercussions.

*By the same token, are you saying that totalitarian regimes cannot be effective?*

The Soviet economy, in its central planning mode, had difficulty producing according to plan. It even had food shortages. Totalitarian regimes are efficient but ineffective. The more democratic they become, the more effective they can be. But then they'd have to give up some political efficiency. They'd to give up on some power and control, which are the essence of a totalitarian regime, and that's not easy for them to do. People usually want something more without losing what they have. They prefer *more* to *instead of*.

To manage, lead, parent, or govern well means to decide and implement, to be democratic then dictatorial. It is not easy. You must decide and implement, be open-minded and resolute at different times. You have to know which frame of mind is correct and at which time. Defined this way, the managing process is all-encompassing, universal, and value-free.

$$\text{Quality of management} = f \begin{cases} 1.\ \text{effectiveness of decisions} \\ 2.\ \text{efficiency of implementation} \end{cases}$$

## External-Internal Integration

Here is another complexity to the leadership process. We already discussed that when you decide and implement your decision, what you are doing is causing change, and that change creates new problems.

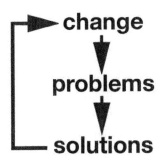

*The new problem could be worse than the initial problem I was trying to solve.*

> *This reminds me of a cartoon I once saw: A man walks into a medical building. In the lobby there is a directory with the names of all the doctors and their specialties:*
>
> *Dr. Smith, cardiologist, suite 202*
>
> *Dr. Horvat, pulmonary diseases, suite 303*
>
> *Dr. Mondlak, internist, suite 404*
>
> *The last one is Dr. Goldber, side effects, suite 1001*

We need to make decisions and implement them, but decisions that will make the situation better not worse.

> *I understand that. We will always have problems as long as there is change, which means as long as we are alive. But how do you make decisions that will not make the situation worse?*

Let us address this important issue. We already discussed that the cause of all problems is...

> *Disintegration.*

So if disintegration is the cause of all problems, what do you think the solution is?

> We will always have problems as long as there is change, which means as long as we are alive.

> *I see where you are going. If the new decision we have made and implemented causes more disintegration then it is bad. And if it makes for integration then it is good. Right?*

Yes and no. A leader needs to adapt the organization to the changes happening in the market. If it is a non-profit organization the same still holds; there are changes out there to which the organization has to respond, or, even better, pro-act.

It is an effort to integrate the organization with the changes out there. But those efforts to integrate the organization with the environment in which it operates cause disintegration inside the organization. As we have said already, all the subsystems do not advance and change in synchronicity. Marketing and sales efforts change to react, or pro-act, to the changes in the market; but operations, production systems, do not change as fast. Accounting changes even slower, and human resources changes the slowest. People do not easily change their behavior and values.

Efforts aimed at external integration cause internal disintegration. To integrate internally, we need to slow down the changes aimed at the external environment. That means that internal integration now causes external disintegration.

You see, this is complex. All this cannot be done simultaneously. A leader, manager, prime minister, or parent has a double role: disintegrate internally to integrate externally; and disintegrate externally to integrate internally. The challenge then is how to keep both orientations integrated.

> If she only integrates internally, there is no growth. If she only integrates externally, it is not a sustainable growth.

If she only integrates internally, there is no growth. If she only integrates externally, it is not a sustainable growth.

*What is the solution?*

There is a sequence. All living systems disintegrate and then integrate. All living systems sleep after being awake. That is true for people, fish, trees—all living systems.

When you were awake you were falling apart dealing with change. Then you stop to sleep for some hours, and what happens when you sleep? You integrate. Then when you wake up in the morning you are fresh and ready to go and disintegrate again.

What happens if you do not sleep, let's say, for a week or longer? Eventually you fall apart. The same holds true for companies if they do not periodically integrate, because all organizations are living systems.

No company should grow exponentially, with its curve of growth going up, up, up. It will eventually collapse; it is only a question of when. Continuously going up will end up going down eventually.

*What do you suggest?*

The revenue or profits curve should go up, then sideways for a while, then up again, and then sideways again, like stairs. Build, consolidate, and build again, to subsequently consolidate again.

But even a stairs function—integrate, disintegrate—is only second prize.

*Why is that second prize? You just convinced me I need to sleep and not be awake all the time.*

Because it reflects discontinuity. To go up requires one kind of leadership, typically very entrepreneurial. To go sideways requires a very different leadership, one that is internally oriented and wants to put order and systems in the organization.

In a stairs function, companies change leaders at the discontinuity points: Too much change and the company is falling apart? Fire the leaders and get a financially oriented person to restore order. But then, after a while, the company is stymied, going nowhere. Fire this leader now and hire a new entrepreneurially oriented one. This causes a lot of wear and tear in the company.

> *Unless you have a leader who is capable of changing orientation: First she is externally oriented and then turns around and is internally oriented.*
>
> *What is the first prize?*

Work on the outside and, at almost the same time, work on the inside. Do not allow too much disparity between the two efforts. In other words, constantly watch the organizational internal-external alignment. Do not allow the disparity to grow too large. Do not chase too many opportunities. They might be a problem in disguise if you are not internally aligned. (Remember opportunities can be problems and problems can be opportunities.)

> *Isn't that too difficult for one person to do?*
>
> *People whose style is to cause change externally are not the ones who are comfortable with integrating internally. And those who are comfortable with putting the pieces together internally are not the ones who like to cause change and integration externally. There is a conflict of roles and thus of styles.*

Absolutely. A well-managed system needs a complementary team. Building a company is like digging for gold in a mine: One person digs, the other person has to build the infrastructure so the mine does not collapse. Growing a family takes also a complementary team. One parent is working outside, earning a living; the other one makes the house a home, integrates. Look at the person you married. You most probably married someone who complements you in style. Someone who is strong in those characteristics in which you are weak, and vice versa. Thus, when we introduce our spouse we might say, "Allow me to introduce you to my better half," and the spouse might say, "No, no, let me introduce you to my better half." Each one is the better half of the other. Together they form the perfection needed to lead a system, in this case a family.

> *But how do I do it in a company?*

> **A well-managed system needs a complementary team.**

In a company you should have one meeting to look outside and another one to look inside. Have strategic meetings discussing what to do with the changing market. Then have a separate meeting about how the company is doing internally. Identify where the cracks are, i.e., what the internal problems are, for example, in the roles people have to perform, in the organizational structure, in authority, in the reward system, in whom you hire, etc., and deal with them.[1]

*Why can't I do them at the same meeting?*

Because you will get confused. Looking at the complications of the inside you will stop having the urge and willingness to deal with the outside. Also, each might require different people attending the sessions.

As a CEO you are the bridge. You should be listening to both sides and deciding how much change on the outside and how much change in the inside is desired when and how. You should perform the balancing act between outside and inside.

*Only the CEO has that role?*

No, it does not have to be the CEO. It can be the head of any strategic business unit. Whoever has the role of making profits or, for a non-profit unit, whoever has the leadership role of getting the results for which the organization exists.

*But these efforts—inside-outside alignment, focus on adapting to market, and then stop changing out there and fix the inside—mean conflict.*

There will be conflict whenever there is a complementary team. The aggressive team member deals with how to adapt the organization to the changing environment. The stable, sensitive one stabilizes and integrates the company. We need the diversity of styles and diversity means conflict. So, there is no management of change without conflict.

There is no change without conflict, period. Change is life, and life means problems, and problems need to be dealt with, which means conflict, and conflict causes pain.

*Life is pain, is that what you're saying?*

Yes, I mean that. No one likes conflict unless they have a mental disorder.

---

1 There is an Adizes Institute program, systematized and structured, to make that happen. We will discuss it later in our conversations.

Conflict takes energy. It is painful and thus people look for solutions where there will be no more conflict. People look for continuous harmony. Love sells. Bookstores are full of books about how to avoid conflict, how to live in harmony. Religions promise that if one follows their belief system they will end up in heaven. The idea that there can be ongoing harmony and no more conflict and no more pain has been the selling proposition of religions, of feel-good gurus, and of political ideologies like Communism. But get real. It will not happen. It cannot happen because of...

*Change.*

> There is no change without conflict.

As long as there is change there will be conflicts. The more change the more conflicts. The faster the rate of change the faster and more chronic the conflicts. Do you realize more people were murdered in wars in the twentieth century than cumulatively in the history of mankind? As change is further accelerating and technology offers more and better weapons of mass destruction, like chemical devices and nuclear bombs, in the twenty-first century we might as well destroy ourselves all together.

Change is life and life is a long string of never-ending problems, and the attempted solutions give rise to conflicts.

*Now I understand why people say: "Life is a bitch and then you die."*

In almost all cultures I know they say: "Little children, little problems. Big children, big problems." We will always have problems as long as we live. We will stop having problems only when we die. On the tomb of Nikos Kazanstakis, the author of *Zorba the Greek*, it says: "No more hope. No more fear. Finally free." We are finally free, no more pain, when we die.

*But conflicts can be destructive.*

You bet. That is one reason, maybe the major one, why people do not like change. They want to change, to solve a problem, as long as there is no change.

Do not avoid conflict by avoiding change. Avoiding change is avoiding life. When there is no change there is death. The idea is not to avoid change but to make conflicts caused by change constructive and not destructive.

> Do not avoid conflict by avoiding change.

*Good idea. How?*

Conflict is energy. It is like rushing water. You can make electricity if you know how to harness it or, if not, it will cause a destructive flood.

How to harness, not dissolve, conflict is an excellent subject for more conversation.

*Great, I'm looking forward to it.*

**26 – MASTERING CHANGE**

# CONVERSATION 3
# Predicting the Quality of Decisions

Now, where were we?

*There is change and it will be here forever.*

*Change causes disintegration.*

*Problems are manifestations of disintegration.*

*To manage or to lead means to solve problems caused by disintegration.*

*In order to solve a problem we need to decide what to do and implement the decision.*

*The quality of management or leadership is a function of how good the decisions we make are, and how efficiently we implement them.*

Good summary.

*But how should we go about making good decisions? How do I know if I am making a good decision? I could analyze a decision after the fact and say that was a good decision. But isn't analysis after the fact too late? You said that the quality of management, leadership, parenting, or governing depends on the quality of the decisions made. Is there a way to know up front if a decision is a good one?*

There is. In order to make a good decision, we need to know how to predict the quality of a decision. We don't want to analyze a decision after it's been implemented, and then judge it by its success or failure. Right?

*Right, but how do you predict whether it will succeed?*

Let's use an example: Say we have a write-up of a problem or a case that contains all the information necessary to diagnose and solve a problem. Assume we give that case to a group of four people. These four people don't know anything more about the case than what's presented in the write-up. We ask them to study the problem together and devise the solution. They are instructed to write down both the problem and the solution, seal the result inside an envelope, and return it to us.

Now let's take another group of four people and give them the same assignment. They too have no additional information beyond what's written up. They have the same case and the same assignment. After the two groups complete their task, we have two sealed envelopes.

Are we going to find that these envelopes contain the same problem and the same solution?

*No. Most likely they will contain different problems and different solutions.*

Right, but why? The case is the same. Both groups have exactly the same information. Why are the problems and solutions different?

> In order to manage well, you have to manage the people who determine the problem and solution, instead of managing the problem itself.

*Because the people are different!*

You have just discovered the key factor in the managerial or leadership process. In order to manage well, you have to manage the people who determine the problem and solution, instead of managing the problem itself.

There are managers who say, "I love to manage. It's people I can't stand!" If you do not like working with people, you are in the wrong profession. Too many leaders open the envelope and say, "Wrong problem! Wrong solution! The right problem and the right solution are..." They think they are leading, when what they are really doing is just working hard. Even if they accept what is inside the envelope, how do they know they have found the right problem and the right solution?

*But if they're the managers they should know better than their employees. That's why they get paid more, isn't it? Isn't that also why leaders get elected?*

They should know better, but do they? Is getting paid more an assurance that a person knows more? Does a leader necessarily know more about every subject he is responsible for?

*Then why is the manager getting paid more? What do we reward leaders for?*

> The role of leadership is to create an environment where the most desirable will most probably happen.

It's not for knowing more about the problem or the solution. They should get paid more for knowing how to find the right people, the "knowledgeables," and for managing the environment in which these people operate, so that the people find the right answers in diagnosing and solving the problem.

If a manager claims to know everything, the organization is in trouble. No one can know it all, especially in the very complex environment we live in now.

If managers want to have the right problem and the right solution, they must match the right people to the case at hand. They must create the environment that will enable these people to arrive at the right problem and the right solution. The CEO of Ogden Corporation said it best: "The role of leadership is to create an environment where the most desirable will most probably happen."

*But as a leader or manager, how do I distinguish the right problem and solution from the wrong ones? If I don't necessarily know more than the people I lead or manage, then how do I evaluate their decision? I could make a mistake, right?*

To know whether the people are proposing a good decision or not, you must ask four questions. If the answer is "yes" to these questions, you have the right problem and the right solution. If the answer is "no" to any of the four questions, you have the wrong problem and the wrong solution.

*What are the questions?*

To understand what those four questions are would take the entire book. But it is worth it, don't you think?

*Agreed.*

At the beginning, our conversations may seem somewhat complicated and overly academic. Later, the usefulness and applicability of these concepts, and how they can lead to the answers to those questions, will become clear.

## The Four Roles of Decision Making

No decision is made in a vacuum. It is made to achieve something. A decision is a good one if it produces the desired results. Thus, if a decision can make an organization be both effective and efficient in the short and the long term, the decision is a good one.

We can present it as a chart:

| Input ⟶ | Output |
| --- | --- |
| **Decision Roles** | **Organizational Results** |
| (P) | effective in the short term |
| (A) | efficient in the short term |
| (E) | effective in the long term |
| (I) | efficient in the long term |

I've studied management practices in several countries and have observed what happens under different conditions. I was like the British Naval doctor who sailed the open seas for a long time and observed that when people's diets were deficient in vitamin C they developed scurvy.

I studied management practices in countries where certain managerial roles were forbidden by law, and I observed and analyzed the managerial "diseases" that emerged.[2] I identified the necessary characteristics—the four "vitamins," which I call the decision roles—that produce healthy organizations that are effective and efficient in the short and the long term:

>Performing the (P) role makes the organization effective in the short term.
>Performing the (A) role makes the organization efficient in the short term.
>Performing the (E) role makes the organization effective in the long term.
>Performing the (I) role makes the organization efficient in the long term.

---

2  See my book *Industrial Democracy: Yugoslav Style*. New York Free Press, 1971. Reprinted by Adizes Institute.

Like a missing vitamin will cause disease, a missing role will produce a pattern of corresponding mismanagement.[3]

I can analyze and predict the outcome of a decision by analyzing which roles were being performed in making the decision and which ones were missing. It is like a medical diagnosis.

Let us have a simplified example: If sales are going down apparently the (P) role is deficient. The (P) role makes the organization perform the purpose for which it exists, and it can be measured by sales. If profits are lower than the competition's apparently the (A) role is deficient. The (A) role makes the organization efficient and thus minimizes waste. If the company is not innovating, not coming up with new products and markets, apparently (E) is deficient. Finally, if the company is too dependent on any one individual to survive or even exist, for example if the presence of the founder is indispensible, apparently the (I) role is missing or deficient.

> *You mean to say you can look at managerial problems as you would medical diseases, and identify which missing role caused them? Then, like you would treat a deficiency in a certain vitamin, "inject" the missing role, or roles, into the system, and lead the organization back to health?*

Yes! I look at an organization as a total system and at what makes it healthy or sick. A healthy system is one that is effective and efficient in the short and the long term.

The Adizes Methodology offers a holistic theory of management, both therapeutic and preventive. It does not focus on solving a specific problem. It focuses on the whole system and how to make it healthy. When the organization is healthy, the problem that is bothering the organization will be solved by itself. As a homeopathic doctor once told me: "I do not treat a specific problem. I treat the whole person."

Being healthy makes the organization successful.

One company helped by this methodology has increased sales from $12 million to many billions in ten years without any dilution of ownership.[4]

> *Is the benefit permanent?*

It can be if the company is constantly nourished and nurtured by repeatedly using the methodology. Otherwise, in the long term, the methodology's effectiveness will diminish, and eventually the organization will lose the benefits. It's like exercising or eating right.

---

3   See my book *How to Solve the Mismanagement Crisis*.
4   Per Stewart Resnick, Chairman and President of Roll International, Inc.

*Why will the effectiveness diminish?*

Because of change. The markets change, the technology changes, etc. If leadership does not manage change properly, the system will become either ineffective or inefficient either in the short or long term.

*Can anyone learn how to engage all four roles?*

Yes, if properly trained.

*How different is it from what traditional consultants do?*

Adizes does not prescribe "medicine," meaning we do not write consulting reports. We empower the organization to release and utilize its own energies to take care of itself. We coach the whole organization as a system, rather than just individuals, to generate those (PAEI) vitamins so it can stay healthy without further intervention from us.

Typical consultants do not teach you how to stay healthy. Usually you need periodic infusions of their consulting services. This methodology is different. While helping the organization change, it simultaneously empowers it to handle future problems so it doesn't develop an addiction to outside intervention. It teaches the organization how to manage itself correctly and continuously. It is more akin to therapy than to medical allopathic intervention.

*How do the four roles work?*

| Input ⟶ | Output |
|---|---|
| Roles ⟶ | Organizational Results |
| (P) | effective ⎫ short term |
| (A) | efficient ⎭ |
| (E) | effective ⎫ long term |
| (I) | efficient ⎭ |

Let us discuss each role, what it is, and how it works—but careful now: Some languages do not have a literal translation for either effectiveness or efficiency. For instance Russian has no good translation for efficiency. They use the words *organized* or *effective* for "efficient," and the word *resultativno* ("producing results") for "effectiveness." It is a bad translation because not all results make for effective systems. Hebrew does not have a literal translation for effectiveness. *Tahliti* ("purposeful") does not mean that what is attempted is achieved, which is the essence of being effective. Thus, let us define what those words mean according to the Adizes Methodology.

## Short-Term Effectiveness

First, a decision must make the organization effective. If the decision doesn't produce effectiveness, then the decision is not a good one.

*What does "effective" mean?*

In the short term, an organization is effective if the decision satisfies the (P)urpose for which the organization exists, thus the letter (P) for this role. There is a purpose to every decision we make.

> Profit should not be the purpose. Profit should be the result of fulfilling the purpose correctly.

When you read a book you have expectations about what you will get out of it. If reading the book doesn't satisfy your expectations, you might feel you wasted your money and time. It's the same with marriage. We marry somebody because we have certain needs and expectations. If those expectations are not satisfied, we might feel we made the wrong decision, we married the wrong person; the marriage is not functioning.

Every decision, whether we are aware of it or not, is made to satisfy certain needs, although we often don't or can't articulate those needs. Every decision is made to function, to produce certain expected results.

*For a business it's profits, right?*

Profit should not be the purpose. Profit should be the result of fulfilling the purpose correctly.

*I do not understand.*

Have you ever seen companies so preoccupied with profits that they're going bankrupt? They're losing money not in spite of, but because of their preoccupation with profits. They cut costs to maximize profits although cutting those costs, like for research and development, will hurt them in the long term.

If you are preoccupied with happiness as a goal and you wake up every morning telling yourself, I must be happy today, you can make yourself quite miserable. The same with health: Obsession with the subject can make you a hypochondriac.

## 34 – MASTERING CHANGE

Profits, like happiness, health, and democracy, are a grand output, a result of doing many things right. Focus on managing right. If you manage well, you will be profitable. Focus on the process to produce the results. Focus on being healthy. If the company is healthy it will be profitable sustainably.

```
Input ─────────▶ Output
Roles ─────────▶ Organizational Results
─────────────────────────────────────────
(P)              effective  ⎫
(A)              efficient  ⎬ short term
                            ⎭
(E)              effective  ⎫
(I)              efficient  ⎬ long term
                            ⎭
─────────────────────────────────────────
                                  PROFITS
```

Too many people watch the score rather than the ball when they're playing tennis. If you have a good tennis coach, he'll tell you not to focus on the score when you're playing. Every volley should be like the first of the match, as if you were starting from zero. If you're preoccupied with the score, you can't play well. Just play the best you can and if you do, the score will tell you how well you did.

> Management for results and by the right process.

It is the same with managing. I disagree with books whose exclusive focus is management by results. It should be management *for* results and *by* the right process. Management by results is mechanistic. It's primarily managing by output, or by the score, with less focus on input and throughput. No primary attention is given to the means of achieving the goals.

Marksmanship is a good example of paying attention to the means of achieving a goal, which is to hit the bulls-eye. To hit the bulls-eye, you must focus on the sights of your gun in the direction of the target. The sights are the means by which you hit the target. If you focus on the target and defocus on the sights, a slight deviation of the sights will make you miss the target.

The human eye cannot simultaneously focus with the same clarity on the target, which is a hundred yards away, and on the sights, which are inches away. Most people focus on the target, on what they want to achieve. In the process of doing so they de-emphasize the sights, the means of achieving the goal. A mistake of one hundredth of an inch in the sights can make all the difference in where the bullet will hit the target, or whether it will hit it at all.

> Train your mind to focus on the means, in the direction of the goal or the results you want to achieve.

One of the "sights" in management is your values. Focus on your values, and manage the (PAEI) roles well in the direction of your goal, and you will score better than if you focus on the goal, compromise your values, and mismanage (PAEI). You might achieve the goal, but it will not be what your real purpose in life is. You will be sorry.

There are people who believe that the goal is more important than the means, so they ignore the importance of the process by which the goal is achieved. Yet a slight misalignment in the process can defeat the desired results, eventually. You must focus on your values and be sure not to violate them. Then focus on what you want to achieve without violating those values even a bit. Focus on the sights and accept the relative haziness of the target. Train your mind to focus on the means, in the direction of the goal or the results you want to achieve. I repeat again, for emphasis, one of the most critical inputs into your decision-making process is values. What are the values that govern your behavior? Which values you will not violate?

The goal does not always justify the means. Rather, it is the other way around: Focus on managing the means in the direction of the goal.

> *I always think more about where I want to go then about how to get there.*

You're not the only one. Goals are exciting. Thinking about means and the values that should govern how those goals are achieved is frequently boring and complicated. And people take them for granted. They are not easy to articulate and operationalize.

> *What should we focus on in managing a company if not on profits? Are you ignoring profits? Isn't the purpose of playing to win?*

Good question. What is the purpose of an organization? Of any system and for that matter of any object?

# The (P)urpose of Business

Look around you. The light that is lighting your room does not exist for itself. It exists to light the room. The pen you are using to write exists to serve you to be able to write. And the table you are sitting at is there to satisfy your need to put something on it.

There is a common denominator to it all. Everything in this world exists to serve something else.

This applies to human beings as well. We are a system of interdependencies. The heart exists for the rest of the body. So do the kidneys. And so does the liver. And, by the way, do not ignore the rectum. Although we degrade its importance and have lots of jokes about it, it has a very important role for the whole body.

> Everything in this world exists to serve something else.

We call leaders "the head" of the company as if the workers are "the rectum." But as I already said, the rectum can cause lots of problems for the head if it refuses to cooperate. You know the expression "a pain in the arse." It can hurt a lot.

*Which means that whoever is a member of the organization, of the system, has a role for the rest of the system and thus is as important as other parts of the system. Okay, go on.*

Everything in this world exists to serve something else. So, what is the purpose of an organization? To serve the clients for which it was created.

> So, what is the purpose of an organization? To serve the clients for which it was created.

This idea has repercussions for personal life as well. You will not find the answer to your purpose in life by focusing on the question "Why am I on this earth?" Exchange the word *why* with *for what*, which is the same thing but has different stimuli: For what do you exist? You must have a client. Someone whose needs you have to satisfy. The more needs you satisfy the more alive you are.

*Not strange that Buddhist monks say: "Thank you for allowing me to serve you."*

*What about satisfying my needs? I am my own client, no?*

You should satisfy your needs, but not exclusively. If there is any component in your body that satisfies no one else but itself what is it?

*Cancer.*

To serve life you have to exist for others as well, not just for yourself. You have to serve. Cancer serves only itself.

Some companies do not serve their market. They only focus on making profits in the short term. They only focus on their needs and forget or ignore market needs, the needs of their clients. You can predict that they will eventually die.

Some governments serve the electorate. Good. Some forget those who elected them, and serve only the needs of the elected. That country is doomed to fail eventually.

Always ask yourself: "Who will cry if I die?" If no one will, maybe you should die. What is the purpose of this organization's existence if it does not serve those it was established to serve?

> To serve life you have to exist for others.
>
> "Who will cry if I die?"

*I see. I should analyze my customers' needs!*

No. I purposely used the word *clients*, not *customers*. Many people confuse the two.

*What's the difference?*

Every organizational entity has clients. These are the individuals or groups of individuals whose needs the entity was established to satisfy. Every organizational unit, even if it does not deal with customers, has clients.

Customers are different. Paying clients are called customers. For the sales department, their clients are the…

*Customers.*

Right. They are the outside, paying clients. But where are the clients of the accounting department?

*Inside the organization.*

You should do with the inside what you do with the outside. With customers you do marketing research, don't you? You ask them, "What do you want? Are you satisfied?" Well, do the same thing with internal clients.

Focus on the clients for whom the entity you are managing exists and was designed to serve. With internal clients, research their needs. You'll learn a lot, just as companies learn when they perform marketing research. Sometimes companies learn that what the customers don't want is being provided amply, while what the customers do want is not provided at all. The same holds true for internal clients.

*Can I measure effectiveness?*

Sure. Usually people measure it by sales, but that is not good enough.

*How should it be measured then?*

How do you know if a restaurant is effective? If it satisfies clients' needs?

*Would you not measure it by revenues? If the customers are buying it means that they are satisfied. No?*

Not good enough. It should be whether the clients come back. If there are repeat sales.

You do not see an animal going back to a dry waterhole, do you? People go to where their needs get satisfied. If their needs are satisfied they come back. Otherwise they do not. So, are your clients coming back?

This metric applies to any organization: a marriage, family, or country. If your spouse is not coming back there is a reason. If your grown children do not come back for a visit there must be a reason. If people want to leave a country, there must be a reason.

Isn't it interesting that they don't check your passport going out of the United States, only coming in? Easy to get out, tough to get in. In the Soviet Union, it was easy coming in but they had guards with machine guns keeping people from getting out. Which country satisfies its people's needs better, the one whose citizens want in or the one whose citizens want out?

Tell me how many people want to join your company versus how many want to leave the company, if they could, and I will tell you how good your company is.

The same is true for a country. Are your entrepreneurs leaving the country? Are foreign entrepreneurs investing in your country? That is a pretty good measurement of how effective the social, economic, and political systems of that country are.

*Okay. I have to satisfy the needs of stockholders. Does not the company exist to satisfy their needs? The company was established to use their investment and give them a good return.*

No. Stockholders are stakeholders. You have to satisfy their need to get a good return on their investment, somewhat more than what they would get from a risk-free saving account.

> Profit should be a constraint goal: Do not have less than so much.

In investing they took a risk, and taking that risk needs to be rewarded or people will not take the risk, will not invest, and there will not be much economic growth and everyone will suffer. But you need to pay them just enough to cover the need of investors to be rewarded for taking risk. This means you should make no less than X% profit for them. It should not be more and more profits. It should be just enough not to lose investors.

Profit should not be a deterministic goal: the more the better. Profit should be a constraint goal: Do not have less than so much.

Where you have to focus is on the market, the needs of your clients. That should be your deterministic goal: the more you satisfy them, the better.

*What about government agencies, the bureaucracies? How does this principle apply to them? They have a monopoly in satisfying client needs in the same way that internal clients in a company have no choice. Everyone has to use, say, the accounting department of the company. You cannot go outside to get the service. You are not allowed to have your needs satisfied by anyone else.*

It's a difficult assignment to really focus on satisfying clients because you could easily avoid doing it. There is no competitive pressure to do it. Some clients have to come back because you have a monopoly over what they need. At best, they will complain. The worst is when you hear no complaints. It seems good because you hear nothing, but apathy is one step away from death. In these cases where you have monopolistic exclusivity, you have an even bigger responsibility to take the initiative and find out if clients are coming back because you are satisfying their needs or because they have to come back.

*What should we do in this case?*

You have to be honest with yourself as a manager, as a leader. Close your eyes and ask yourself, honestly, now: If my clients had a choice, would they come back? Put yourself in your clients' shoes. If you were them would you come back to get the service or the product?

## 40 – MASTERING CHANGE

That is also why in a marriage we should not take our spouse for granted simply because, supposedly, he doesn't have a choice to go outside the marriage to satisfy his needs. We have to pay special attention to the needs of our spouse, to what he expects from the marriage.

Let me now summarize the first role, the (P) role: Satisfying present clients' needs makes the organization effective, (P)roviding for the present needs of your clients.

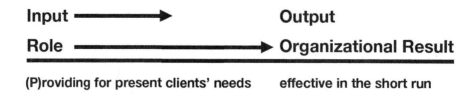

*To perform this (P) role what characteristics must a leader possess?*

To (P) you need what psychologists call achievement motivation. You must want to accomplish things. If you know the client's needs and how to satisfy them, but lack achievement motivation, you could be a good staff person, you could assist managers, write memos, and make recommendations. But for the (P) role, this need to achieve is required.

Achievement motivation is a necessary but not sufficient condition for the (P) role. If you have the motivation to achieve, but don't know what must be accomplished or how, you are dangerous. You're an unguided missile. This combination of qualities is often seen in eager young executives. They are enthusiastic but lack knowledge or experience.

Good leaders, to be functional and make effective decisions, must be knowledgeable achievers, not just knowledgeable and not just achievers.

I disagree with books that say a manager is a manager is a manager. Or a leader is a born leader who can lead anything. This claim, that if you are a leader you can manage anything, is wrong—unless you add three more words: after some time.

*What does that mean?*

When you change jobs, either within a company or when you leave for another company, you come across a new organization, a new set of clients. No two identical organizations exist, just as no two identical people exist. No two identical branches of the same bank exist. They're on different corners of a street, have different parking problems, and attract different customers from different industries. They may be similar, but never identical.

*But people usually focus on similarities. They try to find out whether they recognize anything. They find comfort when they recognize a task they already know.*

*You're wincing. Is this a typical mistake?*

You have to look for the differences too. Only then can you design a custom-made strategy to satisfy the specific needs of that moment.

When you meet a new love in your life, do you look for similarities and say, "You remind me of an old flame," or do you look for what is unique in this new person?

*Better to do the latter, obviously.*

> How is this task different from any other task I know?

The same is true in managing. You should ask, "How is this task different from any other task I know?" To be effective, good leaders, whether supervisors, department managers, parents, or sociopolitical leaders, should know the unique needs of their clients at that moment and then be skillful with their unique capabilities to satisfy those needs.

*Okay: Identify who your internal and/or external clients are. Identify their needs. If you satisfy their needs, measured by whether they are voluntarily, willingly, coming back for more, your organization is effective.*

*What about efficiency?*

That is what we will discuss next!

## 42 – MASTERING CHANGE

# CONVERSATION 4
# Efficiency and Effectiveness

*We discussed that (P)roviding for the satisfaction of present clients' needs will make the organization effective in the short term. Performing the (P) role is a necessary component of a good decision. And making good decisions is half of managing well.*

Why do we have to make decisions?

*Because there are problems, and there are problems because there is change.*

*What about efficiency?*

Efficiency means that you spent the minimum energy necessary to get something done. The shortest route between two points is a straight line. That is efficient. You do not go around and around to get to the point.

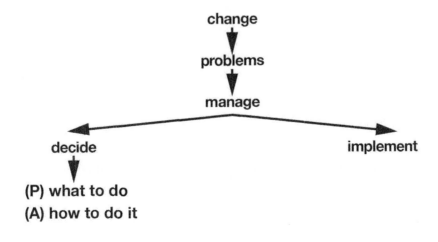

An efficient machine uses less energy than an inefficient machine. This applies not only to machines; an organic system like our body is extremely efficient—ask a medical doctor.

For efficiency you need to systematize the organization. You need to organize and establish policies, standard operating procedures, and rules; you must have law and order and discipline. The right things must be done at the right time, at the right intensity, and in the right sequence. You must do things right, rather than just doing the right things. Instead of reinventing the wheel every time you need to wheel something around, you design the best way to produce wheels by making the process routine.

Back to the tennis analogy, hitting the ball over the net into the opponent's court proves that your hit of the ball was effective. However, in order to be efficient, what do you have to do? You must systematize your volley. You have to learn how to hold your racket and move your body correctly. The coach trains you by sending you the ball in the same direction over and over again. This helps you develop the correct movement and swing, so that you will hit the ball with maximum impact and minimum expenditure of energy.

Systematization makes you efficient. It requires attention to detail, thoroughness, and a good memory. It requires not that you work harder, but that you are more disciplined.

Doing all of this is the role of (A)dministration.

> *That makes sense. A decision should produce effectiveness and efficiency.*

Right, now can a system be effective and not efficient?

> *Come to think of it, yes, it can. A decision may satisfy a need, but at higher utilization of resources than is necessary.*

Right. Let us look at a game of tennis. In order to win you first have to hit the ball over the net into the opponent's court. That is, you have an effective volley. But you can do it very inefficiently: You turned your body too much, or you moved your body the wrong way.

To be efficient you train. You train how to swing the racket, how to hit the ball correctly, and you practice and practice and practice. In your practice, you made the perfect moves but missed the ball. Can it happen?

> *You were efficient but not effective.*

This can happen not only in practice but also in real life. Imagine someone saying to his opponent, "Send me the ball exactly here, to this specific spot, because I am most efficient when I swing the racket here. I know best how to hit the ball from here. Do not send it anywhere else."

*Who makes this mistake?*

Bureaucracies. They go through the motions dictated by their manuals and policies. They are most efficient in what they do, but they miss satisfying client needs, because those needs might have changed since the system was established. They hit the balls that come to the racket rather than bringing the racket to the ball. They serve only those needs that fit their procedures rather than adapt the procedures to satisfy the needs of their clients. That is why "bureaucracy" is a derogatory label.

# The Inevitability of Bureaucracy

Now let me ask you a question: How quickly do you think the location of the ball changes during a tennis game?

> The more change the more bureaucracy there will be.

*Very quickly. It changes location often.*

How long does it take to practice and learn how to hit that ball efficiently?

*A long time.*

In the modern world, market needs change faster than the capability of the company to deliver satisfaction in an efficient way. The needs of clients change faster than the system adapts to satisfy those needs. The system required to satisfy a need changes slowly, while the needs evolve quickly. The result: bureaucracy. Needs are not satisfied.

*Bureaucracy is partially caused by change. The more change the more bureaucracy there will be. I can see that.*

Right. So you have to choose what is more important: to be effective or to be efficient; to be approximately right or to be precisely wrong. Do you want to hit the ball into the opponents' court, although not in the ideal location, or hit it right into the net?

*Obviously, effectiveness is more important.*

In order to be more effective you might have to be less efficient. Efficiency can be detrimental to effectiveness. It is better to be approximately right than precisely wrong.

*When a company is young, it's often effective but not very efficient. It chases the market to survive. Its systems are still in the cradle, developing.*

*As it grows older, it becomes more efficient but less effective. It has systems galore, but those systems change slowly; without change the company responds less and less to the changing needs of the market, which makes it ineffective.*

Yes! To be in the Prime of your organizational lifecycle is to be both effective and efficient, and that takes effort and a lot of organizational learning. It is not automatically forthcoming.

*But, if efficiency is up, then profits are up, and is that not what we want in the business world?*

> Profits should be a measurement of added value. Cutting costs does not add value per se, even if it increases profits.

When you generate profits exclusively through efficiency, profits will go up only by cutting costs. As you continually shrink costs, however, what else might go down? If you cut costs to the point that you can't satisfy your clients' needs well, effectiveness will drop and sales will decline.

*So?*

There is a lag between the time when the clients' needs are not satisfied and when clients find another business to patronize. It takes time to build their satisfaction (sales), and it takes time to lose their loyalty. Now, you can cut expenses faster than clients can move to another supplier. That means that sales decrease more slowly than the cuts in expenses. This time lag, between when you cut costs and when you see sales decline, can make your company look profitable in the short term, while it is actually going bankrupt in the long term. You will be profitable in the short term, but eventually the deterioration in your sales will catch up. You'll have no clients left with which to do business.

Profits should be a measurement of added value. Cutting costs does not add value per se, even if it increases profits.

*You say profits should measure the added value. Can you elaborate, please?*

Needs have a price: A client is willing to pay a certain amount of money to satisfy his need. The value of the need is equal to the price paid (in a free, competitive market).

However, there is a cost to satisfying that need. If you can satisfy that need at a cost that is lower than the price the client is willing to pay, you make a profit. So, profit is a measurement of added value: you are able to satisfy a need at a lower cost than the perceived value of that need.

You should maximize client satisfaction but avoid losing profits. This means satisfying needs within the limits of profitability, rather than maximizing profitability and compromising client satisfaction. Profits are thus a limit, not a goal. In other words, client satisfaction is a deterministic goal, a goal you want to maximize; profit is a constraint goal, a goal you do not want to violate.

*What about non-profit organizations? Like NGOs? They are not profit motivated. So what is their value added?*

Any organization should satisfy client needs with the least energy waste. In the case of non-profit organizations, the result will not be profit. If it is a political party, it will be getting reelected. For a philanthropic organization, it will be financial efficiency and the fulfillment of its mission to the best of its capabilities.

> Profits are thus a limit. Not a goal.

Consider a hospital: Depending on the type of hospital, the method of measuring value added will necessarily be different. For a teaching hospital, added value can be measured by the number of medical doctors it is able to train, while maintaining economic viability. For a research hospital, it can be measured by the contributions the staff has made to professional journals. If it is a service hospital you would look at the quality of medical service provided and whether there is any waste. You would not focus on minimizing expense at the cost of having lower quality medical service, right?

The focus of the non-profit should be first on its function in society, and then on the value it creates by minimizing the cost of satisfying that function or need. The non-profit, like a for-profit organization, must identify the client and the client's needs. They can then measure their effectiveness by repeat demand for their services and ask themselves: Am I providing these services most efficiently, with the minimum amount of energy needed?

The "cost" of satisfying a need is not only money. It can be any other manifestation of energy or time. For example, how long is a client willing to wait in line to have their needs satisfied? How long is a client in a jungle willing to walk to the nearest hospital?

I do not consider managing a non-profit different from managing a business or a country. All should focus on client needs and satisfy them with minimum wasted energy.

*I understand. We need to be both effective and efficient.*

We can add it now to the diagram:

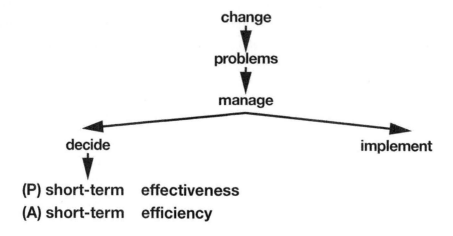

*Now, tell me what we need for long-term effectiveness? I understand that in order to be effective and efficient in the short term, I need to (P)erform a needed service and (A)dminister it. Now how about effectiveness in the long term?*

## Long-Term Effectiveness

Long-term effectiveness means that present decisions will satisfy future client needs.

What we want are decisions that produce effectiveness in the long term, decisions that can predict and satisfy new needs we believe will emerge. We want the organization to make proactive decisions.

*Give me an example.*

Let's assume you need to build a factory today, that will produce gadgets you predict will be needed next year. When next year arrives, your prediction proves to be true and there is a demand for the gadgets. Your decision to build a factory today makes you effective tomorrow.

*You mean I have to adapt my organization to the market changes.*

No. To adapt is reactive, you wait until something happens and then adapt.

*What is wrong with that?*

Every day some bird or flower becomes extinct as our environment changes. Do you believe that they do not want to survive?

*They try to adapt. So what is wrong?*

Their speed of adaptation is too slow in comparison to the speed of the changes in their environment.

*How about the human race?*

The human body can change at a certain speed. However, adapting may have worked a hundred, two hundred years ago when change was slow. The world is different now. Change is accelerating and neither the birds, nor plants, nor the human species is capable of adapting at that speed. You need to be proactive, to predict change and prepare for change, then you have a chance.

*How can I be proactive?*

Let's go back to the tennis analogy. As you hit the ball, what else do you have to do? You must think about where your opponent's next shot will land. You may have to run to the net, to the middle of the court, or to the baseline in order to meet that next ball. This process of positioning yourself now for future demands is called being proactive.

A proactive approach will make you effective in the long term. If you're in the right place when the next ball arrives, you will be ready to hit it again. So, to be proactive means to do something today to position yourself for the future.

I'm not talking about marketing or merchandising. I'm talking about positioning yourself to meet future needs. Are you getting ready with a new product? Are you getting ready with new distribution channels? Are you equipping yourself with a new technology, so that you'll be able to satisfy the needs you predict?

*You mean I should plan?*

Yes. Planning is not deciding what we will be doing tomorrow. That is dreaming. Planning is what are we going to do now, this year, to prepare for what we believe and expect to happen next year.

The mind is like a computer. Or, more specifically, we built the computer to mimic the mind. The computer takes orders literally. You cannot put in one command and expect something else to happen. Our mind works the same way.

If you say to yourself, "tomorrow I will start a diet," tomorrow, when you wake up, your mind asks you: Is today tomorrow? Since it is not, you will not start the diet. You will never diet. It is always going to start tomorrow.

> *Interesting you say that. There is a bar in Amsterdam that has a big sign on the wall: "Free drinks tomorrow." They have never served a single free drink. When, in Mexico, they say* mañana *(tomorrow) it means, "forget it, it won't happen."*

You have to act *today* to prepare for tomorrow. Create your tomorrow today. Create your future now.

> Create your tomorrow today. Create your future now.

The people who *adapt* to a changing environment are the ones who wait until the ball lands in the court. Once they know where it has landed, they adapt, or they react to it. But by then it might be too late. The world is changing too fast. Organizations, just like the earth's flora and fauna, will not survive if they cannot adapt quickly enough to the changes in the environment in which they operate. By environment I mean the market, the competition, the technology, the political and legal environment, the physical environment (air, water, natural resources), social environment, etc.

*Change fast or die slowly, right?*

An organization needs to change faster than the environment in which it operates. It needs to be able to imagine what the future will look like. It has to build scenarios of future client needs, the competition, the environment, and anything else that might affect the organization. It has to be creative and imagine what is going to happen.

*What do you mean by "creative?"*

The future is foggy. Not all information is available or clear. You may not have all the information, and the validity of what you do have changes with time. Indistinct visions appear and then disappear. You have to assemble the available information and then fill in the gaps in the emerging pattern by using your imagination. That's creativity: filling in informational gaps to create a whole picture.

But to be proactive takes more than being creative. After you predict where the next ball is going to land, what is the second thing you must do?

*You have to actually make your move on the court.*

Yes, you must move to a spot on the court where you believe the next ball will land and position yourself for it. But since the ball may not land where you predicted, you must be willing to take a risk.

$$\text{(E)ntrepreneuring} = f \left\{ \begin{array}{l} \text{creativity;} \\ \text{willingness to take risks} \end{array} \right\}$$

*You mean one has to be an entrepreneur.*

No. Here we are talking about the (E)ntrepreneurial *role*. To be an entrepreneur you need more than just the (E) role. You need to be (PaEi).

An entrepreneur needs to be more than just creative. She must be result oriented and (P) oriented too, if she is going to succeed. With (E) alone a person is a dreamer, a creative contributor, and that is it.

Some people are creative but do not take risks. They're not (E)ntrepreneurial or proactive. Usually you find such people in the consulting or business teaching professions. They're creative, they can imagine the future, but they are unwilling to take the risk and act upon what they imagine.

The ideal balance for the (E) role in a leader is both the ability to imagine the future and the willingness to take risks in order to position the organization to deal with that future.

*If you are proactive you will be effective in the long term?*

There is a better chance than if you are not proactive. As the expected needs arise you will be ready to respond.

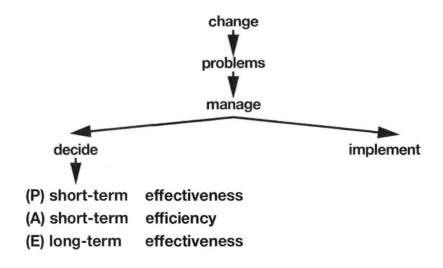

A person who is creative and thus capable of imagining the future and willing to take risks is entrepreneurial. This is the third role of (E). To satisfy present client needs is to be effective in the short term. To prepare to satisfy future clients and future needs prepares you to be effective in the long term.

I repeat: To be effective in the short term you need to be dedicated to the task. You need to be achievement motivated. For the long term, since you have to look at the future and analyze the hypothetical future needs of present and future clients, you have to be creative enough to imagine that future. You have to be willing to take risks, because you have to start preparing today to be ready for the future, although what you project may not happen.

*What then is the fourth role: How to become efficient in the long term?*

# Long-Term Efficiency

In order to be efficient in the long term, one must (I)ntegrate, as summarized below.

You (I)ntegrate, for instance, when you teach people to play team sports. All the participants share emotionally, socially, and sometimes economically from winning. It is not a star system, but an ensemble. When building a team, you build the teammates' support for each other so they will benefit or lose as a team rather than as individuals.

*How do you do that?*

**To (I)ntegrate:**
**Is**
**to**
**change**
**organizational**
**culture**
**from**
**mechanistic**
**to**
**organic.**

Let's explain the terms in our definition above.

"To change" is an important term, because it means that the change we want to have in order to integrate is active. We cannot be passive and expect integration will happen by itself. The opposite is true, as time is destructive by nature. Take a beautiful garden, for example. You could spend thousands of dollars to build one, but if you then do nothing—do not touch that garden for two years—what will happen? It will be like a jungle, with weeds all over. Same with the best car you can buy: do not drive it, and a year later it probably won't start. Time by itself is destructive.

Marriage too is like a garden, like a top-notch car, like any system. It needs continuous maintenance or it will fall apart. A friend of mine's wife asked him for a divorce. He was surprised: "I did not do anything." You have to work to maintain your marriage.

One day I was planning with a client when we would meet again. I suggested March 15. "Oh no," he said. "I am on my honeymoon then." I was shocked. How could it be? Just the evening before, I had dinner with him and his wife. How did he find the time to divorce his wife and remarry all in one short night? He saw my surprise: "No, no. It is with my wife. We have a rule in our marriage: On the anniversary of our wedding we go on a honeymoon every year, because one honeymoon is not enough for a lifetime of a marriage."

All systems need maintenance. Why not organizations? This is why I start the definition of (I)ntegration with *to change*. It means to do something differently today so that tomorrow is different from yesterday.

The next word is *organizational*. This requires a more detailed explanation. What does the word *organization* mean? If I were to ask you how many people are in your organization, where would you look for the answer?

*I would look in the personnel files of the organization.*

As a manager, in order to find out who the people in your organization are, that you're supposed to (I)ntegrate, motivate, and manage, don't look at your organization chart or personnel files. Look for "the rock."

*The rock?*

Let me illustrate what I mean through an analogy. Five friends get together Friday night and have some beers. As they are drinking, someone suggests they go on a hike to the nearest lake the next morning. The rest of the group enthusiastically agrees. The next day, they walk up a very narrow mountain path on their way to the lake. It is so narrow they must walk single file. As they are walking, they're whistling, joking, laughing, and maybe even arguing with each other. For organizational psychologists or sociologists, this is an organization, because they are connected by interrelationships. For those interested in management and leadership, there is no organization until the group arrives at a point on this narrow path where a rock is blocking their passage. The rock is so big that none of them alone can lift it. What does the group have to do now?

*Move that rock.*

Since no one alone can lift it, they have to interrelate for an immediate purpose, to move the rock. The managerial process and the organization, by extension, were not born when they decided to go for a hike to the lake. Drinking beer satisfied the (I) need. Deciding to go to the lake was the (E) role. Now that they need to remove the rock to be able to reach their goal—that represents the (P) role. Now organization, or the (A) role, is needed: They need to get organized because none of them alone can lift the rock.

A commercial organization is born when no single individual can satisfy the needs of the market. If the needs of the market could be satisfied by an individual, there would be no need for an organization. The same applies to noncommercial entities, whether a family, an NGO, a state, or a global society.

The purpose of any organization is to satisfy its clients' needs that cannot be satisfied by an individual alone.

When an organization is very young, the purpose is clearly visible, because a young organization cannot ignore its clients. If it does, it goes bankrupt. The company wants the clients' repeat business, or else it may not have the cash to pay salaries.

As organizations grow older, they focus more and more on the score, on profits, and on measurable output. They forget who the clients are and what needs they must satisfy. They start to focus exclusively on profits. At that point many companies go bankrupt, not in spite of their focus on profits, but because they were focusing exclusively on profits.

> *Why do organizations lose their sight? It's like what happens to vision as people age.*

That is the subject of another book of mine, *Managing Corporate Lifecycles.* You can learn more there if you're interested.

Back to our analogy, imagine that our group of friends cannot lift that rock by themselves and they still want to go to the lake. They see another group of people coming up the path. Our group does not know them, but they need their help to lift the rock. They need them to get to the lake. They need to integrate them into their effort to push and lift that rock.

Are those people in the new group members of the organization? Sure they are, because the original group needs them to fulfill the task on hand, they need them to reach the goal.

Members of your organization are not just those who report to you or who are on the payroll. In order to reach your goal, to move your rock, you have to change the culture of all of those whose help you need in doing so.

> *You mean to say that I need to coordinate, plan for, organize, and reward not just those who directly report to me, but all those I need in order to dispense my responsibility as a manger, as a leader?*

Yes. A manager who says "I can do only what is possible with the people reporting to me; and if I do not have all the people I need to do my job, I should not be expected to be responsible for it," is a bad leader. He does not lift rocks, he lifts pebbles.

There is no leader, manager, administrator, executive, prime minister, or even parent, who has all the people they need for their job reporting to them.

A parent is responsible for raising his or her kids. But teachers do not report to parents. Nor does a sports coach. Certainly, the group of kids down the street, with which a child might socialize, does not report to his parents. Yet all of them impact the raising of a child. They are like surrogate parents.

I have never met a manager who claimed, "All the people I need to carry out my responsibilities report to me." Never! The managers I know always claim the opposite. Their usual complaint is that they have difficulty carrying out their responsibilities because people critical to the tasks do not report to them. Sam Armacost, who was president of Bank of America, had the best response to this situation: "You don't need to own a highway in order to drive on it. You need only a token to get on it." You need the capability to be a team player.

*But surely the presidents of companies have everyone they need reporting to them.*

Do they? The unions do not report to the company president. Neither do the bankers, the stockholders, the clients, or the competitors. From the perspective of those at the bottom, it looks as if presidents have everything under control, but they often only act that way to demonstrate authority. Upon closer inspection, one might find that they are lonely at the top and frequently feel powerless to carry out their responsibility.

*How about the president of a country?*

She is the least powerful of them all, because she has even more people to mobilize, and their "rock" is not a rock, but a mountain.

You are the most powerful when you work alone. But then there is no organization and you are not lifting a rock. You are not managing an organization. You are just managing yourself. (By the way it is not as simple there either. You have all kinds of voices in your head you need to calm down and make cooperate. You are not that "alone" either.)

*I guess we're all lonely and vulnerable, yet some leaders will not admit it.*

If they did, they would scare their constituents. People expect their leaders to be like their parents: strong, knowledgeable, providing security, making them feel safe. If a leader admits that he is not that powerful, it scares people. That is what happened with US President Jimmy Carter, who made a speech about America's crisis of confidence. He lost much of the respect of the nation and is still considered one of the weakest presidents the country has ever had.

It is even more critical in countries that have a tradition of being managed dictatorially. Take Russia, for instance. President Vladimir Putin must act dictatorially, because the people expect him to. If he behaved like Prime Minister Dmitry Medvedev, who is more open, people would consider him weak. The country would feel rudderless. It would be like anarchy.

*Then where should I, as a leader, look to find the organization I am supposed to manage?*

Start by looking at the clients for whom the organization exists. That means being conscious of your responsibility to others. No one exists solely for himself.

*I know people who are totally self-centered and couldn't care less about anyone else.*

The moment you exist exclusively for yourself, you become a cancer. Cancerous cells use energy for non-functional purposes. They serve nothing and no one but themselves. Some people are cancerous entities in an organization, and some organizations are cancerous entities in a society. The world is created so that everything exists to support something else in a functioning totality, which then functions to serve its components. That is the ecological balance we are all so preoccupied with nowadays.

Starting any organization, society, or community means being conscious of this interdependence. It is this spiritual consciousness of *who am I*, which is always answered with *for whom* and *for what am I*.

We could modify Descartes' statement, "I think, therefore I am," to "I serve, therefore I am." Rabbi Abraham Heschel said, "If I am not for myself, who will be for me? And if I am only for myself, then who am I?"

There is no healthy organization without a sense of common destiny linking it to a larger scheme. There must be a consciousness of interdependence, whether the organization is a nation, a business, a marriage, or an individual.

After you identify for whom the organization exists (the clients), you should identify the people whose cooperation you need in order to satisfy the needs of those clients.

Let's go back to the group of friends who are trying to move the rock blocking their path. Assume that in order to remove the rock, to reach the lake for canoeing, you need the assistance of park ranger who does not organizationally report to you. Maybe, as already stated, you need other hikers to help lift the rock. And since you need the whole group in order to achieve your goal, the other hikers and park rangers are all members of your organization, who need to be coordinated, motivated, and, in a word, managed.

*But why would they do it? The ranger gets paid to help. But what about the other hikers?*

Because there is a common goal: The other hikers want to get to the lake too, or at least beyond the spot the rock is blocking. Or they are people who "help forward," they help you in the hope that someone will help them in the future. We all help each other. We are a community.

It is your job to find what their needs are, why they would cooperate, and satisfy those needs so that the rock can be moved.

It is not always clear to everyone where the common good lies. It is your role as a leader, manager, or parent to identify the common goal, the common good, and mobilize the people around it. Moreover, you should reward them for cooperating. Or, even better, you should be sure there is a reason for them to cooperate. There should be a reason that reinforces cooperation.

*What could that be?*

Look at the metaphorical rock you are responsible for lifting. Some of the people you need to help you lift the rock work for you directly. They're on your payroll. They're the employees on your organizational chart. Some people necessary to lift the rock do not work directly for you. They are in other departments. Maybe they're your peers. Maybe they're your superiors. Maybe they're even outside the organization. The people you are supposed to manage or lead are all those people you need to lift the rock (or perhaps find a way to bypass the rock—either way you still need them to get to the lake). All of them need to get satisfaction from moving that rock. Otherwise, why would they cooperate?

> You should feel responsible for serving a totality in order for that totality to serve you.

Some people do it for the money. Some do it because they like lifting rocks. Some do it because of the camaraderie of jointly lifting the rock. Some do it because they want to get to the lake too.

The weakest motivation is of those who do it for the money. The strongest motivation is when people do it simply because they want to help.

When determining whom you should include in your "organization," look beyond the rock, even beyond the lake. How far you look, and thus whom you need to integrate, depends on your consciousness. The organization, to which and for which you feel responsible, might include not only those people needed to move the rock. If you raise your eyes higher, you will realize that the rock is irrelevant and so is the lake. What integrates us changes over time. Today it is the rock, but getting to the lake, as a goal, might change. What is constant is the human race, the needs of which change, whether they are to move a rock or reach a lake. Feel responsible for the human race, for our civilization, but do not stop there. If you continue looking up, you will realize that the world we occupy is inhabited not just by the human race, but also by plants, animals, rocks, practically everything that surrounds us. You should feel responsible for serving a totality in order for that totality to serve you.

*This discussion reminds me of a story: Three people are laying bricks. If you ask the first person what he is doing he might answer, "I'm laying bricks." The second person might respond, "I'm building a wall." The third person might answer, "I am building a temple where we are going to worship the Lord together."*

Only the third person understands the purpose of the whole enterprise and recognizes the benefits to be shared from each person's function. Through prayer, in whichever form it is done, a person becomes (I)ntegrated with the Lord. That (I)ntegration, in order to be fully realized, has to be *within* oneself, *between* oneself and others, and *outside* of the immediate circle into the larger scheme to which one belongs.

We become aware of God when we become conscious that everything and everyone belongs to one large, interrelated system. When we become conscious of that, we realize we are one, although we have different forms, shapes, and textures. The differences are necessary for the functioning of the whole. Through our differences we serve each other in a totality. That totality has consciousness too, a total, absolute, and everlasting one. That is God to me.

*How do I operationally do this—tomorrow morning?*

Look at the (PAEI) codes. Start by asking, who are my clients? For whom do I exist? This is the first group of people or entities, depending on your consciousness, that you need to identify. Next, identify the present needs of those clients and what you need to do to satisfy their needs. That is the (P) role. The next question on which you should focus is, how do you go about doing it with minimum waste?

*That is the (A) role?*

> You love because you are.

You should also ask yourself what the future needs of your present and future clients will be. That is the (E) role. Then determine whom you need in order to satisfy your clients' present and future needs? Do you also need rangers, other hikers, and so on? That's the organization that you need to integrate and you need to make it worthwhile for them to cooperate. That is your (I) role.

Ask yourself what the people needed for lifting the rock or arriving at the lake want from the organization. What is in it for them if they cooperate? To some, the organization pays a salary. To others, it pays no salary, but someone has to take them to dinner and massage their egos. Others are paid commissions. Getting "paid" is different for different people and it needs to be ethical and legal. Your job is to find out how the organization should reward them, so that they cooperate to satisfy the needs of your clients.

The strongest motivation is when you cooperate because of who you are as a human being. You need no reward. You ask for none. You lift the rock because you are a cooperative person. Period. You love people without a hidden agenda, without asking for a reward. You love because you are.

## The Stakeholders

The people you need to lead, manage, and integrate, in order to satisfy your clients' needs are called stakeholders. They should be paid a salary or rewarded in some other way. Like clients, stakeholders have self-interest too. Employees, salaried or otherwise, and stockholders, for instance, are stakeholders. Both groups have something at stake: The satisfaction of their needs should be based upon how the organization performs.

> *What about management?*

They also have needs. That's why they are in the organization. They're stakeholders as well. Be sure their needs and rewards mirror the needs and rewards of the organization. Sometimes they do not. During the financial crisis in the US at of the beginning of the twenty-first century, management took millions of dollars in bonuses, while the banks they worked for were going bankrupt, employees were being fired, and shareholders were losing their shirts.

> *What about the community in which the organization is located? Does it have something at stake?*

The community is a stakeholder too. You must make all stakeholders realize that if they cooperate, their needs will be satisfied. You have to create a win-win climate in which money and salary are not the only means of exchange, and you have to synchronize the satisfaction of the needs of the clients with satisfying the needs of the stakeholders.

A leader is like a transformer in between two patterns of needs: on one hand are client needs that have to be satisfied; on the other hand are the stakeholders whose cooperation he needs in order to satisfy client needs. He must satisfy all their needs.

You are in between two pressure groups: needs of clients and needs of collaborators, the stakeholders. You are in the middle, juggling. Sometimes you cannot satisfy all clients' needs because you do not have the capability to satisfy all the needs of the collaborators you need. You have to align the needs of the two groups.

Try to maximize client/customer satisfaction. Make them want to come back again and again—that is your deterministic goal—with only reasonable profits necessary for giving a competitive return on investment to investors, to stockholders, and whatever else needed for the other stakeholders. You should give competitive income to the employees. They are another group of stakeholders.

But never, ever lose your focus. The focus should always be on the clients, not on the stockholders. Customer satisfaction is the goal. Profits are the constraint.

## Mechanistic vs. Organic Consciousness

*What about the words mechanistic and organic? You used them in your definition of (I)ntegration. What do they mean?*

Imagine a chair with four legs standing in the middle of the room. Why is it called a chair? Why don't we call it a cow?

*Well, if you could milk it, you could call it a cow.*

> You are what you do, and what you do has functional meaning through the needs you satisfy.

Yes! For the purposes of our discussion, we can say that something is what it does, what needs it satisfies, what it is designed to do. If it does not perform the function, then it is not the object. If you tell me the function, I can tell you the name of the object. If you have a piano that is not being played, it's not a piano. It's a piece of furniture. If you have a chair you cannot sit on, it is not a chair. It could be an art piece by the Memphis Group, and the owner would be upset if you sat on it. If I show you a hammer and ask what it is, you should know enough from what I have said so far to answer me.

*Easy: I don't know what it is until you tell me what you do with it. If you pound nails with it, then it's a hammer. If you use it to harm someone, it's a weapon. If you collect different types of hammers from around the world to hang in your garage, then it's a decoration.*

We don't know what something is until we know its function, what need it satisfies. You cannot say you are a father if you have never done anything to satisfy your child's needs. You might be a biological father, but if you're not fulfilling the child's social, economic, and emotional needs, you're not a parenting father. You are what you do, and what you do has functional meaning through the needs you satisfy.

Now, back to the chair: It's a chair because we can sit on it. It fulfills the function of providing a place to sit. The (P) function has been satisfied. What about the (A) role? How would you check that?

*I'd look to see if there is anything unnecessary. Wasteful. Is it easy to produce? Is it easy to clean?*

How about the (E) role?

*I'd look to see if it satisfies other needs, future needs, beyond sitting. Like if it is aesthetically pleasing, if it fits the color scheme of the other furniture, etc.*

Now about the (I) role. What would happen if the right forward leg broke down?

*We no longer have a functioning chair. We have a broken chair. We cannot sit on it.*

The question is, why doesn't the left forward leg move to the center of the chair, creating a tripod, so that the chair can continue to function as a sitting device? The answer is obvious: The chair is like a machine. There is no internal interdependence between the parts. It is as if the left leg says, "I am okay. The problem is with the right leg. I am not broken."

*I can see that. It happens in some organizations. The company is losing sales. The people in the production department say it is a sales problem, not their problem.*

Yes, in managerial lingo, this is called a silo mentality.

In order for the chair to fulfill its role, someone from the outside has to fix it. This chair is dependent on external intervention to function. There is no internal interdependence between the parts of a chair. A multimillion-dollar spaceship can explode in flight and kill seven people because an O-ring does not function. No other part can take the place of that O-ring. This is called mechanistic consciousness.

Now let's look at organic consciousness. Look at your hand. It's a hand because you can grasp objects, it functions as a hand. What would happen if you broke or lost one of the fingers? Would you still have a hand?

*Yes. It wouldn't be as good, but I would still have a hand.*

Why?

*Because the other four fingers would compensate. The hand would continue to function.*

Exactly. What makes a hand a hand is not just the physical attributes of the five fingers. It's that each of the five fingers "thinks" like a hand. If each leg on the chair thought, I'm a leg and part of a chair, then each leg would support the function of satisfying the need to sit. The chair would have an organic instead of a mechanistic consciousness.

Let's look at humans. Why do our legs run when our eyes see danger? It is as if, through organic consciousness, all our body parts recognize the benefits and liabilities of their interdependence, and work to protect the whole. In a mechanistic consciousness each part is "conscious" only of itself. There is no internal sense of interdependence.

In an organization with a mechanistic consciousness, production people worry only about production and sales people worry only about sales. And who worries about whether the totality functions? Outsiders have to worry about the totality and have to intervene because none of the individuals involved worry about it. That intervention is often undertaken by management. In such an organization, employees view and oppose management as if they were outsiders.

An extreme case is when management also worries only about its own interests and not about the totality it manages. In that case, the external intervention is provided by consultants, by the government, or by no one, in which case the organization dis(I)ntegrates and might go bankrupt.

This disintegration does not happen only in business organizations. It can happen in a country where those in a leadership position take care of themselves and not the country. They are corrupt. In essence no one takes care of the country—it is not strange that the country suffers.

In the chair example, if every leg understood and supported the benefits of being part of a sitting system, then the chair would have an organic consciousness. It wouldn't be a broken chair, because each part would compensate for the system's vulnerability and do its best to make the system function. The chair would be less dependent on any one of its parts. It would work like a hand.

# 64 – MASTERING CHANGE

*I think I understand: To be efficient in the long term, an organization should act like a hand in which no finger is indispensable. In an organization, teamwork should be such that each person supports the other, so that no one is indispensable.*

Look at your hand. Which finger is the most important one? Most people pick the pointing finger. It is the most responsive to our instructions. Look at sculptures. The guy is on a horse. Hand is pointing forward and the pointing finger pointing the way.

The pointing finger is the most important finger for leading a young organization. You do not reason too much with a toddler when to go to sleep. You tell him to go to sleep because it is time and take him to bed and that is it. But when this toddler grows to be forty years old you cannot and should not treat him as if he is a baby. Right? Some mothers try to baby their adult children and what happens?

So, in order to have a hand, which finger is the most important one? It is the thumb. Why? Because it is the thumb that makes the four fingers into a hand. In a certain language, the thumb is called "the hand maker."[5] If you have no thumb, you have no hand. That is the integrator, the team builder.

Now look at my hand. Fingers straight up, together, and touching each other. What is that? Go to any church, of any denomination, or Indian temples, and look at their gods and goddesses. What do you see? They all stand with their hand half up and the fingers together. What are they telling us?

Be different, but together. Each finger is different, but to be a hand we need to accept each other's differences and work together. Not in spite of being different, but because we are different. Each finger does something the other finger cannot do as well. There is synergy when they work together.

In the Middle East this is called a *hamsa*. Women carry it as an ornament. People in the Middle East put it on the door at the entrance

---

[5] I am sorry I forgot which language it is—I have lectured in over fifty countries, and I do not remember now who told me this.

# EFFICIENCY AND EFFECTIVENESS – 65

to their home. It is a blessing: different and together.

In the Middle East, when they curse someone they spread the fingers and put it in front of the face they are cursing as if saying: Be different and not together.

The difference between a blessing and a curse is only two inches: Are we different together or different not together? For being together we need the thumb. The (I)ntegrator.

Have you been to New Delhi, India? Over the booth of the immigration officer, as you try to enter the country at the airport, you will see sculptures of hands. Each hand has the thumb touching a different finger. I suggest to you, those sculptures represent the Indian culture, which is very (I).

*That is what we need to do? (I)ntegrate not in spite of being different, but because by integrating differences we can create synergy.*

Yes, you do not want fusion, forcing all to be the same in order to be together.

*Like fascism and Communism.*

Or some religions. Come to think of it, all radical religions reject differences.

What we have here is a struggle between those who accept differences and know how to benefit from them and those who reject differences and are fearful of them. It has been going on for centuries. Sparta and Athens had those differences. Look at who was fighting whom in both world wars. It was democracies against totalitarian or monarchic regimes.

*This struggle will be here forever?*

I believe so, except that now, with advanced weapons of mass destruction, it is becoming massively more dangerous.

*We have gone wide and far off the subject of how to manage a business. Can we get back to what am I supposed to know to lead better?*

Ask yourself: What is my managerial or leadership responsibility? What is my rock? Who are the clients and what are their needs? Who are the stakeholders I need in order to lift the rock, and how do I foster the necessary interdependence between stakeholders? How do I get people to realize that we need each other? For instance, do we have a common mission? Do we have a reward system that nurtures cooperation?

> When clients are satisfied by satisfied stakeholders, you have a system in which no one is indispensable.

If people share a vision and have a reward system that nurtures the pursuit and achievement of that mission cooperatively, then it is likely no one will be indispensable. People will back each other up and not wait for an outsider to fix their problems.

You should create an environment where you (I)ntegrate the clients and stakeholders. When clients are satisfied by satisfied stakeholders, you have a system in which no one is indispensable.

To be healthy means that the organization functions to serve the present purpose for which it exists, (P), efficiently, (A), and is capable of proactively coping with a changing environment, (E), with a consciousness of interdependency so that no one part of the system is indispensable, (I).

(PAEI) is a code that can be applied to many, many situations or needs. Here we are using it to analyze decisions that make organizations healthy or sick. If you study Adizes, you will find the (PAEI) code[6] can be used to analyze leadership styles,[7] organizational structures,[8] and strategies,[9] as well as to predict future problems,[10] and much more. As a matter of fact, at the Adizes Institute every year or so, we find another use of the (PAEI) code. It is like chemistry. In Russia they call Adizes the Mendeleev of management.

Now let us go back to the group of people who, on Friday evening, while drinking beer, decided to go hiking to a lake, came across a rock that blocked their passage, and had to decide to move the rock or to go back. (Or maybe camp there and have a barbecue.)

---

6  See Adizes, I. *The Ideal Executive, Why You Cannot Be One and What to Do About It*. Santa Barbara, CA: The Adizes Institute Publications, 2004.

7  See Adizes, I. *Management/Mismanagement Styles: How to Identify a Style and What to Do About It*. Santa Barbara, CA: The Adizes Institute Publications, 2004.

8  See Adizes, I. *Managing Corporate Lifecycles–How Organizations Grow, Age and Die*, Volume 1. Santa Barbara, CA: The Adizes Institute Publications, in conjunction with Embassy Book Distributors, 2012; and Adizes I. *Managing Corporate Lifecycles–Analyzing Organizational Behavior and Raising Healthy Organizations*, Volume 2, Santa Barbara, CA: The Adizes Institute Publications, 2015.

9  See http://www.ichakadizes.com/paei-code-and-strategy-development.

10  Adizes, *Managing Corporate Lifecycles*, op. cit.

(I) is not of the same quality as the other (PAE) roles. It belongs to a "different league." In a sense, (I) is needed for each one of the (P), (A), and (E) roles to function well. The (P) role is not in a vacuum. You have to sense what needs to be done. Thus, at least a small amount of (I) is needed. However, in this case, the (I) is not oriented to people but to a task. For a (P) person to sense what needs to be done, she must have some sensitivity to the task, to the situation. The (P) role without this sensitivity will be operating in a vacuum.

The same is true for the (A) role. One has to feel the system and its needs in order to administer it.

And the same holds for (E)ntrepreneuring. An entrepreneur feels what he is innovating for and about. A market whiz feels the market, senses it, and is integrated with it. An entrepreneurial engineer feels in her bones the equipment or machine she is inventing. This also applies to artists. They are (E)s too. A good sculptor senses the stone he is working on. He feels the object of his work, as if the two are integrated.

Without (I) the other roles are barren, unproductive, I might even say useless.

> The purpose of existence of any system is (I)ntegration, the (I) role.

In our story about five friends going on a hike to a lake, first note that these five people were friends. Their friendship and sense of belonging expressed itself in a need to do something together. Initially, that need was satisfied by drinking beer, (P). Then, it was satisfied by going on a hike to a lake. New (P). Then, it was satisfied by working together either to lift the rock, another new (P), or to come up with another plan, maybe give up on the lake and go and have a barbecue somewhere else, (E). Relating and interrelating, (I) was at all times present.

If the (P) role is driven by the need to achieve, the (A) role by the need to control, and the (E) role the need for immortality or the fear of death, the (I) role is driven by the need for affiliation.

The ultimate reason we do anything is the (I) role, the interrelationship. (I)ntegration is the ultimate and constant need. It expresses itself by different yearnings, such as to go and drink beer together, hike together, or paddle a canoe together.

(I) is the ultimate purpose for our existence. There is nothing in this world that doesn't exist to serve something else by functionally interrelating with it. The pen I write with has no meaning if it does not leave a mark on paper. Breathing is useless unless the oxygen feeds my body. Nothing in itself is functional on its own. The ability of anything to function is evaluated by how it serves its clients. The purpose of existence of any system is (I)ntegration, the

## 68 – MASTERING CHANGE

(I) role.

In personal life this need to interrelate is called the need for love. I suspect that every problem in our personal life is a manifestation of a lack of love, and the solution is to experience love.

You can see how powerful this need for affiliation is in prison. Why is prison a punishment? Beyond the fact that the prisoner lost freedom to act and power over his life, there is loss of affiliation, and the most severe punishment in a prison is being put into isolation. People go crazy, and some, if isolated for too long, commit suicide. To calm prisoners down, some prisons give prisoners a dog to raise. That dog gives them love and it has an incredible calming effect. In the US, they bring dogs to be petted by the patients in hospitals. It has a healing effect, I am told.

Interrelationship, (I)ntegration, is forever and constant. It expresses itself in different needs we wish to satisfy in the future. It is like saying that spirit is constant and forever. It expresses itself through different bodies when we are born, and it continues to exist when we die. And this (I)ntegration exists as long as we serve each other for a totality that will, in turn, serve us. That's the road to being alive forever, through your deeds and not through your body or thoughts.

The ultimate need, to be (I)ntegrated, to be functionally interdependent, is constant, just as spirit is constant.

> *How does that happen? When does a particular expression of this constant interdependence start? When is an organization born?*

When the founders of a company become inspired to start the company, they call their banker, their parents, and anyone else they need to call. They take out loans and set up the company. Now, what did they see before their eyes that day they were inspired? Did they see profits?

> *I don't think so. When people start companies, they won't see any profits in the first few months, or maybe even years. As a matter of fact, if they closed up shop and went to work for somebody else during that time, they'd make more money.*

So what did they see?

> *An opportunity to make profits.*

Note the choice of words: an opportunity to make profits. That tells you that you have to focus on the opportunity, and if you exploit the opportunity correctly you will reap profits. Eventually. From our previous analogy you can see that the profit is the bulls-eye and the opportunity the sights. What do you think that opportunity is?

*Added value is created by satisfying the needs that someone is willing to pay to have satisfied. So the opportunities we are talking about are the needs in the marketplace that are currently not being satisfied well, or at all, and that could be satisfied by the new company the founder is contemplating. Founders see needs they believe they can satisfy and that should be satisfied. When needs meet capabilities, an opportunity is born.*

> When needs meet capabilities, an opportunity is born.

Right. An organization is born when the interdependence is realized and a commitment is made to satisfy it.

The first thing to note is that the founders were conscious; they were not sleeping. They were conscious, aware, and sensitive to something else beyond themselves. Out of that consciousness of interdependence, the (I) role, came an awareness of specific perceived needs that can and should be satisfied. That need could be for ice cream or a new medicine that will cure a disease. This is the (E) role, identifying the specific need that should be satisfied. Then, the founders get moving on the path towards satisfying that long-term need and, in the process, encounter obstacles (rocks). Removing rocks, (P), is functional when it enables the founders to move closer to their long-term goal, (E), without ruining the grand purpose of the whole enterprise, which is to functionally (I)nterrelate. You can achieve (E) and (P) goals and in the process destroy (I), and when that happens you will feel the whole effort was not worth it.

Take a person who has a dream to build a business empire and works hard, stepping on people, destroying lives, including destroying his family. He might achieve stardom but wonder if the price was worth it.

Drinking beer was the initial way to satisfy (I) needs. The person who suggested a hike noted a new need to interrelate. He is sensitive to what the people aspire to. When the group comes across the rock, this person should still be sensitive to the grand need to interrelate functionally. In light of that, he should lead the process of removing the rock or abandoning the hike.

The problem with some large organizations is that by the time they employ several thousand people, very few, if any, of the employees know why they are walking on that path or where they are hiking to, or where the rock is.

*Because they're all pushing the rock without knowing why?*

Yes, and pushing each other. "You're stepping on me." "No, you're stepping on me." They are preoccupied with turf wars. They spend their time dwelling on the liability, rather than on the purpose and benefit of their interrelationship and interdependence.

*What do you mean by "interrelate functionally?"*

I mean create added value. If the process of removing the rock creates tension and fighting, while the purpose of the hike in the first place was to have experience being together, they might move the rock, but miss the purpose of moving the rock.

The same holds true for a marriage. What is the purpose of being married? Is it to have children or to love and be loved, in which case the children are an expression of the couple's love for one another? What about a couple that cannot have children? Should they divorce, or can they find another manifestation of love through which they can experience their purpose of being together?

What if they have problems in their marriage? Those problems are "rocks," issues like career decisions, what house to buy, how to spend money. How can those rocks be removed? What are the right decisions? It depends on what they are committed to or why they are together in the first place. If it is love, insisting on being right about how to remove the rock correctly and vigorously insisting on it, and fighting to win the argument, can be quite wrong. They may move the rock, arrive at the lake, and find they destroyed the purpose of why they went to the lake in the first place.

In managing, leading, parenting, interrelating in a marriage, and interrelating in general, always ask yourself: What is the purpose of the relationship in the first place? What are you committed to first and above all? The answer, if you are conscious, is love. If you are confused as to how love got into the conversation, relax. It will become clearer later. For the time being, ask yourself as far as you can be conscious, what are you committed to? What are the long- and short-term needs for which the interrelationship of your organization exists, whether that organization is you personally, your marriage, your business, or society? Next, ask yourself how you should satisfy those needs without undermining the interrelationship itself.

The ultimate (I) is love. I found out that people who love what they do succeed better than those who don't. It is obvious, is it not? They are passionate about what they do, thus they succeed. They are integrated with their actions. They feel the object of their efforts, thus success. Do you love your place of work? Do you love your clients? Do you love the product or service you provide?

In all conflicts, all assignments to remove whichever "rocks" there are in your life, if you are guided by love, do it from the heart. You will succeed even if you fail. You will not feel guilty or like a failure, because you did it with all your heart, with love. What else could you have done better? So if it failed, it was supposed to fail. You could not have saved it. It was beyond your efforts.

Do you realize that people who are in love look younger than their age and people who hate look old? What is love, if not total integration, and we already said integration is the sign of health. If you are healthy, you live longer. Love prolongs life.

To have a sustainable, long-lived organization, it should be based on love. Love your employees. Love your clients. Love the product. Just love, and the more you do, the longer the organization will survive, and the more successful it will be.

If you're not convinced, try hating for a change. Hate customers. Hate suppliers. Hate workers, and see how long will you survive. . . .

*Then what?*

The organization does not become effective and efficient in the short and long term by itself. Someone needs to make (PAEI) decisions that will then make the (PAEI) organization produce (PAEI) results. These results produce short- and long-term value added, which commercial organizations measure by profits. Whose role is it to see that (PAEI) decisions are made? That is the role of leadership, management, parenting, or government.

*I'm looking forward to the exercises, because this was really confusing!*

We will have many exercises. In our next conversation, we'll start analyzing what happens when any one of these roles—(P)roviding a needed service, (A)dministering, (E)ntrepreneuring, or (I)ntegrating—is missing. We will learn how to diagnose leaders or managers and companies. If we see something is not working, we will be able to identify what's missing. If we know why it is happening, we should know what to do about it!

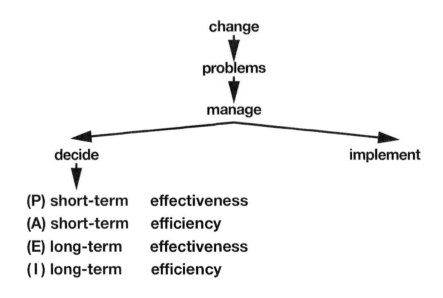

## Summary

*Let me summarize to see if I understand the material. This was very complicated, to say the least.*

It will become clearer through lots of discussions and examples. Trust me!

*Okay. To manage change a decision has to be made and implemented. Good decisions make the organization effective and efficient in the short and the long term. They make the organization functional, systematized, proactive, and organic in consciousness.*

*To be effective in the short term, the organization has to (P)rovide for the clients' needs. The (P) role can be measured by repeat sales out of total sales.*

*Efficiency in the short term means using the least amount of resources, including managerial time, to accomplish something. For that the organization needs to be (A)dministered, systematized, and organized. In order to do that, the organization needs routine and discipline.*

*For effectiveness in the long term, the organization has to be (E)ntrepreneurial, to pro-act. It has to imagine future clients' needs and take action in the present to be able to satisfy those needs in the future. In order to do that, it has to be creative and willing to take risks.*

*For efficiency in the long term, the organization needs to be (I)ntegrated by creating an organic climate of cooperation between and among all stakeholders to satisfy the needs of the clients.*

*If all stakeholders cooperate and no one is indispensable, the organization can be efficient for the long term. For that the organization has to identify and be sensitive to the needs of all the stakeholders and clients, and create and nurture a climate that mutually satisfies those needs.*

Good summary! From now on, we won't have to cover as much theory. Instead we can focus on applications.

# CONVERSATION 5
# The Incompatibility of Roles

*I've been thinking a lot about our last conversation. Let's summarize it again:*

*In order to manage the problems caused by change, we need to make good decisions and implement them efficiently.*

*How well we manage is a function of the quality of the decisions we make and the amount of energy we have to spend in order to implement those decisions.*

*To make quality decisions, we must focus on the present services that need to be (P)erformed in order to satisfy the reason for which the organization exists. This is the (P) role. It makes the organization effective in the short term.*

*We must also perform the (A) role, to (A)dminister, ensuring that the right things are done at the right time. This process makes the organization efficient in the short term.*

*The (E) role, (E)ntrepreneuring, makes the organization proactive by positioning it, in the present, to deal with future clients' needs. This role makes the organization effective in the long term.*

*The last role is the need to (I)ntegrate. This role transforms the organization's culture from mechanistic, where all stakeholders and clients feel isolated, to organic, where people share their sense of interdependence because of mutual interests and values.*

*We need all four (PAEI) roles, which are like four "vitamins." Any time one of these "vitamins" is missing, a certain predictable organizational disease will occur. Depending on which role is missing, the organization could be ineffective or inefficient in the short and/or long term.*

*Now, what are those managerial diseases, please?*

You must understand the (P), (A), (E), and (I) roles very well before we start diagnosing systems, whether we diagnose people, organizations, or societies. Try to answer a few questions.

Assume your two children, say five and six years old, are playing in their room while you are reading the Sunday paper. After a while, there is a commotion and you hear them yelling, "Daaaaddy!" They are fighting over a xylophone. On this day they both want the same xylophone.

The first question is, if they're calling for Daddy to come and solve their problem, is their interdependence mechanistic or organic?

*Mechanistic. They are not resolving their own problem; they expect somebody from the outside to step in.*

Right! Now what would the (P) solution be?

*To take the xylophone away.*

Stop! How should you go about finding the (P) solution?

*You need to identify the clients and identify their needs. You should analyze how to satisfy those needs and then do it. That is the (P) role: (P)roviding the present needs of present clients.*

Right! However, if you took the xylophone away, who was the client whose needs you were satisfying?

*Mine, I guess. I wanted some peace and quiet.*

Yes! This is a typical mistake. Many times in solving a problem, managers satisfy their own needs, not the clients' needs. Try again: Who should the clients be in this example?

*The kids.*

Then what should the (P) solution be?

*Buy them another xylophone.*

That may be the right solution, depending on what you assume to be the children's needs. If their true need is to play the xylophone, to make music, then the solution to buy another xylophone is a good one. But do you believe the two kids are fighting over a xylophone because they really want to play music?

*They might be fighting because they want to make noise.*

Then the solution is to give them some pots and pans from the kitchen to bang on and make noise.

*Maybe they're fighting because of sibling rivalry.*

Then they'll fight over the pots and pans too, because they need to fight until someone yields. The solution to the sibling rivalry could be to let them fight it out, and, unless it gets out of hand, leave them alone. If they're fighting because you're reading the newspaper and they want your attention, then they will fight until you give them your attention.

Please hear what I'm saying: The (P) solution is not easily identifiable. First you have to identify who the clients are. Then you have to try to determine their real needs, because you cannot know the need for sure.

*I could ask them.*

Yes, you can, and many companies do market research and statistically validate what clients needs are, but be careful. Clients often do not know what they want. They know only what they do not want.

*What do you mean?*

The last time you bought a car or a suit, did you know what you wanted and simply purchase it, or did you look around and try different suits until you found what you liked?

*I went shopping.*

In order to have a (P) solution, you have to offer the clients alternative solutions until the clients are satisfied. You will identify the need and verify it only by the fact that the clients are happy, in this case, when the kids are quiet and playing.

It's like selling dog food. You don't know if the food is any good until the dog eats it. The dog does not speak; it votes with its behavior. The same is true of humans. Don't just listen to what they say; watch what they do. Are they buying? The best proof that there is value in what you are providing is if they actually buy it. Never assume what the needs should be and then get upset when clients don't have those needs. Don't patronize your clients. Try and try again until you succeed and you succeed when the clients come for more. You need to try over and over again because—I repeat—clients do not know what they want. They know what they do not want. I mean when they are looking for something new, I do not mean repetitive buying like buying vegetables or bread. I mean something like buying a car. You have to try a few times until the client says, "Aha, that is what I want!" It is like looking for a spouse.

> **People do not buy a product. They buy satisfaction of a need.**

*So we haven't found the (P) solution to the xylophone problem until the kids are quiet and doing something that satisfies their needs, as expressed by their struggle for the xylophone.*

Right! The kids are not fighting for the xylophone. They are fighting to satisfy certain needs that the xylophone represents. The need could be to make noise, to express their sibling rivalry, to get their parent's attention, or perhaps to fulfill an aesthetic need to play music.

People do not buy a product. They buy satisfaction of a need. To make a (P) decision means to a solution that satisfies the clients' immediate needs. To identify what that need is might take several tries.

*How about (A)?*

The (A) role makes an organization efficient. Tell me what the (A) solution to the problem between the kids could be.

*Have some law and order.*

Right, but how?

*Well, we know the (A) role is to make the organization efficient. That means systematizing the organization so we do not have to reinvent the wheel each time we need to wheel something around. In an (A) decision, we should have the same solution for the same problem. That makes us efficient. So, the (A) solution would be to say that one brother gets the xylophone for ten minutes, then the other one gets it for the next ten minutes, and we toss a coin to see who gets the xylophone first. We apply a family rule we can apply in all similar cases.*

But what happens then? When you apply that solution, ten minutes to each child or whatever the rules of the family dictate, who is the client now and what is the client's need?

> *The family, and it needs some peace and quiet. Now the needs of the family come before the needs of any individual in the family.*

The family is the client, and this solution ignores the children's particular needs.

That happens in many organizations. When an organization is young, it looks for the (P) solution, how to satisfy client needs. It satisfies the clients and because of that its sales grow bigger and bigger, and the organization gets messier until it hits a crisis. Then management says, "We need some order here." The organization itself emerges as a needy client. So, the company hires a professional (A)dministrator to organize the place. This person sets up budgets, information systems, organizational charts, and incentive programs. The old-timers might get upset, because the professional manager is not selling, not serving the customers. They do not understand, do not realize, that the (A)dministrator has a different client in mind. The organization and its stakeholders are his clients, not the customers.

In other words, first the organization develops its capability to satisfy its customers, then its focus shifts to satisfy its stakeholders. Then it (I)ntegrates both into a working totality. When this happens, the organization is in the Prime of its lifecycle.[11]

If the switch in focus from clients to stakeholders is abrupt, it can create antagonism within the organization, because the professional manager's focus is different from what the rest of the organization is used to. Now, the long-time employees resist all this internal orientation, and often, the professional manager is fired for doing the job he was hired to do in the first place. "He just sits in his office and works on his computer all day," the old-timer (P)s might complain. "He never sells anything!"

> *How about the third role? What is the (E)ntrepreneurial answer to two kids fighting over a xylophone?*

Would you like to try to answer?

> *Let me see. In order to be (E)ntrepreneurial, I have to be proactive by positioning myself now for the next need. So what do I have to do? I have to find a new need other than the one the children are fighting over. I'll say, "Let's go to the movies!" I bet they'll stop bickering immediately and get ready to go.*

That's what businesses often do. When they note that sales of a present product or service are going down—that client needs are not being satisfied—and when they can't reverse the

---

11  See Adizes, *Managing Corporate Lifecycles*, op. cit.

situation, one solution is to identify and satisfy a newer, stronger client need, the development of a new product or a new market.

What about the (I) solution?

*My guess is to tell them to play together.*

The moment you *tell* them the solution, you are intervening, you are coming from the outside. Is that mechanistic or organic?

*Mechanistic.*

That's why telling them to play together would be an (A) solution, not an (I) solution.

*What do you suggest?*

You should not step in and order the kids to play together, because you would reinforce their mechanistic consciousness. They would continually rely on you to resolve their problems. In the (I) role, the task of management, leadership, or parenting is, as Ralph Ablon, CEO of Ogden Corporation, said, "to create an environment in which the most desirable thing will most probably happen."

*How do you do that?*

In the case of the xylophone, here's what I would do: I would say, "How dare you two fight? Brothers should not fight. I will not be here forever to solve the problems between you two. Who will solve your problems after I'm gone? Lawyers and judges? The punishment for fighting is that you must give me the xylophone. Neither of you will have it. Now go to your room and don't come out until you have solved the problem."

*But you ignored their needs.*

No. Ignoring them would mean not being conscious of my clients, which, in the case of being a parent, are the children. If I ignored their needs I would have probably screamed at them to be quiet and let me have some peace at home and walked away. That would be ignoring their needs. I focused on their needs but did not solve the problem myself. I created a situation in which they had to satisfy their needs by themselves, not by relying on me. A parent can't make a child be anything. A parent should create an environment in which a child can become the best he can be.

*I see. You created an environment in which the most desirable thing would most probably happen. What you are saying is that next time my vice presidents start fighting over a budget I should refuse to resolve the conflict. Give none of them the budget they want. Send them to their "room" and request that they solve the conflict among themselves.*

> A parent can't make a child be anything. A parent should create an environment in which a child can become the best he can be.

Yes, but what happens if the kids come out of their room and tell you that their solution is to burn the house down?

*I will send them back until they come with a solution that is acceptable.*

You should do the same with the two vice presidents fighting over a budget. Send them to redo their solution until they find a solution that is best for the company, not a compromise between the two of them. They should think about what is good for the company, and the kids should think what is good for the family.

*But wouldn't the kids cry and resent the fact that you refused to solve their problem? And would not the vice presidents consider me a weak leader because I refused to solve the problem, and even abdicated my role as a leader?*

You are right; expectations get in the way. People often prefer that someone else makes a decision and then they can resent and criticize the person who made that decision, object to the decision, and complain endlessly about how bad the decision was. It is so much easier for people to do that than to take responsibility and make the decision themselves. In that case, there is no one to complain about or to.

Do not fall into this trap. Force them to take responsibility. They will not like it, sure. They might resent it, but that's the price they have to pay to develop their relationship. That is how they will grow.

Now, how long do you think it would take for the kids to resolve their problem and come out of their room?

*Probably thirty seconds.*

How long do you think would it have taken them if I had said, "Take the xylophone and go to your room to solve the problem?"

*A lot longer! But why?*

Because the (P) and (I) roles are incompatible. It's very difficult to (P)rovide for a need and (I)ntegrate simultaneously. I know this from my own experience. I have attended seminars where they taught us teamwork, interdependence, respect, and listening tools. I always resolved to practice these concepts. But guess what? When I returned to work and suffered about twenty minutes of time pressure and conflict, I decided I'd had enough (I)ntegration. Trying to be (I)ntegrative and at the same time task oriented, especially under time pressure, is extremely difficult. My (I) role declines when my (P) role increases.

*Ah, I know this from my own experience. I have attended seminars where they taught us teamwork, interdependence, respect, and listening tools. I always resolved to practice these concepts. But guess what? When I returned to work and suffered about twenty minutes of time pressure and conflict, I decided I'd had enough (I)ntegration. Trying to be (I)ntegrative and at the same time task oriented, especially under time pressure, is extremely difficult. My (I) role declines when my (P) role increases.*

## (P) and (E) Incompatibility

Any combination of the four roles is incompatible, not just (P) and (I). (P)roducing and (E)ntrepreneuring are incompatible too. How many times have you said, "I'm working so hard, I have no time to think?" What does that mean? Pushing the rock—satisfying present demands—is so overwhelming that you have no time to think about future opportunities. The (P) role actually endangers the (E) role.

> At some point, you have to freeze the planning, the changing, so you can proceed with the doing.

*Yes, I know. I've heard the saying, "People who work too hard have no time to make serious money."*

Conversely, (E) threatens (P) too. (E)ntrepreneuring means change, and that threatens the (P) role. People in production often complain about development engineers or designers, saying, "If you guys don't stop changing things, we'll never get anything done." At some point, you have to freeze the planning, the changing, so you can proceed with the doing.

*Any examples?*

This happens in some countries. There is too much change in fiscal or monetary policies to control a high rate of inflation. In a democratic society, governments might rise and fall frequently, and because the socio-political orientations of different parties vary, these changes in power bring changes in fiscal and monetary policies. At one point, Argentina had a new finance minister making new policy changes every six months. What can people do? People hedge their commitments, and the fewer people committed to a plan of action, the less productivity, savings, and supply there will be. People might even transfer their financial resources to countries with more stability. The result is that inflationary pressures will continue to rise. This in turn encourages more flights of capital and further shaky commitments.

*You mean to say that to control inflation, stability is necessary.*

Right. The Adizes Methodology was used in Brazil during the Cardozo presidency to stop inflation. Clovis Carvallo, who was the de facto Prime Minister of Brazil in his role as Ministro de Casa Civil, and who has been certified in Adizes, told me so.

*That is impressive.*

> To control inflation, stability is necessary.

This incompatibility between (P) and (E) has another application. You cannot have economic growth without political and economic stability. Too much (E) undermines (P) and too much (P) undermines (E). Watch countries with continuous economic performance. They have stable continuous political leadership.

*Like Turkey under Prime Minister Erdogan.*

Or Israel under Netanyahu. Conversely, countries that have turbulence in leadership do not fare well.

*Like France?*

*But I don't see how too much (P) could undermine (E).*

If there is a crisis for survival and you have to (P), you do not have the energy or interest to invest time and money into preparing for the future. You just want to survive the present.

## (P) and (A) Incompatibility

Now let's look at another combination: (P) and (A). They are also incompatible. Remember the tennis analogy we used in our previous conversation? When you want to be very effective, you have difficulty being efficient. In your eagerness to hit the ball, you might ignore how you are hitting it.

#### 84 – MASTERING CHANGE

*That is why, during training, your coach might say, "Ignore the score." In training you focus on how you hit the ball regardless of where the ball lands.*

Thus, sometimes if you are very efficient you end up being less effective. You focus all your attention on how you are doing something and you miss the purpose of what you are doing.

*We talked about this already, I remember: You hit only the balls that come to your racket rather than bring the racket where the ball is. You satisfy only those needs that fit your standard operating procedures or policies. You ignore the changing needs of the client. As if you are saying to the opponent in the tennis game, send me the ball only here, because this is where I am organized to hit it.*

Yes, these are the companies that say "It would be a wonderful business to run, were it not for the changing needs of our customers." They are a bureaucracy. The reverse is also true: Too much (P) can undermine (A).

*That happens in startup companies, I bet. They are so busy trying to make ends meet, (P), that they have no time to get organized, (A).*

Exactly.

## (A) and (E) Incompatibility

*(A) and (E) are also incompatible, right?*

Sure. We know that policies, rules, and institutionalized behavior inhibit change. Thus (A) endangers (E) and vice versa; too much change, too much (E), hinders systematization and order.

*Yes, it is very difficult to innovate, be creative, think outside the box, and take risks when the organization is run by (A), where you must follow rules and predetermined routines and adhere to policies.*

If you manage by (A) do not be surprised that there will be little innovation in your company. Look at Russia today. They want innovation. People are very creative, but somehow innovation and entrepreneurship are not catching on. Why? The reason is the culture of fear that historically prevails in that country. (A) is implemented through fear. I have lectured a lot in Russia and told them that in order to have more entrepreneurs, more middle class, they need to change the culture of fear

*How did they react?*

I believe their leadership is in a trap. If they remove management by fear, people will not understand how to behave in the new reality. They will dismiss the leader as being weak. So the leader must behave in the way people expect him to behave.

It is not easy to change that culture. It's not easy to take a culture that is used to dictatorship and make it democratic. If you remove dictatorship you do not necessarily get democracy. If the foundations of the society are not already culturally democratic, you'll get anarchy.

*You mean to say that only a strong, committed leader can establish democracy?*

Yes.

*Is that all?*

> Corruption is the result of disruptive change.

No. There is another manifestation of the incompatibility of (A) and (E), and it is corruption. Show me a country with high rate of disruptive change and I will show you a lot of corruption.

*Like the CIS countries, those that used to be part of the Soviet Union?*

Yes, but not only them. There are also the developing countries in Latin America and Africa, as well as India and China. Come to think of it, America was quite corrupt at the beginning of its industrialization stage, with the railroad barons. Change can give birth to corruption.

*Why is that?*

When there is disruptive change the (A) becomes a mess. Russia, for instance, has three different accounting systems. Some of the laws are from the Communist era, some are from the Tsarist era, and some are new, from the post-Communist era. Businesses suspect they must be guilty of something, but they do not know what. The court system is overwhelmed.

*Then how do you operate?*

You seek protection. You pay someone in government not to sue you, not to hurt you, or to give you preferential treatment.

Imagine a wall. When there is an earthquake—disruptive change—what happens? The wall develops cracks. Holes. There is a Hebrew expression that says a hole in the fence invites the thief.

## 86 – MASTERING CHANGE

Corruption is the result of disruptive change. (E) destroys old (A) and no new (A) has been established. In the murky water people go fishing, taking advantage of the situation. It doesn't matter whether the change is from Communism to a market economy, or from an agrarian economy to industrialization, or decolonization.

> *They try to find the guilty party and sentence them, sometimes to death. Punishment should stop corruption, right?*

Killing the mosquitos that carry malaria does not solve the problem. New ones are born. You need to dry the swamp where they breed. The same is true here: You need to reengineer the (A) system, clean up the messy (A), bring transparency to the system, improve the court system, and then watch corruption go down.

Another example of (A)-(E) incompatibility, and the disasters that can happen because of this incompatibility is anti-Semitism. Jews are culturally very (E). They train to be (E)s from a young age. In studying the Talmud, they are encouraged to challenge everything all the time, not to take anything for granted.

In a society where (A) is culturally dominant, people resent (E) style with a passion. If there is a crisis in (P), the (A)s accuse the (E)s of being the culpable ones.

Germany is culturally very (A). See how easily anti-Semitism took off in Germany with the rise of the Nazi party. Now in the beginning of the twenty-first century, as Europe is having problems with economic growth—declining (P)—Rightist parties are growing and Right parties are more (A) than (E). (The liberals are the (E)s.) What is happening? Anti-Semitism is on the rise. In which countries? Those with a strong (A) component in the their culture. The UK is more anti-Semitic than Italy, and in France (A) is growing at the expense of (E), and you can see anti-Semitism on the rise there too.

> *What about Greece? Anti-Semitism is very high there, but they are strong in (E).*

It is the disastrous decline in (P). Greece is in a terrible economic mess that causes resentment of any (E)s, including Jews.

(E) is threatened any time (A) is on the rise or (P) is on the decline. (E) stands out and is noticeable, thus it is an easy target to blame for all the ills of society.

*Are you concerned for the Jewish people?*

Yes, I am worried but it is not just anti-Semitism that concerns me. It will be anti any (E)s. The Chinese in Indonesia or Malaysia, the Indians in South Africa, the Armenians in Turkey. All ethnic (E)s are in danger when significant (A) is on the rise or major (P) on the decline.

## (P) and (I) Incompatibility

Another combination is (P) and (I). We have talked about this incompatibility already. While trying to (P)roduce and (P)erform, that is, satisfy client needs, we might have to compromise the needs of some stakeholders. Perhaps we demand more from employees and get the unions upset. That can hurt (I)ntegration. Or if there is time pressure to satisfy an immediate need, attention to interpersonal needs might suffer.

*You are right. No one falls in love while chasing a bus. They fall in love on vacation, walking on the beach at sunset.*

Notice that when seduction is attempted the lights are low, candles, soft music—relaxed. For (I) you need to reduce the (P).

*Does this explain why people claim that in big cities it is more difficult to establish intimate relationships. Finding love is tougher in big cities than in a small city or village.*

> Finding love is tougher in big cities than in a small city or village.

Yes. The bigger the city, the more hustle and bustle there is, the more alienation and loneliness. The more people, the lonelier you will feel.

To find lonely people craving love and a sense of belonging, go to big cities. Show me a city with a rapid pace of work, with lots of stress, and I will show you lots of lonely people. The bigger the city the lonelier the people are.

*And the more pets they have. They get someone to love them unconditionally.*

When there is no pressure from (P), (E), or (A), then (I) comes up and you will be able to experience love more easily.

Note that (I)ntegration or dis(I)ntegration occurs not only between people, or inter-people— we should look at dis(I)ntegration intra-people too.

## 88 – MASTERING CHANGE

*Intra-people?*

Yes. I use that word to describe (I)ntegration within a person, because there is more than one "me." There are several: mind (A), body (P), emotions (E), and spirit (I). Frequently they are in conflict. The mind (A) makes decisions that damage the body (P), and people often push their bodies to extremes while building a career. They work so hard (P) that their emotions (E) suffer.

> **The spiritual is best expressed when the body, mind, and emotions are quiet.**

In modern society the mind receives most of the attention. The mind goes to school and earns a degree. If you measure what percentage of the day is allocated to the mind, you will find it gets the majority of our waking hours. Luckily, we sleep, so our body, emotions, and perhaps spirit enjoy some attention. However, the mind often robs them of their share with sleepless nights spent worrying about something.

Even if the body enjoys exercise, rest, and good food, while the mind goes to school and earns a degree, and the emotions enjoy heart-to-heart communications, the spiritual part could still be deprived. The spiritual is best expressed when the body, mind, and emotions are quiet. If you fast for a while, the body becomes quiet. If, at the same time, you meditate, the mind and emotions become quiet. Then you will get a deep sense of who you are. Your spirit will express itself. You will have a sense of unity within yourself and with the world around you. This could be a spiritual experience.

> **Experience love without trying to understand it.**

Notice that spiritual leaders like Moses, Jesus, and the Buddha all had fasted and meditated when they discovered God.

On a smaller scale, going to church or synagogue or a mosque does that too. There is no (P), (A), or (E) activity while praying. It is all (I).

*I still do not understand the (I) role, or how to get it.*

The (I) role is difficult to explain because understanding one's spiritual nature is 100 percent experiential. For now, why don't you enjoy some poetry, music, or art? Or just watch nature. Experience something that doesn't speak to your mind, something that you don't try to understand. Experience something that makes you feel part of it. Experience love without trying to understand it. Love is not a cerebral, physical, or emotional experience. In its true form, it is a spiritual experience, expressed in intimacy with something, someone, or oneself.

*What does this have to do with (PAEI)?*

Well, the mind, body, emotions, and spirit correspond to (PAEI).

Mind?

*(A).*

Body?

*(P).*

Emotions?

*(E).*

And spirit is (I).

Since these four roles are frequently in conflict, one of the roles might emerge as dominant in our behavior. We might focus mostly on our body, mind, emotions, or spirit—whichever wins the internal battle—at the expense of the others.

Change fuels our internal conflict. The more hustle and bustle in our lives, the less the four roles are in balance. The higher the rate of change we experience, the more the mind, body, emotions, and spirit get scattered.

Depending on a person's preference, usually expressed as habit, one of the four roles might win, while the other three are neglected. For example, some people make their mind the master. These are the technocrats, the robot-like people with no emotions or spirituality. There are others who dedicate their lives exclusively to their bodies. Exercise and healthy food are their religion.

> *And the third group dedicates itself to some form of art, feeding mostly their emotional side. What about the exclusively spiritual group?*

They flock to the religious orders. The higher the rate of change in society, the more we see of such groups.

> *Where does this lead us?*

The higher the rate of change, the more inter- and intra-dis(I)ntegration, and that is expressed in lack of inter- and intra-love.

> *Lack of inter-love—what is that?*

Aggression, hostility toward others.

*Then lack of intra-love is aggression and hostility toward oneself?*

Yes. The higher the rate of change, the higher the rate of depression and suicide.

*So should we stop change?*

No one has ever succeeded in doing that. People have slowed down change only to have it erupt with a vengeance later. Don't try to stop change. Learn how to deal with it instead.

*How?*

> You should love your friends as you love yourself.

That's what our conversations are about. To start, note that (I)ntegration in its highest form is love, and loving others starts with loving yourself. That does not mean loving your mind or body or emotions or spirit, but loving your mind and body and emotions and spirit. Next, it means caring for the needs of others as if they were your own. You should love your friends as you love yourself. This is the essence of the Bible, says one of the Jewish sages: *Ve ahavta le reeha kamocha*, love your neighbor as yourself. It is also one of the foundations of Christianity, Buddhism, and all truly spiritual religions.

*Religion is supposed to be providing the (I) role for society.*

Unfortunately, religions also have a lifecycle and, over time become an organized religion. Over time (A) grows to the degree that (I) declines and spirituality is lost all together. That brings us to discuss the (A)-(I) incompatibility.

## (A) and (I) Incompatibility

Let's explore this one with an example. Which country has the fewest lawyers per capita?

*Japan, I think.*

Correct. That means their need for (A)dministration is low, and that is because their (I)ntegration is high. In Japan there is a great deal of loyalty and interdependence in business. Corporations offer lifetime employment and a family environment. They take care of each other; they are guided by their culture, not as much by their legal institutions.

Now which country has the most lawyers per capita?

*The United States?*

Yes! It seems as if everyone is suing someone. (A) is very high and growing; our court system is overloaded. We rely on external intervention to solve our interdependency problems. Our (I) is lower than that of the Japanese.

Years ago, when Japan was the envy of American business and Japan was very competitive, I recommended, tongue in cheek, that the way to beat them is to export our (A) to them. That would undermine their (I), which is their competitive advantage.

*How would you export (A)?*

> To (A)dminister a problem is so much easier than to (I)ntegrate a relationship.

Teach them American traditional management theory on hierarchies, span of control, the role of the CEO as a sole ruler, etc.

By the way, the United States doesn't have to export (A). It can grow indigenously in Japan. As change accelerates, dis(I)ntegration could occur and they might attempt to control it with (A)dministration. They are not immune to such development because they have not articulated and systematized their cultural advantage of (I) to the point that they can nourish and reproduce it. They are enjoying it while it lasts.

*Why would they use (A) to control dis(I)ntegration and not (I)?*

Because to (A)dminister a problem is so much easier than to (I)ntegrate a relationship. With (A), you make a set of rules and your task is finished. Expression of (I) involves education and nourishment of culture and values.

*It is easier to punish children than to teach them values of cooperation. I can see that.*

(A) and (I) serve the same function. They are the "glue" of organizations. (A) is the mechanistic glue and (I) the organic glue. We can use one or the other and often confuse the two. People should not substitute one for the other.

*Give me an example?*

Where do you find more crime? In large cities with no community spirit or in small places where people know each other?

*In metropolitan areas.*

If large cities where people are alienated suffer more crime, is it due to a lack of (P), (A), (E), or (I)?

*(I), I presume.*

What is usually the attempted remedy?

*More (A).*

> Show me a country with a high rate of change and I will show you a high rate of divorce.

Right! More law and order. More punishment. More prison time. Isn't it bizarre that they give people three or four life sentences when a person has only one life to give? They electrocute or hang or inject lethal chemicals into the sentenced criminal. Does this approach work to reduce crime?

*No, it doesn't.*

Because crime is not an (A) problem. It is an (I) problem. It is not a legal problem. Inter- and intra-dis(I)ntegration are causing it, whether it is the individual who is dis(I)ntegrating mentally or emotionally, or the surrounding socio-economic and political subsystems that are disintegrated.

# (I) and (E) Incompatibility

*What about (E)-(I) incompatibility?*

The more change, the less time and energy we have to pay attention to each other. There is a psychological test that measures stress. Each life event is assigned points of stress, losing a job, so many points, divorce, so many points, going on vacation, so many points. The common denominator is change.

The more change, the more stress, and the less integration within ourselves and with others. Show me a country with a high rate of change and I will show you a high rate of divorce.

> *Right. There are more divorces on the east coast and west coast of America than in the middle of America. And the higher the rate of change, the more people will be in prison, and the more acute the problem of crime will be.*

All are manifestations of dis(I)ntegration. (E), change, causes disintegration, i.e., negative (I), which people attempt to solve with more (A).

Instead, solve disintegration with integration. For instance teach prisoners to meditate and see how they change. Let them raise puppies. Let them experience love and see how that impacts them.

## (PAEI) Code to Analyze Organizational Structures

*How does this code relate to business?*

Can you give me the (PAEI) code for the marketing function?

*Well, first it should have an (E). Marketing has to analyze the future, how the clients and their needs will change. And since you focus on needs to be satisfied, the next in the code is the (P) role. So it is (PaEi).*

> (E), change, causes disintegration, i.e., negative (I), which people attempt to solve with more (A).

Right. Notice that there are no zeros in the code. There must be some (A) to deliver the marketing message well, and some (I) to be sure all those necessary to deliver the new strategy are aligned. Moreover, a large (I) is even better. You try to integrate the company with more than its market.

Take the Body Shop chain of cosmetic stores under the leadership of the late Anita Roddick. They were not just selling soap or shaving cream. Every store was an outlet for social activism, caring for abused children or battered women or exploited people, etc. They were not selling a product. They were promoting who they were, their values. They were integrated with a bigger vision than just making money or selling good products.

*Were they successful?*

For a while, but by ignoring commercial (E) they had no marketing department. They considered marketing to be a dirty word, akin to exploitation. They lost their competitive advantage to a better merchandizing company who copied their (I) but added better (E).[12]

Without consciousness of needs, without a spiritual sense of interdependence and oneness, without caring for the clients' needs as if they were our own, we satisfy pseudoneeds. We might satisfy the client with pseudoneeds, and in the process we could make money, but we would also sabotage the total system. In the end, our efforts would come back to sabotage us.

---

12  See Adizes, *Managing Corporate Lifecycles*, op. cit.

Drug pushers are extreme manifestations of this phenomenon. How many people push something they know is damaging, but continue to do so nevertheless? The proof that they know it is damaging is that they would not give it to their own children. The owner of a factory that pollutes the air does not let the family she loves live near the pollution. But we pollute the air for each other don't we? We must not do to others, what we don't want others to do to us, or to those we love.

> Without consciousness of needs, without a spiritual sense of interdependence and oneness, we satisfy pseudoneeds. Our efforts would come back to sabotage us.

*"Love thy neighbor as thyself," right?*

Yes, and: Don't do unto others what you don't want done unto to you. Thus, true marketing, to be effective in the long term, has to be (I) based.

The (I) is in the heart. (I) is love and love dwells in our hearts. It is very important that business leaders do not work only with their brains but with their hearts as well. It is not only good for the world in which we live, but it is good for the company as well.

*Unfortunately, leadership training is focused on the brain, on the mind, and very little on the heart.*

*What else? Can you give me the (PAEI) code for the sales function?*

Can you do it?

*First, it should be (P). Second, (E).*

Why do you have (E) second?

*Don't we want creative, forward-thinking salespeople?*

Yes, but that's not what we're talking about. We are not talking about a trader, contractor, or developer. We are talking about the sales *function*. On a personal level, a salesperson's personal style should be (PaeI): sensitive, client-focused (I) and still sale-oriented (P). Since (P) and (I) are very incompatible, outstanding salespeople are rare.

Now, what is the (PAEI) code for the sales department? The sales function?

*(P) is the most important role because in order to produce sales, a sales department has to demonstrate how the product or service satisfies needs.*

What should the second role be? Should the sales function be flexible (E), sensitive (I), or efficient (A)?

> *Efficient. That's why we have sales territories, scheduling, itineraries, and routes. We want the maximum bang for the buck.*

Right! That's why the sales function should be (PAei), like a production function.

> *Come to think of it, sales is like production. Marketing designs the plan—what should be sold at what price and how it should be sold. Sales goes out and implements the plan. Stylistically, marketing is like process engineering and sales is like production.*

**An excellent marketing person does not necessarily make an excellent sales person.**

This (PAEI) code shows you the incompatibility between the styles and functions of marketing and sales. Marketing should be (PaEi), while sales should be (PAei). Marketing should look at the long term and make requests regarding what should be done to prepare for the future. Sales should be short-term oriented and efficient.

Marketing is change oriented and can disturb the order sales needs for short-term efficiency. So it's normal to have conflict between the sales and marketing departments in an organization.

> *You mean an excellent marketing person does not necessarily make an excellent sales person, and vice versa?*

Right.

> *Then we sure make mistakes! In my company we usually promote the best salespeople into marketing.*

To avoid conflicts, many companies put marketing and sales under the same manager. When that happens, which orientation, which role dominates do you think?[13]

> *When marketing is put under the same vice president that is also in charge of sales, marketing has difficulty performing its function of providing leadership for change. It ends up performing mostly a support function, such as preparing sales collateral material. (P) will take precedence over (E).*

Why is that?

---

[13] See Adizes, *Managing Corporate Lifecycles*, op. cit.

*Because when you have a choice—should you do long-term impact work or short-term—the short term pushes the long term out.*

Right, when you have one VP for marketing and sales, most probably there is no marketing function. There is the name but not the function. The marketing department does sales-support functions and calls it marketing.

When production and engineering are combined, the same phenomenon is repeated. (P) dominates at the expense of (E). Engineering usually performs a maintenance function. Thus, don't have one VP for sales and marketing, or for engineering and manufacturing. The (P) orientation will kill the (E) orientation.

*Any other examples?*

How about the (PAEI) code for motivating?

*(- - - I)?*

Why just (- - - I)? That says you don't care what we do, or how or why we do it, just as long as we agree? That's not motivating. That's surrendering.

> Don't have one VP for sales and marketing, or for engineering and manufacturing.

*Is it (P) and (I)?*

What about the (A) and (E) roles? It's important that you not forget any role. Any deficiency will haunt you, because all four "vitamins" are necessary. Whenever one role is missing, one of the desired outcomes won't happen. The organization is going to be either ineffective or inefficient in the short or long term. Sooner or later, you will have to address the absent role if you wish to produce a healthy organization.

The Little League "one game" coach who inspires the kids with rah-rah-rah motivation saying, "Let's win this game!" is using a (P -- I) approach. Without (A), there is no systematized plan for how to win the game. Without (E), there is no plan for how to deal with future games. It is only, "Let's unite, play hard, and win." Obviously, that could be enough for winning a game, but not the season.

*Okay. All four roles are necessary. Got it. What about (pAeI)? What kind of motivation would that be?*

You tell me.

*It would be a system that motivates people, like a bonus or an incentive program.*

Right! How about (paEi)? What kind of motivation is that?

*When people have a vision of the future or a mission that motivates and unites them.*

What type of motivation do we use most in the Western world?

*I believe (pAeI).*

Right again. Modern society is becoming increasingly (A) oriented. Jacques Ellul elaborates on this in his book *The Technological Society*.[14] Think about it, there is a manual for everything—how to listen, talk, dress, eat, or make love. There is hardly a field of human endeavor for which there is no how-to manual. Even these conversations of ours can be converted into a manual on how to manage, lead, parent, or govern.

The strongest motivation is not (pAeI); it is (paEI). That's what people go to war for and die for. That's one of the reasons why Japanese productivity is so strong. People are hired there for the long term, so they identify with the long-term vision. They know they will benefit from achieving the goals. They are motivated and thus dedicated.

*This code is like shorthand, like the DNA of any organization or any system. What I've learned is that although all four roles are necessary, they are incompatible, and because of that, what?*

A role could be missing, squeezed out, threatened into extinction, or never fully developed.

> Happiness is not a destination, nor is it a journey. It is the *condition* of your journey.

*Got it. And what happens then?*

Now that you understand the code, we are ready to explore one of its applications, to understand and predict managerial styles, the difference between management and mismanagement, and management and leadership. Management is when all (PAEI) roles are dispensed. Mismanagement is when one or more of the roles is missing. Leadership is when three roles are present one of them is (I).

---

14  Jacques Ellul. *The Technological Society*. New York: Knopf, 1964.

*Got it. But you have not told me yet how to predict the quality of decisions, the four questions I have to ask.*

We will get to it, and when we do, you'll see the trip was worth it. Happiness is not a destination, nor is it a journey. It is the condition of your journey, to be precise. The same is true of learning.

# CONVERSATION 6
# Management, Leadership, and Mismanagement Styles

The (PAEI) code has multiple uses. Today we will apply it to understand managerial or leadership styles. But first please let us review what we have covered so far.

*Okay. To manage is to decide and implement. To decide, we need to focus on effectiveness and efficiency in the short and the long term. For that we need the (PAEI) roles to be performed. The problem is that the roles are incompatible.*

*What happens if a role is not performed?*

To understand what happens when a role is missing in managerial styles, I created archetypes of some extreme cases. In these cases, instead of having one role missing and three performed, I have three roles missing and one performed. Once we understand these extreme cases, we can better understand the less extreme ones.

## (P- - -): The Lone Ranger

Let's take the first case, in which (P)erforming is the predominant role. It is the doing, the achieving, the single-minded fulfillment of the purpose for which the organization exists. (A), (E), and (I) do not exist in this (P - - -) style, which I call the Lone Ranger style.

How does the Lone Ranger manage or lead? I emphasize the word *how*. We're not interested in why the (P - - -)'s style is as it is. We are not psychologists who want to know what happened in someone's childhood to cause certain behavior in adult life. We are interested in how someone actually behaves as a manager and what we can do about it.[15]

*But it is tough, if not impossible, to change a person's style.*

You are right. I do not believe I can change style totally. I can, however, make it more flexible and able to relate to others.

Now, think about how the Lone Ranger rose through the ranks to become a manager.

*That's easy, diligent, hard-working (P)erformers are often promoted to management.*

> The Lone Ranger is neither a LIFO nor a FIFO, but a FISH: First In, Still Here.

But now that several people are reporting to the Lone Ranger, what's happening?

*There will be problems. (A)dministering, coordinating, and supervising are not a (P- - -)'s strong points.*

Neither are new ideas, change, and vision. (I)ntegrating people is also missing from the (P- - -)'s repertoire. This (P) excels exclusively in (P)erforming, in (P)roducing results.

*I think I know this person.*

Let's examine the Lone Ranger's style. Does he work hard?

*Certainly! Very hard.*

When does the Lone Ranger arrive at work?

*First, before anyone else.*

When does he leave?

*Last.*

In inventory control, the terms LIFO and FIFO stand for Last In, First Out and First In, First Out. The Lone Ranger is neither a LIFO nor a FIFO, but a FISH: First In, Still Here. The (P- - -) works all the time. At eleven o'clock at night, what does the (P- - -) take home?

---

15  I suspect there are physiological causes to behavior, having to do with hormones and glands–for example, the (P) role could be driven by the adrenaline gland, and the (E) by the thyroid gland–but this is so far from my expertise that, for now, let us skip it.

*A briefcase full of work.*

Right. The exhausted Lone Ranger might not have the time or energy to even open the briefcase, yet it's there next to the bed. Some Lone Rangers travel the world lugging their briefcases. They don't have time to open them, but they carry them just in case. They're like alcoholics who are never far from a bottle. That's why some people call (P- - -)s workaholics, who are never far from work. You can identify them in seminars. First of all, do (P- - -)s willingly attend workshops or seminars?

*No. They go only if ordered to. They have no time for meetings, there's too much to do.*

At seminars, where do you find them during the break?

*On the telephone to the office, asking, "Any problems?"*

It's as if they're saying, "I've been here for two hours with, God forbid, no problems. Please give me a problem to solve." They're like alcoholics saying, "Two hours and I haven't had a drink. Please, have mercy. Give me a drink."

*I know this type. When they are forced to attend a meeting and a secretary walks in with a stack of papers, they're the first to ask, "Anything for me?" They like to do work. (P- - -)s measure themselves by how hard they work. They worry if they're not worried.*

That's why it's dangerous to have a (P- - -) around after an organization has outgrown him. This person is like an unguided missile. Let's say the founder has a (P) style and he shows up at the office because he doesn't know how to fill his time any other way. If he has nothing to do, he will find something that may only stir up trouble. He might cross organizational boundaries and ignore organizational charts. You might even find him at the shipping dock telling people how to load a truck. Worse, he might call a customer and make a deal that violates company policies. Why? Because he has to do something. If you don't give a (P- - -) something to do, he's going to do something you may not want done.

*Like a child.*

Lone Rangers work very hard. They complain that the day is too short and that there is too much to do. If someone asks, "Why don't you delegate some work to your staff?" what's the answer?

*"They can't do it. They're not ready yet."*

"How long have they worked for you? Twenty-five years? Why don't you train them?"

*"I have no time to train them!"*

"Why don't you have time?"

*"Because I have no one to delegate to."*

(P---)s go in circles and can't delegate. That's why I call this person the Lone Ranger.

Next, how does the Lone Ranger's desk look? Clean?

*No, it's crowded with papers. If one desk is not big enough, there's a credenza behind it, also crowded.*

If that's not enough, there are papers all over the floor and along the wall. If you ask the (P---) how he is doing, what will the answer be?

*"Oh my God! There's so much to do. I've been working so hard lately."*

And if you ask how long "lately" is?

*"Twenty-five years!"*

Their behavior is compulsive. Imagine asking an alcoholic, what should I do with this bottle of Chivas Regal? What would he say?

*"Put it on my desk."*

Likewise, when you ask a Lone Ranger, what should I do with this problem, what will be the response?

*"Put it on my desk."*

> If you want to see a depressed Lone Ranger, clean up his desk overnight.

When you look at the desk of a Lone Ranger, what you see is not work but "a wine cellar." If you want to see a depressed Lone Ranger, clean up his desk overnight.

*I knew a manager who had a subordinate who worked extremely hard but always complained she had too much to do. The manager decided to help her out by not giving her any new assignments until her desk was cleared. The cleaner the desk got, however, the more depressed she became. Instead of feeling relieved, she felt rejected. Now I understand why.*

# MANAGEMENT, LEADERSHIP, AND MISMANAGEMENT STYLES – 103

Good example. Now let's look at the people who work for a Lone Ranger. They come to work most of the time after him and what are they doing?

*Waiting for an errand to run.*

In organizational parlance, the Lone Ranger's employees are called gofers: they go for this, go for that. They're untrained, unprepared, and undirected. They are expected to get it done and then ask what's next.

Does the Lone Ranger hold staff meetings?

*No. There isn't any time.*

Suppose the Lone Ranger is told he must have staff meetings because a good manager should have them. What would the meetings be like?

*Very short. The Lone Ranger would tell the staff what to do, then send them on errands. Few questions would be asked. No debate. No discussion. Then the (P- - -) would proudly announce, "We had a staff meeting!"*

Does the Lone Ranger train people?

*No. A Lone Ranger would say, "I have no time to train," or "Why train people? All they have to do is watch me do it, work hard, and get the job done."*

The Lone Ranger sees the world in a simplistic way, the problems are simple and the solutions are simple. The problem is you're not working hard enough. The solution is to work harder. That's all. The (P- - -) confuses quantity with quality.

*More is better for a Lone Ranger. All you have to do is do more: If we tried harder, we wouldn't have any problems. Our problem is that people are not working hard enough.*

Function is everything; form is ignored. From the (P- - -)'s perspective if you work hard enough, success is assured.

## (-A- -): The Bureaucrat

Now let's proceed to the next deficient style: (-A--).

The (-A--) is not a (P)roducer of results or a (P)erformer. She doesn't focus on the needs that must be (P)rovided by the organization, but solely on (A)dministration, systematization, and routine. The Lone Ranger looks exclusively at what is being done, never mind how. The (-A--) is looking exclusively at how it's being done, never mind what it is.

This person is not an (E), who would move in new directions, take new risks, and initiate change. Neither is this person an (I), who tries to bring people together. I call this person the Bureaucrat.

*A Bureaucrat manages by the book and looks exclusively at how to make the organization efficient, right?*

> A bureaucrat sometimes ends up running a well-controlled disaster.

Yes, and the book, by the way, doesn't have to be written. It may be all in the (-A- -)'s memory. She runs the organization on precedents. A system exists and you are expected to follow it. Everything must be documented. The Bureaucrat suffers from a disease called "manualitis," everything must be put into manuals.

When does a Bureaucrat come to work?

*On time.*

When does she leave?

*On time.*

When do the Bureaucrat's subordinates get to work?

*They'd better be there on time.*

When do they leave?

*On time.*

What do you think they are doing in the meantime?

*That's not important. What's important is that they get there on time and leave on time. To them the form is more important than the function. I have seen this many times.*

That's how a Bureaucrat sometimes ends up running a well-controlled disaster. The company's going broke, but on time. Everything is very efficient and by the book. What does the Bureaucrat do with free time?

*Write that book!*

Yes! The Bureaucrat is always looking to control violations. The (-A- -)'s function is to make new rules, new standard operating procedures, and new policies. That's why in bureaucracies the book of procedures and policies grows larger and larger from year to year. The more violations the (-A- -)s find, the more rules they have to make. More rules, however, mean more violations, which means more rules are needed. The book grows over time without bringing more control.

Does a Bureaucrat have staff meetings?

*Of course. Probably every Monday, Wednesday, and Friday, from nine in the morning until noon.*

Does the (-A- -) have an agenda?

*Absolutely, with details regarding how, not the what, or the why.*

> The Bureaucrat wants to do things right and cares less about whether they are doing the right things.

Subordinates in an (A)-dominated culture learn that if they don't make waves, if they do everything by the book, and lie low long enough, they might become the president.

The classic Bureaucrat is the character of Captain Queeg in the novel *The Caine Mutiny* by Herman Wouk. In the middle of World War II, what worries Captain Queeg most?

*Who stole the strawberries.*

A company managed by a Bureaucrat may be going broke, but they will call a meeting about who stole the strawberries, or who did not fill out the proper forms. The Bureaucrat wants to do things right and cares less about whether they are doing the right things. She would rather be precisely wrong than approximately right.

*I can see that the Bureaucrat also confuses form with function, except that in contrast to the Lone Ranger, the Bureaucrat believes that if the form is carried out, the function will follow. An (-A- -) perceives that all that is needed to achieve results is to go through the motions faithfully and sometimes blindly.*

Consider Captain Queeg. A typhoon was about to sink his ship unless he ordered a change in course. But what did he say? "I'm not disobeying orders on account of some bad weather."

> *This reminds me of a story about Bureaucrats. I was on a plane flying over the Amazon River and an accountant was seated next to me. He asked, "Do you know how old this river is? It's one billion years and seven months old." That figure sounded strange, so I asked, "How do you figure one billion years and seven months?" He said, "Seven months ago somebody told me it was a billion years old."*

Bureaucrats will give you a budget balanced to the last cent, but in the wrong direction. They can be precisely wrong.

Your story reminds me of another one, two friends were riding in a hot-air balloon and got lost in the clouds. They began to descend, trying to figure out where they were. When they spotted someone on the ground, they shouted to him, "Where are we?" The person shouted back, "In a balloon." One friend said to the other, "That guy must be an (A). His information was accurate, precise, and totally useless."

> *Oh, this joke has a continuation. The guy on the ground goes home and tells his wife, "I just met two top-level executives, (E)s. They are up there in the clouds and have no idea where they are, where are they going, or where they're coming from.*

You are alluding to the third type of mismanagement, or misleadership, the men in the balloon: (- -E-).

# (- -E-): The Arsonist

Describe for me this style as you understand it.

> *The (- -E-) has zero (P). He doesn't pay attention to providing the immediately needed service. He also has zero (A). The details of how something gets done are unimportant. Zero (I) means interpersonal relationships, team building, and organizational climate are not important either. This person is an exclusive (E). This style is looking primarily to the future and identifying what he considers to be new opportunities.*

Right. I call this style "the Arsonist." He likes to start fires.

An Arsonist is usually very dangerous on Monday mornings or upon returning from a plane trip that lasted more than three hours. The (- -E-) has had time to dream up new strategies, new priorities, and a new direction. The (- -E-) is very excited as he unloads these ideas on the employees.

When do the employees come to work? What will happen if the Arsonist shows up at seven in the morning and the employees are not there?

*The Arsonist wouldn't like that. He would feel they're not committed enough.*

When do the subordinates leave?

*Right after the Arsonist leaves!*

Yes, they have to be at work before the (- -E-) and leave after he does. The time people arrive at and leave work is one of the behavioral characteristics that identify managerial or leadership styles. The Lone Ranger is first in, last out. The Bureaucrat is in on time, out on time. When does the Arsonist come to work?

*Who knows!*

When does he leave work?

*Who knows!*

But since people don't know when the Arsonist will appear or disappear, and they must be at work before him and leave after him, what happens? They are on-call practically twenty-four hours a day, 365 days a year. It is not unusual for the Arsonist to call a staff member in the middle of the night from Paris to discuss a sudden idea.

*I've seen companies with a big (- -E-) in charge. The subordinates are vice presidents who make huge salaries, but they sit in their offices until seven or eight at night just watching their fingernails grow. They have little to do, but they're afraid to go home, because the Arsonist might call a meeting. They never know when that might happen, but everyone must be ready. Nobody knows what the agenda is either. Even if the Arsonist does have one, he is the first to violate it. The staff is supposed to be able to answer questions according to whatever agenda the Arsonist has in mind. People attend meetings with their entire office in a mental briefcase.*

Let's compare this style with that of the Lone Ranger. The Lone Ranger is called a workaholic, but she might also be called a firefighter, since the Lone Ranger responds to problems after they occur. When a fire flares up, she extinguishes it, then waits for the next burst of flames. Another term for the Lone Ranger is "manager by crisis." In fact, the Lone Ranger is managed by crisis.

Now, if the (P- - -) is a firefighter, the (- -E-) is an Arsonist. If the Lone Ranger's style is management by crisis, the Arsonist's style is crisis by management. The Lone Ranger gets ulcers, the Arsonist gives them.

> If the Lone Ranger's style is management by crisis, the Arsonist's style is crisis by management. The Lone Ranger gets ulcers, the Arsonist gives them.

That's why when the Arsonist returns from a trip, people whisper, "Here he comes." They know the Arsonist will call a meeting and start new fires. The Arsonist enjoys seeing people run around frantically, working harder than usual, as if the organization were on fire. That's why when an Arsonist asks you how you're doing, you should answer, "I'm working so hard, I'm falling apart. I haven't seen my family for weeks." The Arsonist might respond, "Good, good."

In a company managed by an Arsonist, who does all the talking in a meeting?

*The Arsonist!*

Here's another joke to make the point. Italians are known for their food and their music, but not for their military accomplishments. In the First World War, some Italian soldiers were in the trenches ready to attack. Out of the trenches emerged a commanding officer in a beautiful blue uniform with a red sash, gold epaulets, and many decorations. He pulled out his saber, raised it to the sky and shouted, "Avaaaantiiiiiii!" The soldiers in the trenches looked up, clapped their hands, and shouted, "Bravo!" But nobody left the trenches!

The same happens in the organization managed by an Arsonist. Upon returning from a trip, the Arsonist calls a staff meeting and starts waving his saber in the air, enthusiastically presenting ideas that he is excited about. He exclaims, "We have this opportunity, we have that opportunity! We are going to do this, we are going to do that." The subordinates look at each other and mentally clap hands while thinking, "Bravo! Here we go again." But nobody gets out of the trenches. Why?

> *Because next Monday the Arsonist is going to change direction again. An Arsonist never tells you to stop what you're doing, but continues giving you new things to do. When people get out of the trenches, they soon realize they're running in circles. So what happens? They learn to stay*

> It's difficult to soar like an eagle when he is surrounded by turkeys.

*in the trenches, clap their hands, and await the next avalanche of "absolutely top priorities." They pray and hope the boss will forget them. Maybe he doesn't really mean it. What does the (- -E-) really mean anyway?*

You are right. Subordinates spend an enormous amount of time trying to understand where their Arsonist boss stands. They waste energy trying to interpret directions and hold off on acting because they don't know if the decisions are for real or just ideas.

This frustrates the Arsonist, who has dreamed up more and more fantastic new ideas designed to make changes. Staff people cheer "Bravo!" yet they don't move. Nothing, or very little, gets done. From experience they believe it is just another idea and he will change his mind soon thereafter or forget the idea because a new one came to replace the old one.

Unfortunately for all, in this case it was not an idea, but a real decision. The Arsonist grows impatient, since nothing is happening. He is thinking it's difficult to soar like an eagle when he is surrounded by turkeys. The organization is not moving, (- -E-) concludes, because the employees don't support what he wants. Paranoia and suspicion of sabotage set in. He looks for the culprit. (- -E-)s usually have someone whom they accuse of not being up to par. There must be someone who carries a bell around his neck like the lead bull. Someone who is the reason why nothing is done as the (- -E-) wants. If that person quits, almost instantaneously the (E) choses a new person to become the scapegoat.

> It's too late for you to disagree with me. I've already changed my mind.

The Arsonist fails to realize that people can't follow because they don't understand what is wanted. Arsonists themselves frequently don't know what they want either. They might even say, "It's too late for you to disagree with me. I've already changed my mind."

*Sometimes subordinates think a decision is real, so they act on it. Then the Arsonist gets upset, asking, "Why did you do that? I was only thinking out loud." In another case, when the people don't follow his directions, the Arsonist becomes outraged. "Why didn't you carry out my decision? That was a final decision!"*

It is funny but sad. People really have difficulty knowing what's going on with an Arsonist. They lose whether they work on an assignment or not. Without an easy way to carry out, or even catch up with the latest idea, they constantly feel like losers.

> Arsonists don't realize that they are their own worst enemies.

The Arsonist too suffers from a sense of failure. His mind rushes forward faster than the accomplishments of the organization, leaving him unfulfilled. Over time he feels disillusioned, and deeply disappointed. He feels people have let him down. Arsonists don't realize that they are their own worst enemies.

An organization is like a series of gears: A big wheel causes a succession of smaller wheels to turn. When the big wheel makes one turn, the small wheels must make many.

If the "big wheel" is an Arsonist, it changes direction frequently and abruptly. It goes forward a full circle, then backward a half circle, then forward again a half circle, then back two full circles. What happens then to the small wheels? For every little bit the big wheel turns, they have to make a full circle. They turn a little and then in mid-turn they have to reverse. Before they even have a chance to follow the last instruction, they have to change direction. Finally, the gears break down. Nothing or very little gets done. When that happens, the Arsonist feels this proves his suspicion that the staff is not to be trusted. They did not do what they were supposed to do.

*But Arsonists are charismatic. They're dreamers, and they attract people who believe in their dreams.*

Only to become disillusioned later, because people cannot fulfill the Arsonist's ever-changing dreams.

*How about the subordinates?*

Each of the extreme styles has a typical subordinate. As I mentioned, the Lone Ranger's subordinates are gofers. They're untrained and must be always ready to carry an assignment, trained or not. The Bureaucrat's subordinates I call yes-yes clerks. They follow the rules and don't make waves. The Arsonist's subordinates are called claques, after the people hired by an opera house manager to start artificial applause on opening night. An Arsonist's subordinates are paid to clap hands and cheer.

*When an Arsonist calls a meeting and presents ideas, can you object?*

It's dangerous, because Arsonists will take it personally and hold it against you. Arsonists hire employees to clap hands, not to boo while they sing their high C. Tread lightly when disagreeing with Arsonists, because the big (E) also stands for Big Ego.

> Never have an audience when you have a sensitive meeting with an (- -E-).

The moment you express doubts about an (- -E-)'s idea, he will interpret your reaction as disagreement. It would be better to preface your comments with "I agree with you that..." and watch how you use the word "but." The Arsonist may get annoyed. Try to avoid saying "I disagree." It really can infuriate them. Say instead, "I have a different opinion for your consideration." And always have a discussion in "four eyes." If there is a third person attending, the (- -E-) will defend his position and fail to be logical. He will fight you. He has to win the argument. Never have an audience when you have a sensitive meeting with an (- -E-).

*You are absolutely right. I have to watch whomever am I working with. Each has a different style and I can upset them badly if I do not know how to handle their style.*

I recommend my book *Leading the Leaders*. It will tell you in detail how to handle different styles. It can help your marriage too.

Now, let's look at the last style of mismanagement.

## (- - -I): The Super Follower

What do you think happens when you have only (- - -I)?

*This type of manager's exclusive focus is on who, never mind what, how, or why. They look at people and how they're dealing with each other.*

Let me give you an analogy; four people are looking out the same window, but they see four different things. One of them sees birds, mountains, lakes, and sailboats. Who is that? Who sees only the big picture?

*The (E).*

The second person looks out the same window and sees no birds, no clouds, no sailboats, only that the frame is dirty. Who is that?

*The (A).*

Right. This style is obsessed with details. For instance, you could write a major report about how and why your company should enter the New York market, and the (A) might return it with small corrections and objections over minute details. You suspect the Bureaucrat missed the whole point of your report. You saw the big picture, and the (A) missed it by focusing on the details.

The third person sees neither the big picture nor the details. Instead, this person is busy figuring out how the window opens and how it is cleaned. Does it allow enough air in? Is it facing the right direction? The functionality of the window is what interests this person most.

*That's the (P).*

Right. Finally, the last person isn't even looking at the window. This person is looking at the other three people and wondering what they're looking at. Examining people and their interdependence is the primary concern of (I). She is interested exclusively in who is with whom. I call this person (- - -I), the Super Follower.

*Why "Super Follower?"*

Look at it this way. In a meeting managed by a Super Follower, who speaks?

*Everybody else.*

What does the Super Follower do?

*Listens to which people said what, who did not say what, and why they didn't say what they could have said.*

> **(I)s know what's going on politically better than everyone else in the organization.**

She focuses on people and their interrelationships. (I)s know what's going on politically better than everyone else in the organization. They have a good political nose. They don't show their cards easily, because they want to know where the group is going before committing themselves. They don't communicate clearly, because they want to find out first what other people think. They might send up a weather balloon by saying, "I have an idea, but I'm not that sure about it." They might say, "I recommend we declare dividends, but I don't feel too strongly about it."

They want to know what the consensus is so they can join it. (- - -I)s do not lead. They follow the followers.

There is another name for this style. When my book *How to Solve the Mismanagement Crisis* was translated into Spanish, the translators called this style *pez enjabonado*. That's Spanish for "soaped fish," something so slippery you can't hold onto it.

In trying to corner the Soaped Fish, you might say, "You said this," to which she would respond, "You didn't understand what I really wanted to say." A Soaped Fish always wiggles out. How? Because she is more politically astute than anyone else. She feels the vibrations and underlying political currents of the organization before anyone else. Group dynamics and power politics are her focus.

Employees of the Soaped Fish are called informers. They find out what's going on, who said what, why they said what they said, and what they meant when they said it. Through these informers, the (- - -I) hears and understands the organizational drum signals.

*But aren't we painting an extreme picture?*

Each one of these styles is an extreme case. It is extreme because one role is being performed and the other three are not at all. That is why those are exaggerations. I have exaggerated on purpose to be able to see the contours of behavior clearly. In reality people are not that extreme. They have some of the above style characteristics but not all.

## Managers vs. Mismanagers

When you have a big (P) and small (aei) it means the person is primarily a (P)roducer of results, but also has some ability in the other roles. He doesn't excel in them, but isn't blind to them either. A (Paei) is not a Lone Ranger, but a (P)roducer, and usually a first-line supervisor. A manager.

By the same reasoning, a (pAei) is not a Bureaucrat, but an (A)dministrator, and a (paEi) is not an Arsonist, but a creative contributor. (In order to be an entrepreneur, she needs to be (PaEi).)

In life there are many combinations of (PAEI) roles, with different degrees of strength and weaknesses producing styles that combine the archetypes described here.

Each style has strengths and weaknesses. We should not say that (E) is bad in itself. It's bad if the other roles are zero. We always have to ask ourselves if there is a full code. Does a particular person have a one-track style or a well-rounded style?

If a style has a blank in the code, that person is a mismanager. If the person has all the letters of the code, how large each role should be depends on the task, on the responsibilities that person has. If a style has no blank in the code, that person is a manager; and if he has two roles in capitals and one of them is (I), that person is a leader.[16]

---

16  For an in-depth discussion of this subject of styles, see my trilogy: *The Ideal Executive: Why you cannot be one and what to do about it, Management/Mismanagement Styles,* and *Leading the Leaders,* all op. cit.

We can sum up this conversation about managers and mismanagers with this chart:

| Mismanagers | Managers | Leaders |
|---|---|---|
| (P---) = Lone Ranger | (Paei) = Producer | (PaeI) = Shift Leader |
| (-A--) = Bureaucrat | (pAei) = Administrator | (pAaI) = Administrative Leader |
| (--E-) = Arsonist | (paEi) = Creative Contributor | (paEI) = Statesman |
| (---I) = Super Follower | (paei) = Integrator | (PaEI) = Productive Statesman |
| (PA--) = Slave Driver | (PAEI) = Commanding Officer | (PAeI) = Directive Leader |

If you assume that each role can vary in intensity from zero to a hundred, you will have more permutations of styles than people on earth. So, we are all different and, at the same time, we are all similar.

To summarize, we have learned that when any of the (PAEI) roles is missing, mismanagement will occur and the resulting style of mismanagement will be somewhat predictable. Conversely, when two roles are capitalized and one of them is an (I), a leadership style will emerge.

> We are all different and, at the same time, we are all similar.

*This means that there are different leadership styles: (PaeI), (pAeI), (paEI), or, even better (PAei) and (PaEI)?*

Absolutely. Whether a person is a leader is a question not only of style, but also of what the organization needs at that time. The founder of a company needs to be a (PaEi), or, even better a (PaEI) leader. If her style is (PAeI), it will not work for a startup company. She will suffocate the "baby." But that could be exactly the leadership style needed for a company in the aging stages of the lifecycle.[17] We all can be leaders as long as we have (I), but what style of leaders we will be depends what the system needs at that point in time.

Next, we'll discuss what happens when all four (PAEI) roles are missing, and when all four (PAEI) roles are performed equally well.

*That should be easy.*

It isn't, and you'll see why!

---

17  See Adizes, *Managing Corporate Lifecycles*, op. cit.

## CONVERSATION 7
# What to Do About Change

Would you like to summarize our last discussion?

*Sure.*

*Change is constant.*

*Problems emerge because of change.*

*To solve problems caused by change we need to decide what to and implement our decisions.*

*You said we need all the (PAEI) code roles performed in order to make good decisions.*

*If one or more of the (PAEI) roles is missing, a predictable mismanagement style will emerge.*

*We have already discussed the four extreme mismanagement styles: the (P- - -), (-A- -), (- -E-), and (- - -I). We also touched on managerial styles and leadership styles.*

*Now, what about a person who has zero (P), zero (A), zero (E), and zero (I)? What type of style would four blanks indicate?*

## (---): Deadwood

I refer to a manager with none of those roles as Deadwood. Deadwood mismanagers are not interested in what, how, why, or who, but only in survival. Low managerial metabolism and low energy are their trademarks. They say "uhm hm" and "yes, yes" a lot, but never actually do much.

Deadwood does not show resistance to change either. Remember how the other mismanagers resist change? If Lone Rangers are told to change something, they'll say, "How can I do it? My desk is full," or "I'll get to it when I have time."

> Deadwood does not show resistance to change.

Bureaucrats resist change, because they know the cost of everything and the value of nothing. They dwell on the repercussions of change, so they say it can't be done. "It's too risky," or "It's too costly." They think from an implementation point of view and perceive opportunities as problems.

Arsonists resist change when the idea is not their own. Super Followers oppose new ideas, because those ideas could be politically risky: "People aren't ready for it yet. This is not the right time." The "right time" for them is not when the market demands it, but when the internal political climate will allow it.

> Bureaucrats resist change, because they know the cost of everything and the value of nothing.

Deadwood has a different attitude about change. If you tell a Deadwood manager, "Let's move Paris to the Sahara," he'll say, "Sure." No up-front resistance. But a year later when you ask, "Where are we with the project to move Paris to the Sahara?" he'll say, "We've been studying it. Here's a preliminary report. We're still working on it." You see, he didn't move one pebble to the Sahara. However, the Deadwood spent plenty of his time just protecting himself for not moving one pebble anywhere.

It's very difficult to get rid of Deadwood, because they always agree with you and accept any assignment. They always say, "Everything's okay! Whatever you say! Sure!" But they don't do anything and feel perfectly all right about it. When someone gets fired, the Deadwood might say, "I don't know why they fired Lisa. She didn't do anything."

Another characteristic that distinguishes the various types of mismanagers is their typical complaint. For instance, what do Lone Rangers say?

*"Too much work to do. I'm not catching up."*

Right. And Bureaucrats?

*"It's not being done the way it should be. It's not properly organized or under control." They emphasize the word* should.

You got it. How about Arsonists?

*"People are not following the priorities. They're working on the wrong tasks." Arsonists complain even though they constantly change the priorities so that nobody knows what the latest priorities are.*

Beautiful. What about Super Followers?

*"We don't communicate well. You must have misunderstood me. What I really meant to say was…"*

In contrast, the Deadwood doesn't complain. When you ask how it is going, they say: "Fine." Any problems? "No."

Look again at the characteristics of the Deadwood style: no resistance to change and no complaints. Deadwood looks like the perfect subordinate. He never says "no." He has no problems. All is fine. We love the guy. Now notice, what makes Deadwood really dangerous is that the Deadwood phenomenon spreads. Deadwood multiplies.

*What do you mean?*

Every one of these mismanagers has a typical subordinate, and who do you think works for Deadwood?

*More Deadwood.*

Yes. My greatest fear when diagnosing an organization is when I ask how it's going, and everyone answers, "Everything is fine. No problems." Remember, the quietest place in town is the graveyard; nothing happens there; no one has any problems because there is no change. That's death. Being alive means change, and change means working on problems, and growing means working on larger problems.

But why does Deadwood multiply?

Deadwood doesn't grow in managerial capabilities. He doesn't move on or delegate. This keeps the people under Deadwood from growing as well. When Deadwood dies managerially, the people below will eventually die as managers as well. Efficiency and effectiveness disappear and no one knows why, because no one is complaining. When managers tell you everything is okay, and when no one is trying to improve or change anything, the organization has too much Deadwood.

*But why does Deadwood appear? What can we do about it?*

If you look at the previous four mismanagement styles—Lone Ranger, Bureaucrat, Arsonist, and Super Follower—you can see that the difference between those styles and the Deadwood is the number of blanks they have in their (PAEI) codes. The former styles have three blanks; Deadwood has four blanks. Thus, the first four styles are three-quarters Deadwood already.

Lone Rangers become Deadwood when they lose their exclusive capability, which is to (P)roduce results.

*How does that happen?*

Lone Rangers work very hard and claim they have no time to train subordinates, but who else do they not have time to train?

*Themselves.*

So, what happens after twenty years? They are not people with twenty years of experience, but rather people with one year of experience repeated twenty times. They still work hard, but they are obsolete. The world has changed and they haven't adapted.

*How do Bureaucrats become Deadwood?*

They manage by the book. If you want to "kill" them managerially, change the "book," for instance, computerize systems that were previously done manually, or install new budgetary systems—in other words, change. If the Bureaucrat can't adapt, a major change could transform him into Deadwood. They do not learn the new "book."

*How about Arsonists?*

They burn out when they start one fire too many and can't control the fires anymore. Soon they lose the trust and respect of the people who work for them. The organization eventually stops listening to the Arsonist, who still has ideas but no followers. Eventually Arsonists lose faith in themselves and stop trying.

*And Super Followers?*

They become Deadwood when a crisis demanding immediate resolution arises and they cannot solve it the (I) way, because (I)ntegration of people requires time and there is no time. What usually happens since the situation calls for action, not negotiation, a small revolution erupts from below and they are pushed aside. They still might try to (I)ntegrate, but nobody will listen to them anymore.

Do you see the common denominator in all four cases?

*Let me think. Lone Rangers becomes Deadwood when there is change and they don't adapt. Bureaucrats become Deadwood when the system of implementation changes and they can't handle it. Arsonists become Deadwood when they spur too much change and lose control. Super Followers become Deadwood when a crisis requires immediate action and they lose control of the political process.*

*The common denominator is change!*

Exactly. Show me an organization with a high rate of change and I will show you a growing heap of Deadwood. While the situation changes, they do not change. The faster the situation changes externally, the faster Deadwood develops internally.

*But that's not a typical bureaucracy where change is slow, although I would expect to find Deadwood mostly in bureaucracies.*

Bureaucracies have latent Deadwood. In their case Deadwood becomes apparent when the organization experiences change. In a regulated environment everything appears to be under control. The Deadwood beneath the surface bursts forth when regulation is removed and change is introduced rapidly.

Actually, the type of organization that is subject to the highest degree of Deadwood is rather a young company going through tremendous change, a high-tech company, for example. Unless it invests heavily in retraining, it will have either a high turnover or growing Deadwood. It changes so fast that some people cannot keep up. They die managerially.

On the macro level the same phenomenon might occur. Show me a society with a high rate of change, and I will show you a society with many homeless people. Their plight is not due to unavailable employment. When a society changes rapidly, many people cannot keep up. They cannot work effectively and gainfully in such an environment. They simply give up.

Why are there so many homeless people in the United States, the richest country in the world? Because the USA is undergoing tremendous change. The same is true of developing nations. Countries that are industrializing rapidly have streets full of beggars.

*But the USA is already industrialized.*

The USA is moving into the post-industrial age, the information age. There is a change from manufacturing and service industries to knowledge-based industries. These fields require more brainpower than muscle, and some people cannot link up with those changes.

*Do you suggest we stop change?*

No one can stop change, although many individuals, political parties, and religious movements have tried, and are still trying, and will try forever. The way to handle change is not by slowing change down, but by learning how to solve the problems of change faster.

*Any suggestions?*

That is what this book is about, as an introduction.[18]

I have found that change follows a predictable pattern, which means that problems have a predictable pattern too. Change follows a lifecycle, and certain problems are indigenous to each phase of the lifecycle.

Some of these indigenous problems are normal and some are not. The role of management is to remove the problems inherent to the phase of the lifecycle the organization is in, and prepare the organization to deal with the problems that will come with the next stage.[19] What is clear for our discussion now is that decisions need to be made for solving the problems that emerge with change. Those decisions must provide solutions that will make the organization effective and efficient in the short and long term. This means we need a (PAEI) decision.

The styles we have been discussing constitute mismanagement because they are missing one or more of the (PAEI) roles. What do we need in order to make good decisions that will make organizations effective and efficient in the short and the long term?

*To get a (PAEI) decision we need the (PAEI) roles to be performed, which means we need a (PAEI) style.*

We need someone who is task-oriented, who performs the (P) role, and is organized, systematic, and thorough to perform the (A) role. He must have also have a global view and be creative and willing to take risks, thus performing the (E) role. Further, he must be sensitive to other people's needs, a person who is a team builder, who makes himself dispensable, thus performing the (I) role. In other words a (PAEI) person who can perform all roles simultaneously, at the same time, forever, on every decision, and on every problem.

*But such a person doesn't exist.*

---

18  To really be professional in leading change for exceptional, sustainable results using this methodology, I invite you to study at the Adizes Graduate School for the Study of Change and Collaborative Leadership, or at affiliated universities that offer the Adizes program. AGS grants a doctorate in Organizational Therapy with the Adizes Methodology.

19  To learn more about organizational lifecycles, see Adizes, *Managing Corporate Lifecycles,* op. cit.

Exactly! This (PAEI) person exists only in textbooks. By the same reasoning, there is no perfect parent, manager, or leader, and for that matter, no perfect follower. Nothing is ever perfect in itself when it is subject to change. Perfection occurs only when time is irrelevant. That's why we say that art is timeless, but business and life are subject to change. None of us is perfect.[20] Now you can relax. You and I, and all of us, are imperfect. So what's new?

People have been chasing this myth of the perfect manager for years by raising salaries, increasing stock options, and giving all kinds of special rewards to CEOs, all in a quest to find this incredible faultless genius.

> The managerial process is far too complicated for any single individual to perform alone.

This utopian expectation gives rise to the errant direction of much management education in the United States. The existing programs describe what managers should do, although in reality they cannot do it. Open any textbook on management theory, and you will find that the most repeated word is should. The manager should plan, should organize, should communicate, should discipline, should lead. The fact is no one can excel in everything. The managerial process is far too complicated for any single individual to perform alone.

*Because the (PAEI) roles are incompatible, no one can be (P), (A), (E), and (I) at any one time, let alone forever. That makes sense.*

If the (PAEI) executive exists only in textbooks, does that mean every organization will be mismanaged?

*No. Although no individual can be the perfect manager, leader, or executive, we can have a team.*

But watch out; not just any team.

*It must be a complementary team.*

Right. What is necessary is not a single omnipotent genius, but a complementary team. I emphasize the word complementary. Often, when I use the word team, people say, "Right. I need a team of people like me." That's not team building. That's cloning.

Look at your hand again. A hand is five different fingers, which together act like a hand. If all the fingers were alike, you wouldn't have a hand.

---

20   See Adizes, *The Ideal Executive: Why you cannot be one and what to do about it,* op. cit.

In management, we need a complementary team with a sense of united differences. If all the components were the same, the organization would be vulnerable. If they were different, the organization would still be vulnerable because the differences would work at cross purposes. Strength comes from united differences, different fingers with different distinct capabilities that work together.

> In management, we need a complementary team with a sense of united differences. Strength comes from united differences.

The same holds true for a society. The society that is going to handle change best is one that has complementary cultures. I'm not talking about complementary abilities and knowledge, but complementary styles and judgments. This is what has made the USA so successful: Not its resources—other countries have no less, if not more. Not size—other countries are as big, if not larger. It is a culture that nourishes diversity and a population that is diverse, very diverse.

*But don't these differences create miscommunication and conflict?*

There are many reasons for miscommunication. This is one of them. When people's styles are different, they can miscommunicate easily.

*So how can united differences give strength? Differences lead to conflict, and conflict is a weakness.*

On the contrary, differences can give strength.

*Please explain that one.*

Differences are a strength if, when united, they compensate for individual weaknesses.

*I understand: I compensate for your weaknesses with my strengths and vice versa. Now, jointly, we have all strengths, but how do you handle the conflict that diversity generates?*

Let us slowly deal with this important question, because you are right, diversity can be a strength and it can be a weakness. It can be a disaster. It can generate destructive conflict, breakdown of nations, marriages, and partnerships.

Although people will tell you no one is perfect, they do not walk their talk. They still try to be perfect, and they expect others to improve and overcome their weaknesses. People work on their own weaknesses and get frustrated when others do not change. You are born with a personality style, and when people criticize you on your weaknesses, you get hurt and upset. This is because you have this hidden assumption that you could be perfect if only you could fix your weaknesses.

This is a common mistake. You are what you are. You have strengths and you have weaknesses. Normal stuff. So, focus, capitalize on your strengths, and for your weaknesses, find someone you trust to complement you and work as a team.

> *But if I hire someone to complement my weaknesses it means that a person working for me is better than I am.*

In some style characteristics, true.

> *Assume I am the (A) type and I need to hire someone to complement me who is creative, visionary, willing to take risks. That person will scare the daylights out of me; I won't hire her. Or the reverse, I am the (E) type and to complement myself I should hire an (A), who will frustrate the hell out of me.*

Right. People want to believe they are better than the people working for them. This assumption that managers must be better than their subordinates is the source of the hierarchy and elitism that characterizes managerial behavior. Think differently.

> *How?*

You must adopt the attitude that they do not work for you but with you.

> *How do I keep this working together stuff from creating a conflict that will make me frustrated and make me lose sleep? This is the sort of problem married people face all the time. Marriage is a complementary team, but, boy oh boy, is it hard work. How do you prevent the conflict from being destructive?*

Let us think about what makes conflict constructive.

> *This is paradigm shift I would love to understand.*

## Constructive vs. Destructive Conflict

There is change, and change means disintegration, and disintegration means problems.

*So far, so good. Got that.*

Problems need to be solved.

*And in order to solve them we need to decide, and not deciding also constitutes a decision.*

A good decision is one where all (PAEI) roles are performed.

*And there is no individual who can perform all (PAEI) roles simultaneously, on every problem, forever.*

Thus we need...

*We need a complementary team. A complementary team, however, will necessarily entail conflict, because it is composed of differences of styles.*

So conflict is necessary and inevitable in the management of change, and change is inevitable and constant.

Any time we try to eliminate conflict, we're not managing well. We're like the would-be sailor who says, "I would like to cross the ocean and visit foreign lands, but I don't like big waves." So this "adventurer" stays at home, sits in the bathtub, and reads travel magazines.

> Conflict is necessary and inevitable in the management of change.

It's the same phenomenon when managers or political leaders say, "I love to manage or lead. It's people I can't stand." They are sitting in their managerial bathtub, avoiding the real task of management or leadership, which is?

*The harnessing of conflict.*

The higher the rate of change is, the higher the rate of conflict.

*And if we try to stop conflicts, we will be stopping change. Got it.*

One thinker missed this point, which cost millions of people their lives and many more millions their quality of life.

*Who is that?*

I am referring to Karl Marx. He lived during the Industrial Revolution, a time of rapid change in Europe. He witnessed the conflict it created, the pain the working classes were experiencing, and developed an economic philosophy to stop conflict. How? He preached what he called the dictatorship of the proletariat, which is the absolute rule of the workers. That meant one political party, the Communist party. With only one party, there would be no more discussion, and thus no more conflict.

Another source of conflict is a lack of common interests. (We will cover that in future conversations.) Marx preached to stop that source of conflict too, with what he called a classless society. Everyone gives according to his capabilities and gets according to his needs. Thus, there is no more conflict.

This philosophy, called the Communist philosophy, attracted millions of people who were ready to die or kill for it. Why? Because it promised heaven on earth. No conflict. Absolute justice and truth, words that people associate with lack of conflict.

> "If you can't take the heat, get out of the kitchen."
> —PRESIDENT TRUMAN

What happened when the Communist system was applied? It stopped change. The Soviet Union began to fall behind technologically, socially, economically, and even artistically. Mikhail Gorbachev led the process of change and the moment he did, what else had to occur?

*Conflict.*

Right. There is no change without conflict, and if you try to stop one, the other will stop too.

*This is very interesting.*

If you don't like managing conflict, don't try to be a leader. If you don't like people or handling differences of opinion, then get out of the manager's hot seat. As Harry Truman, the President of the United States during World War II, said, if you can't take the heat, get out of the kitchen.

Leading is, in large part, dealing with people who have different styles, people that who have different opinions and interests that must be united. But that will cause conflict.

We can now add this element to our master diagram.

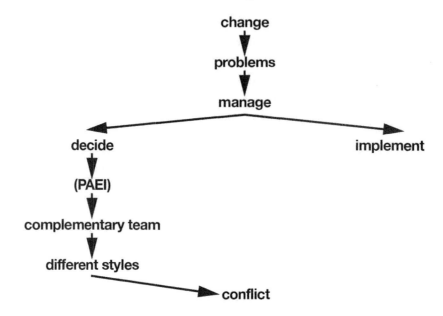

> *I understand that conflict is necessary, but I am still waiting to learn how to make it constructive!*

What does the word "constructive" mean to you?

> *Constructive means to create something new that was not there before.*

That happens when we learn something new. When do we learn? When confronted with an opinion different from ours. We learn from differences.

Imagine you come to someone to tell her of your decision and ask her opinion, and she agrees with everything you say, 100 percent. What did you learn? Nothing new. Maybe you learned that someone agrees with you, but no new knowledge content wise has been created.

Now assume you go to someone else with the same decision and ask his opinion, except this person has a different style from yours. Let us say you are an (E) and he is an (A). You see the big picture. He, on the other hand, notes the details you missed and he starts criticizing your idea, your decision. It is conflict all right, and it is often painful, but if you are open-minded and listen, and willing to listen, you learn something you did not think of or already know. Thus the conflict was...

*Constructive. But to learn from someone who disagrees with you, you must be open-minded.*

---
**It is respect that causes you to be open-minded.**

---

Yes, there must be mutual respect. It is respect that causes you to be open-minded. Without respect for differences of opinion, you do not learn. Respect needs to be mutual so both parties learn. What makes conflicts of style constructive is the existence of mutual respect between the parties involved. It means both parties cherish each other's differences.

*You mean they tolerate diversity?*

Mercy, no! Do you want to have a marriage where you *tolerate* each other's differences? That is the way to suffer, no? You should appreciate each other's differences, because you learn from each other. You enrich each other with your differences.

The word *respect* should not be interpreted as how nicely you talk, and look at the other person, and nod your head. Respect means to value the other, appreciate the other for teaching you and enriching you.

In your previous example where you were an (E) and you hired an (A) to work with you, this (A) can save you a lot of money, right? He can tell you what the barriers are to implementing your dream, helping you avoid having a nightmare instead of a dream. Or if you are an (A) complementing yourself with an (E), this person can make you a lot of money you would not make by yourself.

> *Now I understand what it means to be a colleague. The word comes from Latin:* colegum, *to arrive together. They started from different points of view, and through respectful interaction, learned from each other and came to joint conclusion.*

That is why when true colleagues have a discussion, one might say: "May I respectfully disagree with my learned colleague?" Notice the word *respect*, the open-mindedness, and the willingness to learn.

> *What you are saying is that every leader, manager, or executive should compose her team of people who are colleagues. People whose styles are different, but whom she respects, because she learns from their disagreement.*

Beautifully said. Notice that how we arrive at a conclusion, in a climate of mutual respect, is an asset that can be reapplied. The conclusion or solution can change with time. As President Dwight D. Eisenhower once said, "Plans are useless. Planning is priceless."

Mutual respect is a foundation. The topic can change, the conclusions, and the solutions can change, but the foundation must remain intact.

In Hebrew, the root consonants of the words colleague and confrontation are the same: *amit* and *imut*. Therefore, a colleague is someone with whom you are necessarily in disagreement. Colleagues teach each other by disagreeing respectfully. The relationship is synergistic, full of growth, and constructive when learning happens and when you learn from someone who disagrees with you.

*That happens only when I respect what that person has to say?*

> A colleague is someone with whom you are necessarily in disagreement.

Right. You must be willing to hear and learn from disagreements. Any time you are grappling with a complicated subject—regarding your career, business, or personal life—you consult someone for an opinion. However, you cannot learn from just anyone. Would you consult with someone who is just like you, who always agrees with you, or look for someone you respect who has something different to say, something you did not think about?

*Obviously the latter.*

If you find someone who is different from you, but you don't respect that person, again you will not learn. When seeking advice, you should look for someone who disagrees with you, but whom you respect, because from experience you know you can learn from them.

*We have here a chicken-and-egg problem: You say I should find someone whom I respect, because I learn from them. But in order to learn from them, I have to first respect them. What comes first?*

You must start with respect first. Give them a chance. If you repetitively, repeatedly, do not learn anything from them, or their judgment is wrong, disconnect. I did not say respect everyone. Choose your colleagues.

The same applies to choosing your spouse. Carefully choose your complementary team to compose your marriage. Chose someone who is different from you, whom you respect because they teach you.

> *Interesting. In the Jewish tradition every Friday evening, at the start of the Sabbath dinner, the husband will sing a song of praise for his wife. It is called the "Valiant Woman," (Eshet Hayil). In this song, there is one sentence that always bothered me. It says that a valiant woman is "Ezer ke neged," which in literal translation means "helpful against."*
>
> *I always wondered how she could be helpful if she is against. Now I get it. It depends on* how *she is against.*

If she starts criticizing and putting her husband down for his decisions, she is not helpful, is she? But if she says, "Honey, have you thought about this or that?" etc., and points to the holes in his argument, and complements his style respectfully, it is helpful.

> *The husband learns from his colleague wife.*

Usually (E)s marry (A)s; differences attract, as they complement each other. However this marriage will only be growth-full if there is mutual respect between them and if they are open-minded about each other's point of view, so that they learn from each other. And thus, they will make better decisions together.

You want a partner, a spouse, or a colleague who knows how to disagree without being disagreeable.

Conflicts are synergistic when they are growth-full, when they are constructive. They are growth-full only when learning occurs, and that happens only when there is mutual respect.

Respect is not how nicely you speak or pay attention to the other person. It is necessary to be civilized, but that is only how not to be disagreeable. Respect is a question of values and attitude. To paraphrase Voltaire, I disagree with you but I am willing to sacrifice my life for you to have the right to disagree with me. That is respect, to me.

Let's go over this one more time. When you have a problem you cannot solve alone, you should consult someone whose decision-making style is different from yours. But would you go to just anyone who disagrees with you?

> *Obviously not, I would consult only someone whose opinion I respect, when I believe I can benefit from their disagreement because there is something for me to learn from their differences. I read somewhere that when two people agree on everything, one of them is dispensable.*

There's a similar Zen saying: "If everyone in a meeting agrees on everything, none of them is thinking too hard."

> *Interesting. Now I understand why the Jewish people are considered to be very smart. It is because they never agree with each other. Talmudic scholars are taught never to take anything for granted, to challenge everything.*

Being Jewish means constantly having to argue and defend your position. "Three Jews, five opinions" is an expression you will often hear.

> *That is why Jewish people are sometime a pain to deal with, because they never agree with you? They always challenge you and seem to claim to be superior to you. Honestly, it pisses me off.*

You are not alone—this is one source of anti-Semitism, in my opinion.

Nevertheless, you learn from difference of opinion. If you go to someone who has a different opinion, but find you haven't learned anything that changed your position, then you will feel you wasted your time.

> What makes you a leader is not what you know... it is what you are.

There are those who have something to say. Seek them. There are others who have to say something. Avoid them.

This discussion brings me to the subject of management training or, what is now in vogue, leadership training. Management training should teach people how to handle the pain of harnessing conflict.

> *I notice you are not saying "resolving conflict," but rather you say "harnessing conflict."*

Yes, I do not want to delegitimize conflict, I want to make it constructive. To be a better leader you have to learn how to live with conflict and use conflict constructively. What makes you a leader is not what you know or how much, it is what you are. It is your style, your attitude, and your way of relating to others.

> *Got it.*

Now, I'd like to broaden the focus of the discussion by examining the importance of respect in modern society.

I believe the world stands at a major intersection on the path of history. Because of change, the problems facing society and individuals are increasingly complex. Differences between styles and cultures, and different opinions on how to solve society's problems, cause conflict between countries, between groups, and within individuals.

Whether a person or a society—our global society—will emerge stronger or weaker because of change depends on how we handle our differences. If we build a society of colleagues who respect and capitalize on each other's differences through democracy, we will emerge stronger.

Democracy cannot function without mutual respect. The decisions a democracy makes are not as important as the method used to make them. If a decision turns out to be a mistake, a democratic system that encourages criticism and debate can rectify it. The system enables change, and what it means to be a democratic society has to change democratically too. The higher the rate of change, the more democratic the system must be at every level.

Unfortunately, companies are not run democratically, and as they become bigger, more bureaucratic, and increasingly disempower individuals, I see them as a danger to democracy on macro level.

*Why?*

> Democracy cannot function without mutual respect.

Because if people are disempowered in their working environment, where they spend most of their waking time, why would they feel empowered to impact the decisions made by their political leaders? Democracy has to be all encompassing.

*This is a very ambitious goal.*

I agree, but what is the alternative? Growing bureaucratization. An increasingly disempowered population. Democracy is very vulnerable. It faces threats from increased regulation, increased government intervention—increased (A). It can become democracy in name only, where citizens vote every so often, but feel impotent to effect change via regular channels. Citizens in the US and France already feel they have to occupy Wall Street or to burn tires instead.

*This is depressing enough, but how does respect apply at the individual level? You mentioned the internal conflict change causes within a person. What is that?*

Individuals should have respect for their own internal differences of opinion. They have to recognize and accept the fact that no personal decision is permanent. Keeping an open mind with oneself and with others is essential to making good decisions. Being one's own colleague is the essence of personal success. For that you must have self-respect. We all have a "parliament" inside our head, both conservative thinking and liberal thinking. We should honor and respect these different voices when making a decision. We should respect our own indecision and see if we can learn anything from it.

> *Let me ask a question please. I understand we need a complementary team in which the team members respect each other's differences and make decisions based on mutual respect. But does the team need to have four people representing each of the four (PAEI) roles?*

*Being one's own colleague is the essence of personal success.*

Not necessarily. You can have as few as two people. For example, one person who is (PaEi) and another who is (pAeI) can make an effective complementary team. By the way, this combination is often called a Mom and Pop store. Traditionally, the "Pop" is the (PaEi) in a small family business, the one who opens new stores, brings in new products, and decides on new prices. The "Mom" traditionally keeps the books, an (A) function, and performs the (I) function. She might warn someone who needs something from Pop, "Come tomorrow. He's a little bit crazy today."

There are times, however, when the Mom and Pop roles overlap, or they even exchange roles. Remember, men are not inherently (P)erformers and (E)ntrepreneurs, and women are not inherently (A)dministrators and (I)ntegrators. Mom can be the (PaEi) and Pop the (pAeI).

It takes a complementary team to build a store or to build a family. Show me a successful company, and I'll show you a complementary team. Show me a successful society and I'll show you different cultures working together in a climate of mutual respect.

I suggest that the United States is successful, not just because of its vast physical resources, there are countries with just as many resources, but because it benefits from its sociopolitical culture of mutual respect and trust. It recognizes and respects cultural differences. Have you ever seen a street celebration of America's heritage? Every nationality that makes up the American population is represented, including nations with which America has been at war.

Equal opportunity is the law. Oppressed people from around the world come to the United States for opportunity. In order for equal opportunity to succeed, discrimination on the basis of race, creed, or sex is prohibited by law. If discrimination should increase in the United States, its strength would diminish.

We have to legitimize differences and unite them through a system of mutual respect. We are then enriched because of these differences, not in spite of them. Learning is nurtured because mutual respect encourages the cross-pollination of ideas.

When will differences be constructive and synergistic? When will they produce a learning environment? When there is mutual respect. Without it there is no learning, and with no learning, conflict is dysfunctional.

*Without mutual respect, disagreements are pain with no gain.*

Let us repeat the whole argument from the beginning to be sure you understood me. To recap: Conflict is inevitable because a complementary team is needed for making (PAEI) decisions.

(PAEI) decisions are necessary for any system to be effective and efficient in the short and long term, whether it's an organization or a society.

There is no textbook manager who can perform all the (PAEI) roles simultaneously, just as there is no perfect political party, religion, or culture. A complementary team, or society, or a political system, by definition, comprises individuals or cultures who think and behave differently. That creates conflict, which is desirable when it is constructive, and it is constructive when it is based on mutual respect.

Good decisions, therefore, are a function of a complementary (PAEI) team working with mutual respect.

$$\text{quality of decisions} = f \begin{Bmatrix} 1.\ \text{(PAEI) roles performed} \\ 2.\ \text{mutual respect} \end{Bmatrix}$$

*I think I've got it. In our earlier exercise we imagined a group wrote down the problem and the solution and sealed it inside an envelope. The first two questions I should ask before opening the envelope from this exercise are: Who worked on the problem and how did they work on it?*

Right, and if you don't have a (PAEI) complementary team, or they did not work with mutual respect?

> *Don't open the envelope. You have the wrong problem and the wrong solution.*

If the team was made up of four (A)s, you could predict they would see the problem as a lack of control systems, and their solution would be to institute more standard operating procedures.

> *If there were four (I)s, they probably decided to appoint a subcommittee to study the issue further. They would wait to see which way the wind was blowing.*

Or they will make a decision that is acceptable to those in power in the organization, but not necessarily the right decision for the situation. They will compromise.

> *If they were four (P)s, the meeting was very short. The solution would also be simple: fire, sell, or something like that.*

And if they were four (E)s?

> *Don't even go near the envelope!*

Right. Their solution would probably create twelve more problems. Arsonists' solutions create side effects.

But if you had a complementary team of two or more, in which all four roles were performed, what would the next question be?

> *How did the team work together?*

Right. If they say they disagreed a lot, but compromised to meet a deadline?

> *Don't open the envelope. There was no mutual respect.*

If they say they disagreed, but learned from each other, so that by the end they came up with a solution they all supported?

> *Then, great, open the envelope. But do they vote or must they have a consensus?*

We'll discuss this later. The important thing to note, for now, is that we can predict the quality of decisions based on the styles of the people making them and the quality of their interactions. To produce good decisions, we need a complementary (PAEI) team that works with mutual respect.

## CONVERSATION 8
# Responsibility, Authority, Power, and Influence

*Since we started discussing the (PAEI) roles, now I look at people and say that lady is a (P) or that guy is an (A).*

Wait! That's not right. You're branding people like cattle.

*What's wrong with that? Don't you have tests to measure (PAEI)?*

We have.[21]

*If these tests exist, what exactly is your objection to testing and, as you say, "branding" people?*

I believe that behavior is conditioned mostly by environment. If you assign someone an (A) task, that person will behave like an (A) even if he or she is an (E) at heart. So what good is it knowing what a person is at heart? I am interested in the impact someone's behavior has on others. The best approach is not to test, but to be aware of a person's behavior or your own style and its impact on others.

*Wouldn't you want to know someone's personality type for hiring purposes? An interview might not give you enough data as to their style.*

---

21  The tests are called Management Style Indicators and are available from the Adizes Institute: www.adizes.com.

Absolutely. People who make staffing decisions should use tests, but staffing is not the concern here. I try to change behavior, rather than personalities, by changing the environment in which people work. For instance, don't say that someone is a (P), rather, say that person behaves like a (P). Instead of administering a test, watch how a person behaves.

*What's wrong with labeling people?*

If you start labeling people, your tendency will be to change the people rather than the environment that causes their behavior.

*Okay. Now, can we move on to another subject I have been waiting to get to, how to predict implementation?*

In order to predict whether or not a decision will be implemented, certain factors must be analyzed. First, you cannot implement a decision that's not well defined. If the decision is ambiguous, it's not going to be implemented the way you want.

> If you start labeling people, your tendency will be to change the people rather than the environment that causes their behavior.

*How do you know whether a decision is "well defined?"*

You cannot have an *almost* well-defined decision. It either is well defined or it isn't. A well-defined decision is one that fulfills the four imperatives of decision making.

These imperatives correspond to the (PAEI) roles. Fulfilling them gives you a (PAEI) decision.

The (P) role fulfills the first imperative: what to do. Can you guess what imperative the (A) role fulfills?

*How to do it.*

What about (E)?

*Why it should be done?*

Yes, but (E)'s imperative is *by when*. The timing of a decision is derived from the reason for making that decision in the first place.

*Then is (I) imperative who should do it?*

Exactly, and the big (E) is driving it all the way: *why*.

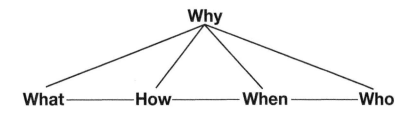

*I see. Why drives what to do, how to do it, by when to do it, and who does it.*

Right. Once we make our decision we need to decide:

(1) what to do, which is fulfilled by the (P) role;

(2) how to do it, fulfilled by the (A) role;

(3) when to do it, fulfilled by the (E) role; and

(4) who should do it, fulfilled by the (I) role.

We must satisfy the four (PAEI) roles if we want to have a well-defined decision.

Frequently people believe they've made a decision, but in reality they've decided only one of the four imperatives. Usually they decide what to do without deciding how. Later on, they may discover that how the decision was implemented has undermined what was decided. The *how* destroyed the *what*.

*Give me an example.*

You probably know this from experience with your kids. They ask if they can do something, and you say yes. Later, you find out that they did what you approved of, but how they did it makes you wish you had never approved the decision in the first place.

*That's true. Sometimes my spouse doesn't tell me what to do, only how to do it. But by the time she finishes telling me in full detail how to do it, she has told me de facto what to do. The* what *and the* how *are interrelated.*

*By when* is also important. If the decision is not carried out in time, the decision will no longer be valid.

*Who* should do it is also important. Sometimes, the person to whom you assign a task determines how the decision will be implemented. Different people interpret decisions to fit their style.

*You mean a decision is not well defined until what, how, by when, and who are communicated and understood? Only then is the decision clear?*

If you decide only one of the (PAEI) imperatives, the person who is assigned to implement the decision will have to provide his own interpretation of the other three imperatives. Then he will do it according to his own style. As a result, you might not like the way the decision was carried out. For example, you tend to have a (P) style and will want it done now, but you did not communicate this at all. The (A) to whom you delegated will assume it is okay if it is done in a year's time. This can create a lot of miscommunication, unhealthy conflict, and mutual accusations between you two.

*So, if I want to predict whether a decision will be implemented correctly, I should check whether the four imperatives were clearly stated and understood. This sounds logical and reasonably simple.*

*Why don't people follow this procedure when making decisions?*

Because people have different (PAEI) styles. Lone Rangers, or (P- - -)s, usually look at the *what* and don't invest time to articulate the *how*. For them the *when* is usually now and the *who* is probably whoever is available right then and there.

Bureaucrats, or (-A- -)s, usually look at the *how*. The *how* drives what to do and when it should be done.

Arsonists, or (- -E-)s, are interested in the *why* (or *why not*) and the *when*. They give you the general idea and usually want it done yesterday. Ask them *what* you should do and they will answer you with why they want it done.

(- - -I)s, or Super Followers, are more interested in *who* is going to do it than *why* it needs to be done. For them, the *what*, *how*, and *when* are driven by *who*. They are very "political."

Because no one is a (PAEI), a decision will usually have one imperative decided and finalized, while the other imperatives remain ambiguous or not expressed at all. The imperative adopted depends on which style dominates the decision-making process.

In order to have a good decision implemented, all four imperatives must be finalized and communicated. This requires a true complementary team that works with mutual respect. (It also requires discipline in decision making, which is covered in another book.[22])

---

22  See Shoham Adizes and Nir Ben Lavi, Ph.D. *Empowering Meetings: A How-To Guide for Any Organization Based on the Adizes Methodology.* Santa Barbara, CA: Adizes Institute Publications, 2014.

*So I must have a decision for which the (PAEI) imperatives are communicated and understood. Is that all there is to having a well-defined decision?*

Not quite. The decision must be bound, too.

*What does that mean?*

Visualize a decision as a square. In each of the four corners is one of the (PAEI) imperatives that define a decision.

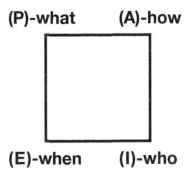

But a square is more than four corners. It has another physical characteristic: It binds space.

The inside of the square represents what we can do, how we can do it, when we should do it, and who should do it. Anything outside the square represents what not to do, how not to do it, who should not do it, and when it should not be done.

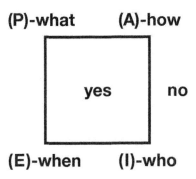

*What are you saying?*

I'm saying that you don't know what to do until you know what not to do.

Consider this example given by Professor Herbert Simon, Nobel Laureate in economics. Jennifer is trying to teach Tom how to lace his shoes. A curtain separates them. Tom does exactly as Jennifer directs, but he misinterprets it in every possible way. Jennifer says, "Take the shoelace and put it through the first hole, and then from below, through the second hole." Tom does exactly that, except he passes the shoelace around his shoe first. Jennifer cannot tell Tom how to lace his shoe correctly, unless she realizes what Tom is doing and can also tell him what not to do.

Any time something new is attempted, people must learn what not to do, as they attempt to do it correctly. A person really only knows what to do, when he also knows what not to do, and that knowledge comes with experience.

It is the same with the *who* component. We learn from experience who should perform a task after we make the mistake of assigning it to the wrong person. We know better who should perform a task after we learn who should not do it.

*Is that why, for some people, their second marriage is better than their first?*

It is, if they learned from their experience. It also tells you not to hire consultants who tell you only what to do. You will never really learn. When they leave, you still do not know what to do because the situation probably changed, and what you were told to do at that time no longer applies. A consultant should remain during implementation, so that she can tell you what not to do and you can learn.

Good experience comes from good decisions. Good decisions come from good judgment and good judgment comes from bad experience.

What I'm saying is that you do not learn from what's expected, but what is inspected. Through inspection you get feedback. That's how you learn from mistakes.

*I know which people manage by expectations only: the Arsonists. They make a decision and expect the task to be accomplished. They hate to inspect, follow through, and make corrections.*

Right. Managers should analyze the results of their decisions. Inspect them and learn from experience. Analyze them until they know what to do and what not to do, how to do and how not to do, when to do and when not to do, and who should do it and who should not do it. Only then can they have a decision that is fully defined and understood.

*But by that time, most probably, the decision is obsolete. They'll have to start all over again.*

You live and you learn, constantly! There is really no such thing as a good decision, it's only a good decision for the time being.

It takes time to experiment with a decision until it works. But even then, don't become too attached to it. Its life span is short. The higher the rate of change, the shorter the time span for the validity of the decision.

> There is really no such thing as a good decision, it's only a good decision for the time being.

A decision has to be depicted graphically as a square. It has to be bound, and it must have four imperatives. The square represents the decision that is supposed to be implemented or the defined responsibility to make a change. A person can't be really responsible until she has a well-defined (PAEI) task, which means a square of responsibility.

*But many times, even if we know the four imperatives, the decision will still not get implemented. Why?*

The (PAEI) imperatives are the first factors that predict implementation, but not the only ones. We also need leadership energy to carry the decision through.

Often we know what needs to be done, but we can't carry it out without authority, power, influence, or any combination of these three.

*Please define these concepts for me.*

There are many definitions of authority. I use sociologist Max Weber's definition, which is the legal right to make certain decisions. It is independent of what the person knows and whom he knows. It is independent of his personality. It is determined by the position in the organization, and anyone who holds that job has the formal right to make the decisions associated with that position. It is the formal authority.

But what if we eliminate the phrase "the right to make certain decisions" and substitute it with "the right to say yes…"

*Or no!*

You've made a common mistake. The word "or" is misleading.

*Why?*

There are many organizations where people can say no, but cannot say yes to suggestions that lead to change.

*So?*

In a bureaucracy, you will find many managers who possess the authority to say no, but only rarely do the same managers have the authority, the legal right, to say yes to decisions that cause change. Only the person at the top has the right to say both yes and no to decisions that cause change.

*I see. When organizations are young, founders have the right to say yes and no. They have full authority; there is no question about where one needs to go for approval of a decision that involves change.*

> In the Adizes Methodology, authority is defined as the right to say yes *and* no.

As organizations grow and become too complex for founders to manage alone, they have to delegate authority. Usually they hesitate to delegate the right to say yes for fear of losing control. As a result, they delegate only the right to say no.

As organizations grow, the right to say yes stays with the president and more and more layers of no-sayers separate the yes-sayer from where the action is.

*That's very dangerous, because authority to say only no prohibits change and bureaucratizes an organization. If authority is the right to make decisions about change, then authority should be the right to say yes* and *no.*

In the Adizes Methodology, authority is defined as the right to say yes *and* no. If managers cannot say yes, neither should they be able to say no.

*That means I should propose change only to the person in the hierarchy who is allowed to say yes. If my boss is not permitted to say yes he should not have the right to say no. He must pass the suggestion up to the person who has the right to say yes. That's how to keep an organization young and capable of dealing promptly with change.*

Careful though, when you try to implement this methodology there is going to be lots of resistance, because lots of problems that need solutions are going to go all the way up the ladder to the president. This is because authority is centralized with the CEO or the founder of the company, especially in an aging corporation or a Go-Go company.[23]

*I do not understand this. Shouldn't the problem or the solution that needs approval be given to the person responsible for dealing with it?*

Not in this methodology. We assign problems to the person who has the authority to solve them, not necessarily to the one who has the responsibility for it.

*Why?*

As organizations advance on their lifecycle, and especially after the Go-Go stage, authority and responsibility get bifurcated. Responsibility is delegated, except for the authority to say yes to changes. As a result, many people have responsibilities, but lack the authority to make a change in order to solve the problem.

So, we assign problems to where the authority lies, where the person can say yes to a solution. When you do this, the president has so much to do she must either take on responsibility to solve the problems or she must delegate authority to the person with the responsibility.

*You are integrating, I see. You are integrating authority with responsibility. You are healing the organization, because disintegration was the cause of their bureaucratization.*

Exactly. If decisions are depicted as a square, next I'm going to depict authority as a circle.

---

[23] See Adizes, *Managing Corporate Lifecycles*, op. cit.

## 144 – MASTERING CHANGE

*I get the idea. The circle also encloses space. The circle's boundaries define the authority I have, or, in other words, what decisions I am legally empowered to make. The space outside the circle represents the areas over which I have no authority.*

Now, superimpose the circle of authority on the (PAEI) square of defined responsibility. What do you get?

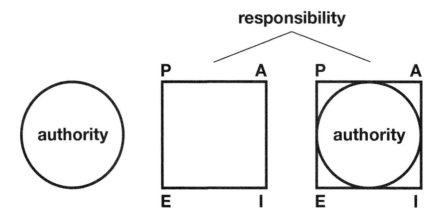

*But the square and the circle can never fully overlap. That means authority will never be equal to responsibility. How can that be? We just discussed the integration of responsibility and authority.*

They should be integrated or together, but not equal.

I purposely depicted authority as a circle and responsibility as a square, so that they would never equal each other. You may have authority beyond your defined responsibility at times, and at other times you may have more responsibility than authority.

*Most people would call this bad management. How can someone be responsible for something, yet not have the necessary authority to decide and carry out that responsibility. All management textbooks say authority should equal responsibility. That makes sense to me. It is logical.*

I think differently. I think the worst possibility is that the two are equal. They should be almost equal, but not absolutely.

*If there are areas where I have responsibility without the authority to carry out a task, how can I perform the task and be evaluated fairly? I am lost now.*

What I have given you so far is an optical illusion. Can you really draw responsibility as a square with distinct lines that absolutely define what is included in your responsibility and what is not? Can you do that in reality?

*Obviously not.*

Why not?

*Because change is a constant. Whatever we decided yesterday might not be applicable today. Responsibility is an approximation.*

The same is true of authority. It is subject to change. You cannot delineate it perfectly. Its boundaries—with respect to time, people, and situations—change.

The square and the circle can never fully overlap. That means that, in reality, authority will never be equal to responsibility. Responsibility and authority would be better depicted like this.

*When do you know exactly what you're responsible for and exactly what authority you have? When do you have both responsibility and authority such that you can stabilize and make them equal to each other?*

Only when there is no change. And when does that happen?

*When you're dead.*

Right. Sometimes you have more control than you need; sometimes you don't have enough. That's life. Not knowing your precise authority and responsibility in a constantly changing world is normal and even desirable.

*Desirable? How do you figure?*

Because it means you are alive, and the more alive you are, the more you run into situations where you are not in authority or control.

*How do I handle that?*

Since authority cannot equal responsibility all the time, you will sometimes have responsibility without commensurate authority. What should you do then to carry out your responsibility?

*Ask for the authority. Go and get it.*

What if you have authority without responsibility?

*Take on more responsibility?*

Right. In a young company, say 40% of the responsibility and authority is given, 60% is taken. In an older company, 60% is given, 40% is taken. (Don't take these numbers literally, like an (A).)

The day when 100% of the authority and responsibility is given and none is taken, the organization is dead. That's why it is desirable not to know your precise authority and responsibility. It means that the organization is young, alive, and changing.

*But how can people function with this kind of uncertainty?*

If you believe it's your responsibility, then it's your responsibility.

> If you believe it's your responsibility, then it's your responsibility.

*But I might invade someone else's territory. What if my responsibility overlaps with someone else's?*

What is wrong with picking up the phone and saying, "We have a problem. Is it mine or yours?"

How do you play doubles in tennis? Do you draw a chalk line down the middle of the court, saying this is your area, and this is mine? When the ball comes at high speed, do you wait until you're sure where it's going to land before deciding who is responsible for hitting it back? Obviously not. You both watch for the ball. Part of the area is yours, part of the area is your teammate's, and whose part is the middle?

*Ours!*

If the ball comes down the middle, you both might make a move. Therefore, you should watch the ball and each other.

*But if we both make a move for the ball, that's not efficient, right?*

Yes, but in order to be effective in hitting the ball, we might have to sacrifice some efficiency. Both of us may have to make a move for the ball, even if it's just our eyes that move.

Have you watched bureaucracies operate? To maximize efficiency they say, "This is your area. Don't step into anyone else's." Everyone has a precisely defined domain of responsibility, so that no one wastes energy doing someone else's job. It is very efficient, but what happens when things change? Say, a problem develops in an area where it's not clear who is responsible. The ball has landed between two players, and neither is sure whose ball it is. What does a bureaucracy usually do?

*It appoints a third person to stand in the middle.*

Yes. Now there are two new areas with potential for uncertainty as to who is responsible. One year later, what will the bureaucracy do?

*It appoints two more people to cover the new uncertainties. Soon there will be a hundred areas where people overlap and feel uncertain about who is responsible. The court will be overrun with players.*

> Bureaucracies are ineffective because they try to be too efficient.

By then nobody is playing tennis. They're watching each other instead of the ball. "Don't step over this line. This is my territory." "No! This is my territory!" It's called turf wars. Nobody even notices the ball unless it hits him smack between the eyes. Everyone is too busy protecting his domain.

*You mean that in a bureaucracy, people focus more on how and who, than on what and why? Or, in the (PAEI) code, a bureaucracy is more focused on (A) and (I), than on (P) and (E)?*

Haven't you seen that in your experience? Bureaucracies are ineffective because they try to be too efficient. To maximize control the assigning of responsibilities is very precise and detailed, eliminating uncertainties. Have you seen job descriptions in a bureaucratic organization? It would take a battery of lawyers to interpret them. Have you looked at their manuals? They contain pages and pages of how to do something rather than why to do it.

As a result, bureaucracies grow in size with change. Change creates more uncertainty. More uncertainty creates more demand for more people to handle it and for more policies and rules, which create even more uncertainty with change, etc.

*Bureaucrats have responsibility but no authority to make changes. It is the elected politicians who have the authority to decide through legislation.*

That makes it very inflexible, very slow to change. Thus, the word bureaucracy has a negative connotation.

*Sometimes when dealing with areas of overlapping responsibility, they appoint a committee. Bureaucracies have lots of committees. Isn't that a solution to the overlap issue?*

Not necessarily, because a committee usually doesn't feel responsible for solving the problem either. No one on the committee has authority to say yes. They only make a recommendation.

A bureaucracy has an (A) culture where people would rather be precisely wrong than approximately right. (A)s ask permission. (E)s ask forgiveness. For (A)s, everything is forbidden unless expressly permitted. For (E)s, everything is permitted unless expressly forbidden.

> A bureaucracy has an (A) culture where people would rather be precisely wrong than approximately right.

In government it is this attention to precision and avoidance of risk that fosters bureaucratic growth. Some societies reinforce this risk avoidance out of fear that government may overstep its bounds. By limiting authority, society prevents government agencies from taking initiative.

*But this could be fully justifiable. You don't want government officials overstepping their authority. That can endanger the control a society wishes to exercise on its public servants. Government officials are there to serve, not overrun—I mean manage, decide for the people.*

Good point. Do you know what the root of the word administer is? It is *to serve*. That's why we say public administration instead of public management. We use the terms arts administration, education administration, and health administration. Public servants, as the name suggests, are supposed to serve the artists, teachers, medical personnel, and the people in general. They are there to facilitate, not manage.

We want public servants, as (pAeI)s, to stay within their defined responsibilities. The artists, teachers, and medical personnel are the (PaEi).

*Then how do you keep public servants from becoming bureaucrats and bureaucratizing the organization?*

There must be complementary management. They must work together, co-decide with the artists or scientists or whomever they serve.

*Who performs the (E) role in government, then?*

The politicians.

*I can see why there is no love lost between the governmental machinery and the political machinery. It appears to be the typical (E) versus (A) conflict.*

Integrating the political structure into the governmental structure is a difficult process. It can be done, and I have done it.[24] But let's not digress anymore. Let's go back my recommendation that authority not match responsibility exactly. I say that responsibility should equal authority, more or less.

*You're claiming that all management textbooks that say the opposite, that authority should equal responsibility, are wrong.*

Yes they are. The parity they prescribe doesn't occur in the real world. Have you ever met a manager who claims to have all the authority she needs for her responsibility? In my experience all managers, leaders even administrators complain they don't have sufficient authority to carry their responsibilities.

In young companies authority is clear, and responsibilities are ambiguous. In aging companies, responsibilities are clear, and authority is ambiguous. Only when an organization is in its Prime does authority equal responsibility, but even then it is more or less. Both are functionally somewhat ambiguous. That is the reality.

*Because of change, right? Both the square (responsibility) and the circle (authority) are changing. They always shift and thus rarely, if ever, fully overlap.*

Yes, the relationship of authority to responsibility must be more or less rather than perfectly equal, because of the reality of change. They could equal only when you stop change, which means when you are dead.

*You mean to say we are fully in control of life when we are dead. This is funny.*

---

24   See my manuscript "Confessions of an Organizational Transformationalist" (Santa Barbara, CA: Adizes Institute Publications, forthcoming).

*But how do you handle more or less? How do you handle the areas of uncertainty? The higher the rate of change, the higher the uncertainty, right?*

Both teamwork and influence, which is another source of energy, must be used to get things done.

The gap between responsibilities and authority, caused by change, should be covered with a lot of influence. The greater the rate of change, the greater the level of uncertainty, which, in turn, requires more influence.

The greater the rate of change, the greater the level of uncertainty as to who has the responsibility and who has the authority. The greater the uncertainty, the better the teamwork will have to be, or in a chronically changing situation, bureaucracy will mushroom.

*You mean my success depends, to some degree, on others?*

> The greater the uncertainty, the better the teamwork will have to be, or in a chronically changing situation, bureaucracy will mushroom.

You are most vulnerable when you fight this reality and attempt to negate your interdependence. Just remember, the organization was born with interdependence, and this interdependence was tested when you all came upon a rock blocking your way, a rock none of you alone could lift. The organization was born when the need for interdependence was recognized. There is no organization and no management without interdependence. If you do not accept this, you can't manage. You cannot lead.

*What else do we have beyond authority to get things done, to cause implementation to happen?*

Power. It is the capability, not the right, to punish and/or reward. If I can hurt you or make you happy, I have power over you.

*When does that happen?*

If you need anything from me, I have power over you, because I can either give it to you or not give it to you.

*Makes sense.*

Now, would you agree with me that to withhold expected rewards is a punishment?

*Yes.*

If you expect something from me and I deny giving it to you, I'm punishing you. I might claim that I'm not punishing you and that I'm just not giving you what you want, but that's a punishment, isn't it?

*I've seen that happen in some bad marriages.*

You want to punish people? Promise them something and then don't deliver it. They will be upset and hurt. You let them build expectations that are not met. And the way to punish yourself is to expect too much of yourself. When you can't deliver, you'll really come down hard on yourself. The road to happiness does not go through expectationsville.

*Are you telling me then, to be a vegetable, someone who wants nothing?*

I didn't say to want nothing, although wanting too has its negative repercussions. When you want something it means you are not happy with what you have. You are negative about your situation. The more ambitious you are, the more frustrated you become and the harder you are on yourself and on others.

> The way to punish yourself is to expect too much of yourself. The road to happiness does not go through expectationsville.

*What should be the right attitude then, without expecting and wanting?*

Do what needs to be done. That is all. Do what the situation dictates. Do the best you can, and leave the rest to God to take care of. If you do not believe in God, let the probabilities in life dictate what will happen.

It is important to understand that you cannot control outcomes. All you can do is your best.

*Without expecting or wanting a specific outcome. Just let it be. Is that it?*

Expecting and wanting assumes you are in control. We all know from experience, which comes with age, that we are not in control. We try to be in control at tremendous expense to our happiness.

You will be happier in life if you just do what needs to be done, do your best, and that is all there is to it.

*As far as organizations are concerned, you said that power is the capability to punish or reward, and that withholding expected rewards is equivalent to punishment.*

Right. Since you cannot lift the rock alone, you need the cooperation of others. And since there are many rocks on the path to the realization of any goal, anyone you need to assist you in lifting the rocks (your responsibility) has power over you. Power is the capability to grant or withhold needed cooperation.

*Let me see if I understand. If I could do the job by myself, there would be no organization, because I would not need others. Since I can't carry out my responsibility alone, anyone I need has power over me.*

The measure of their power is a function of how much you need them and how much of a monopoly they have over what you need. That's why falling in love or being infatuated with someone is an overpowering experience. We say, "I need you so much. I can't live without you. You're the only one for me." That situation can be extremely painful or gratifying, depending on the response.

> Power is the *capability* to grant or withhold needed cooperation.

*So when am I totally free?*

When you can say you don't need anybody for anything.

*But you're going to tell me that will happen only when I'm dead!*

In a prior conversation we mentioned the epitaph on the headstone of Nikos Kazantzakis, author of *Zorba the Greek*: "No more hope, no more fear. Finally free."

As long as you hope for or fear something, that thing has power over you. Being a member of a civilized society, living in a highly interdependent environment, means relying on others. Thus, the more developed the society, the more powerless the individuals in it will feel. Whomever you need, for whatever reason, has power over you. They're as powerful as the importance you attach to whatever you need from them.

*Now let me ask you a question. As a manager, as a leader, where is the power?*

Good question. Is it above, below, or beside you? Whom do you need the most?

*The power is above me. My boss has the most power.*

You have confused power with authority. In the upper strata of the organization, there is more authority than power. Maybe there is some authorized power, but raw power with no authority is in the hands of those you need most to accomplish your responsibility. Who are they?

> It's the people on the line who make a company flourish or die.

*The employees.*

They can withhold cooperation without having the authority to do so. If they do, you can't carry out your responsibility. You will have difficulty lifting the rock of your managerial responsibility without them.

One time I was consulting for a shoe manufacturing company. We were doing strategic planning, what kind of shoes, at what price, style, and quality, etc.—high-level planning. At the break I wandered into the shipping department of the company. They were putting shoes into boxes. I wondered what if a worker, just a minimum-wage worker, was upset with the company, what damage could he do? Take one shoe of one size another shoe of another size, put them in the same box, and send them out. Who would know? Who would catch him doing it? I visualized the strategic planners, consultants, and top executives working hard, making marketing and product-differentiation decisions. Then here's this guy, making minimum wage, who's capable of ruining their whole strategy by not cooperating.

What is the value of a managerial decision if the employees sabotage it? Uncooperative flight attendants can ruin an airline's multimillion-dollar advertising campaign just by being rude to customers. When does a military organization lose a war? When the generals have not been in the trenches for a long time. When they ignore the soldiers on the line.

It's the people on the line who make a company flourish or die. Many people believe the way to power is to climb the organizational ladder. They climb and bloody themselves as they fight their way up, pushing others over the cliff in order to be the only one to get to the top. Finally when they reach the top, exhausted, they find a sign saying, "It's down there."

Many good leaders have learned that the higher they go, the more they have to respect who is "down there," because that's where their dreams and plans will be either fulfilled or dashed.

*What about influence?*

# Influence

Influence is the capability, not the right, to make another person do something without using authority or power.

*Give me an example.*

What I'm doing right now, I hope, is influencing you. I have no authority to tell you what to do. I have no power to withhold future information or cooperation from you if you don't do what I am teaching here. I don't even know whether we will meet again. Thus, if you manage differently starting Monday morning in light of these conversations, it is because you have been persuaded. You believe in it because it makes sense to you.

When people take our input and *make their own decisions* based on this input, we have influenced them. When people are free to act of their own volition, they have been influenced. Anything other than that is not influence; rather, it is a combination of power, authority, and/or influence.

Here is how you can test yourself to see if you have used influence on people or not: Assume you are alone in the room with the focal person, the person you are trying to influence. Assume no one knows what you are telling him to do. There is no record, no tape recorder, and no minutes are being taken. Now assume when you finish talking to him, you have a heart attack and die. Right there.

No one else beyond the focal person knows what instructions you gave him. Only he knows. Will he carry them out or ignore them? There is no record of what was said, so he is free to choose. If he will do it, it means he now "owns" that decision. He was influenced. If he ignores your instruction, you have not influenced him.

Whenever you try to influence someone imagine this scenario. Is the person convinced to the point that he owns the decision and will act on, it even if you change your mind, or not?

When I lead organizational restructuring, I want to test whether or not I have influenced the organization. Are they going to do the restructuring out of their own conviction or because they are just following my recommendations? Do they own the new structure or not?

When the redesign of the structure is done, I take the floor and start criticizing the structure and find problems with it. (It's not too difficult to do because nothing in this world is perfect. The structure is the best we can do. That is all.) People then get upset with me, "We like the structure and we are going to implement it, whether you like it or not. It is our company so please relax."

When they say something like this, I know the decision has been based on influence and not on being overpowered by a fast-talking consultant. I know that they own the structure and will implement it whether I come back or not.

*But power, authority, and influence aren't separate. They are inter-related.*

Absolutely. Let's look at the combinations by considering authority, power, and influence as circles that overlap.

# Authorance

The diagram below is a Venn diagram, the type used in symbolic logic to show relationships between sets. When authority and power overlap, what do you get? Authorized power (ap). That is the right to punish and/or reward. For instance, when someone has the right to promote, to increase salaries, and to approve vacation time, she has authorized power.

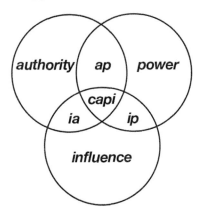

*When they're not overlapping, that's authority without power. What does that mean?*

It means you have the right to tell someone what to do, but if he doesn't do it, you can't really do anything about it. You don't wish to stir up a hornets' nest. This might be the case, for instance, with a talented researcher in a company insists on working differently from all the other scientists. Because she is valuable to you, you leave her alone, even though you have the authority to order her to conform. The cost of using your authority might be higher than the long-term value. That's authority without effective power.

*What about power without authority?*

Power without authority occurs in situations in which you can withhold cooperation without being caught. Consider the difficulty of trying to catch the worker who put the wrong shoes in the box. If you can catch and punish such workers, then they don't have power. However, if you can't catch them, they do have power. Another example is postal workers, who can easily misdirect the mail. You can't monitor every postal worker. As for sales people on the road, you can't accompany them and control exactly what they do and how they do it. They have the effective capability to withhold cooperation if they want to. That's why we control salespeople mostly by results. If you try to control the process, it's often more expensive than it's worth. So you had better motivate them to do it right. This is where influence comes in.

*What about the situation in which power and influence overlap?*

I call this indirect power (ip). If somebody tries to influence you, but you don't feel you have the freedom to decide, that person has indirect power. You read the influence as a threat, as power. Reading between the lines you realize that you had better do what the person says. He is not threatening you, he is rather nice, but you are worried.

*Give me an example.*

A staff vice president from the corporate headquarters visits a factory and gives the production line some suggestions. This person has no authority to instruct, but the production manager knows this staff person is close to the president. She has his ear. She can do damage to the production manager if she wants to.

The VP "suggests" something to be done. The line manager does not believe in the suggestion, but is frightened by this executive from headquarters that can do him harm, and follows the suggestion. If the decision results in a disaster, the production manager says, "Corporate staff told me to do it."

The corporate vice president will respond, "Not true. I only suggested it."

The line feels no responsibility, since it feels it was threatened into submission. The corporate person feels no responsibility, because she didn't authorize the line to do anything. After all, this person had no authority to decide. She just "suggested." The end result? No one feels accountable for what happened.

*You just used the word "accountable." How is accountability different from responsibility?*

In the first edition of my book *Managing Corporate Lifecycles* I wrote a whole chapter about it. For now it's enough to understand the difference is this: responsibility is what the organization expects from you, accountability is what you feel can truly be expected from you. That is what you feel accountable for. For that you need to know your responsibility well, have the authority, power, and/or influence to carry it through, and feel rewarded for doing it. Otherwise, although you are responsible, you would not feel accountable.

*What about when influence overlaps authority?*

I call it influencing authority (ia). That's what the late business author and statesman Chester Barnard called authority by acceptance or professional authority. The person with authority has the right to say what to do, but can also convince people of the validity of what he says. That's when we say, "My boss is an authority on the subject. I think she's right and I'm going to do what she says." That is accepted authority.

When authority, power, and influence overlap, you get a new combination.

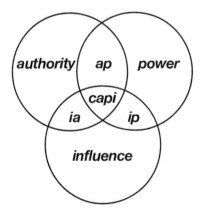

I call this *capi*, which is an acronym for coalesced authority, power, and influence. You have the authority to tell people what to do, you can influence them as to the validity of what you want done, and if they are in doubt and do not listen well, you have the power to punish or reward them, and that assures they will listen and comply.

There is no reason, when you have capi, why people would not follow your decisions. You have the legal right to decide, they know you have the power to punish and reward, and they're persuaded by the content of your decision that it is the right one. You have control.

*I like that.*

Hold your horses. In our next conversation you might find out that it is not the best situation at all. The dream might be a nightmare.

The total managerial energy—which is the totality of authority, power, and influence, plus the union (μ) of authority and power, the union of authority and influence, plus capi—I call authorance, symbolized by a sigma, which is the mathematical notation for summation. In mathematical symbols, it can be written like this:

**Σ = a+ p + i + μap + μai + μip + μapi**

Capi is the core of the Venn diagram, where authority, power, and influence overlap.

**capi = μapi**

Now, we have learned that to implement decisions they must first be well defined, and that means. . .

> *That all (PAEI) imperatives should be fully expressed.*

Which, in terms of decisions, means?

> *What, how, when, and who.*

And also?

> *What not, how not, when not, and who not.*
>
> *Further, in order to carry out this well-defined decision, we need authority, power, and influence, or any combination of the three.*

Next we'll discuss how to predict the effectiveness and efficiency with which a decision will be implemented.

## CONVERSATION 9

# Predicting the Efficiency of Implementing Decisions

*I now understand authority, power, influence, and their combinations. I have a well-defined (PAEI) decision and a square of responsibility. Now, will you tell me how to predict efficient implementation?*

Let's superimpose authority, power, and influence, as depicted in our diagram, on the square of responsibility and see what happens. We'll take three situations.

In the first case, managers have authority, power, and influence, or any combination of them; they have authorance, more or less equal to responsibility, with which to carry out that responsibility. But the capi component, the core of the diagram, where the three overlap, does not cover the responsibility. It is too small. What does this mean?

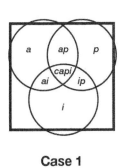
Case 1

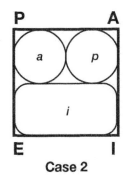
Case 2

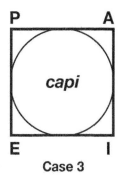
Case 3

*These managers have enough (more or less) authority, power, and/or influence to carry out their responsibility, but don't have control (capi) over all of their responsibilities.*

They are the type of managers who juggle. Over some areas of their responsibility, they have only authority. They will have to decide and then hope their decision is carried out. In other areas, where they have no authority but they do have power, they say to those whose help they need, "Help me out and I'll help you too. Otherwise. . . " In the third area of their responsibility, they have only influence. They have to convince others to help.

They have control only over a very small part of their responsibility: where they have capi. In that area, they make decisions and things get done without much doubt, because they have authority and power and influence.

*But the circles do not fully cover the square. In some areas of responsibility, these managers have no authority, no power, and no influence.*

That's normal because of change, remember? The square and the circles move. They are rarely equal anyway. When responsibility is larger than authority, the person will have to try to get more influence. That should be easier than to get more authority.

Because of change, the composition of authorance has to be such that influence is bigger than the square, influence is bigger than the responsibility. That means a person should have influence over what he is responsible for.

Authority should be more or less equal to responsibility. Since influence is bigger than responsibility, whatever is not covered by authority is covered by influence.

There should be some area in which there is authorized power. Power is inside the authority circle. That is power over what is really critical. This is reserved for transgressions of values, quality, or policy.

By the way, this symbol is the logo of the Adizes Institute Publications.

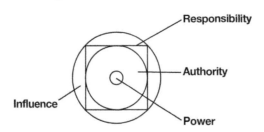

*What about when authority is bigger than responsibility? That can happen too.*

In areas where authority is bigger than responsibility, leaders should just take the additional responsibility on themselves and see that they are not crashing into someone else. Later on, we'll discuss how to do this.

For now, let's proceed to the second case, in which the authority, power, and influence circles do not overlap, although they cover, more or less, the square of responsibility. There is no capi. How does that look graphically?

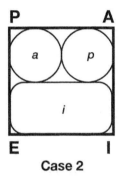

Case 2

*Can managers implement their decisions in this case? Can they be responsible?*

It's going to be more difficult this time. Authority without power isn't worth much. What can one do with authority and no power? How about power without authority? Power without authority is very dangerous. It works in the short term, but backfires sooner or later because it is not legitimized.

*How about just influence?*

Influence without authority and power works, but it takes a long time to build influence. Each of the components—authority, power, and influence—have different rates of effectiveness, i.e., how they impact those to whom they are directed.

162 – MASTERING CHANGE

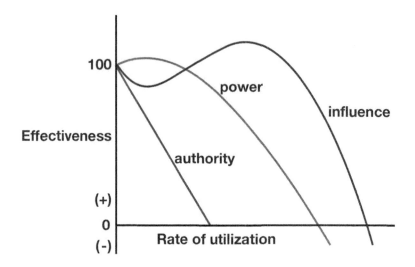

Assume you measure effectiveness on a vertical line. What impact will the use of any of these energies have on the direction of the line?

Place the rate of utilization on the horizontal line. Start with power. If you have never punished, nor rewarded, then the utilization rate is zero.

*Then why is effectiveness above zero?*

It is called assumed power. People assume how much damage you can do to them by punishing or withholding reward before you do anything.

What happens when you use power for the first time? Effectiveness will go up, because the first punishment is the most painful. It is not assumed anymore. It is real. It will be somewhat equal to the assumed effectiveness, but if you continue using power more frequently, what happens to effectiveness? Whoever is using power will have to use more and more to get the same effectiveness. In absolute terms, power loses effectiveness the more it is used.

*You are right. The first time you punish a child it is very traumatic. If you abuse a child often, the abuse increasingly has less and less effect.*

Yes. I worked in a prison. Punishments did not work well. The inmates had been hurt so badly all their lives that another punishment was just another event. Love, however, has enormous effect. That is why some prisons give prisoners a dog to raise. Now take that dog away, take that love away, and you will see grown man cry.

If you use too much power it backfires. The people against whom you are using power, will use power back at you. It has negative effectiveness.

*How about influence?*

Start with zero utilization. Effectiveness is still positive. Why?

*I would guess it is assumed influence, assumed effectiveness.*

Yes. Realize that when you start using influence, at first it might go down in effectiveness. Why? Because the listener is testing you, to see if she can trust your influence. If you prove to be constructive and trustworthy, effectiveness goes up, but not endlessly. At a certain level of utilization, you might be out of your depth, as they say. For instance, you might know economics, but what do you know about psychology and marriage counseling?

*What about authority?*

That is the weakest of managerial energies. People erroneously believe it is the most powerful, and thus seek more and more authority, but it is weak if it is not backed up by power and/or influence. Just imagine you tell a subordinate, do this because I am your boss. If you cannot back it with influence or power, how many times can you use this source of energy?

*Not many times, I agree.*

So what do managers do when they have responsibility with authorance but no capi?

*They can be effective, but I bet they won't sleep very well. They'll spend sleepless nights thinking of ways to enforce their decisions. They will not be efficient in how they use their energy.*

Now let's take the third case: The leader has authorance over responsibility (more or less) and this authorance is entirely composed of capi. How will that diagram look?

The three circles will overlap completely so that you have total capi, and it will almost cover the square.

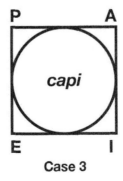

Case 3

## AΣ capi ≅ Responsibility

*For almost every part of their responsibility, the leaders have authority, power, and influence reinforcing each other.*

Can they implement their decisions now?

*You bet! They have the right to decide and can back that right with influence and power, both of which are legitimized and in their possession. Managers in this situation decide, and it happens. They are in control of their responsibility.*

Right on. Let's look again at these three cases.

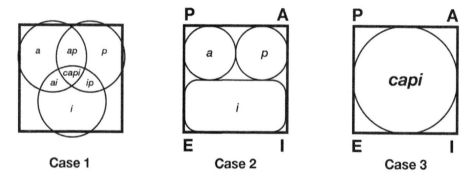

Case 1   Case 2   Case 3

Can the managers in each of these three cases carry out their responsibilities?

*Yes, as long as they have authority and/or power and/or influence. As long as they have more or less sufficient authorance, they should be able to get their managerial job done.*

Which means they are equally effective in each case, but are they equally efficient? Efficiency measures how much energy they have to use to get their responsibility carried out. Who sleeps best at night?

*The managers in the third case!*

Right. All they have to do is decide and it will get done. They have full capi, full authority, power, and influence over their responsibilities.

Who is the least efficient? Who sleeps the least at night?

*The managers with zero capi.*

You have just discovered a very important concept: managerial effectiveness and efficiency. Effectiveness is measured by the capability to get the job done, to carry out ones responsibility. Efficiency is measured by the energy leaders have to expend in order to implement their decisions, to carry their responsibility.

Managerial effectiveness is a function of authorance in relation to responsibilities. Managers are effective when they have sufficient authority and/or power and/or influence for their responsibility. You can be effective as a manager as long as you have sufficient authorance to carry out your responsibilities.

$$\text{Managerial effectiveness} = f \left\{ \frac{\text{authorance}}{\text{responsibility}} \right\}$$

Managerial efficiency is a function of the amount of capi held by the managers, out of the total authorance they have. The more capi, the less energy they have to spend to get things done.

$$\text{Managerial efficiency} = f \left\{ \frac{\text{capi}}{\text{authorance}} \right\}$$

*I believe I understand: The only thing managers need in order to implement decisions effectively is to have sufficient authorance. It means they should have all the authority, power, and influence they need to carry out their decisions. In order to be efficient, with their use of energy in carrying out their responsibility, they need capi.*

So which of the three above situations would you prefer?

*Without doubt situation number 3. I have all the capi I need to get my job done. Easy.*

That is the dream of every leader, manager, executive, and macho man. But let me tell you, what starts as a dream ends as a nightmare.

*What?*

How often do you find people with full capi, full control, over their responsibilities? Rarely, if ever. There is a reason. The situation may exist in a dictatorship, but only for a short while.

*Why?*

Imagine having complete authority, power, and influence. Which source of total managerial energy (authorance) would you be inclined to use most? Which is the most efficient? You use it and it has impact, almost instantaneously.

> *Power! I can see that with children. When I don't have the time to persuade them to do something, I threaten punishment.*

That's why power corrupts and absolute power corrupts absolutely. Power gives instant results, but over time higher and higher doses are necessary to achieve the same impact. It's like a drug.

Power corrupts because it is effective and easy to use. When you have all the capi for your responsibility, you will tend to use the power you need to carry out your responsibilities, because it is so effective and it is available. There is a good chance you will be tempted to use it exclusively. True, it is backed by authority and influence, since it is part and parcel of capi. However, as you use power, not only will the effectiveness of power start to wane, but influence is going to decline too. It will undermine your influence and diminish your authority. As people get punished, they start questioning influence and eventually authority. The result is that capi starts to diminish and there might come a day of a revolution, an uprising. Dictators get assassinated.[25]

Full capi is very rare, and even then, if it is in use, it is not a stable situation. Dictators spend years building capi, only to lose it over time. By assassination or revolution.

We have to learn how to increase the efficiency of what we do under normal circumstances. Stop dreaming of becoming a dictator with full capi over everything. Too many leaders in the dead of night mumble to themselves, "Oh, if only I had all the power I need. If only we could destroy our opposition. Then I wouldn't have any problems. Things would happen then!"

I have news for such leaders. In the long term, dictatorial powers will not provide control. They have to stop dreaming of total power and dictatorial management. Instead, they must learn how to work under normal circumstances, in which they don't have all the power and authority and influence they need.

> *But if no single individual has capi over her responsibility, does it mean that all decisions will be inefficiently implemented?*

---

25  As Voltaire reportedly said, the best government is a benevolent tyranny tempered by an occasional assassination.

*Wait, I think I know the answer—this is the same conclusion we reached about (PAEI). We need full capi, but since no one person has it alone, for full capi, we again need a team.*

Right! Back to teamwork, but this time, we need the team not to make a decision, but to implement one.

If managers do not have capi for the totality of their responsibilities, they need to seek the cooperation of others. They must take into account the interests of the people whose cooperation they're seeking, those who have power and/or influence.

*That makes sense. But people can't manage through a team all the time. Do managers call a meeting every time they want to change anything? That would paralyze a company.*

Let's see if we can figure out a solution. Which of the three cases is most frequently encountered?

*The first, I think, in which a manager has capi over some responsibilities; authority, power, or influence over other responsibilities; and a combination or none of them over the remainder.*

Assume that this first case is a dartboard. (My associates call it an Adizegram.) Let's play a dart game on our circles and square and see what happens.

A problem comes to you, usually through email, telephone, or the door. How are you going to solve it? Take a dart and throw it at the board.

Let's assume that the dart lands far away from the square, as I've drawn it here. What should you do?

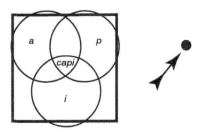

*Obviously, this problem is not my responsibility.*

How would you like going to a restaurant, sitting at a table, and waiting for a long time to be served. No one approaches you. Finally you get the attention of a waiter and ask him for service. He says, "Sorry, you are not at my table," and walks away. Would you come back to this restaurant?

*No way.*

You want this waiter to say: "Let me get your waiter right away," and not to stop until he finds the right waiter and sees to it that you are served. Same here. When an issue comes to you for whatever reason, even if it is out of your responsibility, it is still your responsibility—not to do it, but to find who should do it.

It is not the customer's responsibility to wander the corridors of your company trying to find out who should take care of him.

If the problem, for whatever reason, lands in your lap, it is your problem, not to solve, but to see to it that it gets solved. Got it?

*Got it. It is a matter of organizational culture.*

You bet, and you as the leader should work on creating this culture, nurturing it. It does not happen by itself. What do you think is the best way to create it?

> Every employee should think like the leader. Like in a military, where every soldier should feel as if the security of the whole country is his responsibility.

*To give a personal example?*

Absolutely. As a matter of fact, that is your job as a leader in the company. If you are the leader, you have no box. You are responsible for everything that happens in the company, although you do not do anything yourself. You see to it that the organization does it.

You should feel responsible for everything, although you don't have to handle it all personally. You should care for everything as if it is all your responsibility.

US President Harry Truman had a sign on his desk that read "the buck stops here," meaning there is no one to whom you can pass the responsibility to absolve yourself of it. You are it. You can delegate, but delegation does not mean you are no longer responsible.

> *But that's true also for sociopolitical activists who are socially conscious and fight for what they believe in. They will behave the same way even though they're not the president.*

Good point. That's why in a democracy, every citizen is not only a possible candidate for the presidency, but every citizen should think like a president. Every citizen should be involved in caring for the totality.

The same holds true for a well-managed organization. Every employee should think like the leader. Like in a military, where every soldier should feel as if the security of the whole country is his responsibility.

## The Problem

Now let's throw the next dart. This time, the dart hits smack in the center of your square, in capi. Is that problem your responsibility?

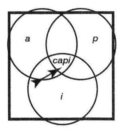

> *Yes. It is in my square of responsibility.*

You have authority, power, and influence? You have capi?

> *Yes.*

What should you do about this problem? It's your responsibility. You have all the necessary authority, power, and influence. What should you do?

> *Decide! Make a decision and carry it through.*

Right. It's your problem! Don't call a meeting, there's no need. If you do call one, it would be to inform others of your decision. If they don't like it, you'll accept resignations. We don't need participative management here. It's your responsibility and you're in control. Do it!

The fact that you have influence means that you know what the right decision is and are convinced of it.

Now, throw the next dart.

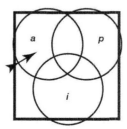

This time, as you can see, it falls inside the square and in the authority circle, which means it's your responsibility, but you have only authority over the matter. You have no power and no influence. Are you responsible?

*Yes.*

But you only have authority. What should you do without power or influence?

*Now is the time to call a meeting.*

Right, but why?

*Because authority without power and influence won't take me far.*

In fact, if you only have authority, you are in a "managerial overdraft."

*What's that?*

Let me show you—it's too important to miss.

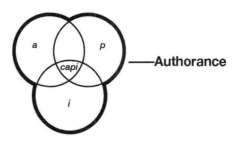

Let's look at this managerial task. A mother is trying to convince her child to eat spinach. First, she says, "Eat, it's good for you. Popeye eats spinach. Look how strong he is. If you eat spinach, you'll be strong like Popeye." Where is she on the authorance diagram? What part of authorance is she using?

*Influence.*

Right. But the kid says, "No! I hate spinach." So the mother tries again, saying, "When Daddy comes home, I'm going to tell him you were a good boy. If you eat your spinach, he'll take you to the zoo." She has moved out of influence. What is she now using?

*Influencing power.*

Yes, by referring to the potential rewards or dangers, she is using influencing power. But still the kid refuses to eat. If the mother gets very upset and punishes the child, what is she using?

*Authorized power.*

But if the husband comes home and says, "What have you done? What are you punishing the kid for? If he doesn't want to eat spinach, he doesn't have to."

> Certain facts should never be spoken. After you say them aloud, you're left with nothing.

*Then she was using unauthorized power.*

This is likely to happen in modern families in which parents share authority. No one can claim exclusive authority.

The kids still refuses to eat spinach, and he's crying. So the mother starts crying, too: "You never listen to me. You never do what your mother tells you to do. What's wrong with you? Listen to me, I'm your mother!"

*Now, she's using authority.*

Right. That's the point! But doesn't the child already know that she's his mother? The day you have to remind people of your authority, when it should be obvious, is the day you are in managerial overdraft.

The day you tell your employees, "Do it because I'm the boss," what are you reminding them of? Don't they know you're the boss? If you have to remind them of such an obvious fact, you're in trouble.

When somebody says, "But I'm your husband," or "I'm your wife," he or she is saying something equally obvious. It means that all sources of authorance, of managerial energy, have been exhausted. The person is down to the last gasp of breath. This is very dangerous because certain facts should never be spoken. After you say them aloud, you're left with nothing.

Authority in itself is very weak unless it's backed with power and influence. You probably can't use just authority alone more than once or twice. If you plead repeatedly with your children, "But I'm your father," they eventually might say, "So what?" In that case there is really nothing else you can do.

*What should you do then, if you have only authority?*

Call a meeting. Why?

*To coalesce power and influence.*

Whom should you have at the meeting?

*Those people with the power to sabotage my solution, the people whose cooperation I need, and the people who wield influence, who have the knowledge. They can convince other people because of their knowledge.*

I don't call this situation a problem; I call it a pre-problem, because you cannot solve the problem until you solve the pre-problem.

*What is the pre-problem?*

# The Pre-Problem

When you call a meeting, you can't be certain everyone will come. You might call a meeting, and people won't come because they don't work for you. Maybe they do work for you, but the trade union doesn't want them to come for fear they'll be co-opted. Or maybe they don't trust you, or don't respect you, or think it is not their problem. Even if they do come, you can't be certain they'll cooperate.

*So what do I do?*

You have to solve the pre-problem first. The pre-problem is to persuade them to cooperate. You have to create a cooperative environment, before you can solve the problem for which you need their cooperation.[26]

---

26  For my thoughts on how this approach is applied to the problem of the Middle East see my article "What should be done by Israel: A Vision" in the Huffington Post (http://www.huffingtonpost.com/dr-ichak-kalderon-adizes-/the-israeli-palestinian-c_2_b_7471496.html) or on my blog (http://www.ichakadizes.com/israeli-palestinian-conflict-what-to-do-a-vision/).

*How do I do that?*

A joke will illustrate the point: A hen and a pig were very good friends. One day the hen said, "We get along so well, why don't we start a business together?"

The pig answered, "Good idea. What do you have in mind?"

The hen said, "Well, I've studied the current market conditions and looked for opportunities in which we would have synergistic capabilities. I have what you do not have and you have what I do not have. Together we have a value proposition for the market. We should start a restaurant serving an American breakfast of ham and eggs."

The pig looked at the hen, took a big deep breath and said, "It's a great idea, but what is a mere contribution for you is a total sacrifice for me."

Many decisions are for the good of the organization, but they're not in the interest of the people needed to implement the decisions.

Each component—authority, power, and influence—reflects the different self-interests of the different people involved. Authority usually reflects the self-interests of management. They have the authority that flows from the stockholders to the board of directors to management. Management possesses the legal authority.

*Who has the power?*

The subordinates, labor.

*Aha! If they're unionized, it's authorized power.*

The employees have power, and their horizon is different from that of the management. Management wants to make the company grow, to get the biggest return on investment. They want the organization to be strong in the long term and management is rewarded through stock options and bonuses. What is labor interested in? In the short term: in take-home income, fringe benefits, working conditions, etc.

*That doesn't seem very loyal.*

It's normal though, and to be expected. Employees don't know if they will stay with the organization long enough to benefit from long-range plans. They don't participate in making them. Sometimes they don't even know what those plans are. Frequently, those long-term plans exclude them. They might be fired on short notice. They have no control, no stock options. Management, on the other hand, could benefit in the long term with profit sharing and golden parachutes.

Each group is naturally interested in that from which it can benefit. What is so surprising about that? The United States was built on the notion of self-interest and the pursuit of happiness.

> *Now I understand why employees are more committed and supportive of change when the company is committed to them for the long term, and through profit sharing or stock options, they benefit from their cooperation.*

Yes, but be careful. Some countries, like Sweden or Germany, have long-term employment and participatory management required by law, but it produces different results. It depends on how you conduct such management. The Japanese have participatory management and lifetime employment as a manifestation of their (I) culture. The moment you do it by law, as in Sweden or Germany, it becomes not (I) but...

> *(A).*

Right. By law you can't fire people, and by law you must have participatory management. By law employee representatives sit on the board of directors.

> *Will that have an impact on the (E) role?*

It could but not necessarily so. In Germany, I suggest, the codetermination model is partially responsible for their economic success. Workers are dedicated and the relationships are less antagonistic. In the former Yugoslavia, on the other hand, the government also forced participatory management by law and the economy virtually collapsed. The (E), and then the (P), fell apart.[27]

When (P) goes down and the economic conditions worsen, (I) can go down too. They had a political mess in addition to an economic one and Yugoslavia fell apart. It dissolved.

It depends on how much (A) is part of the culture or how much it is a forced and alien component.

> *I think we have digressed. We were discussing how people with authority and power have different interests. Who has influence in an organization?*

Influence is usually represented by the technocrats, staff people, and professionals. What are they interested in? The biggest R&D budget, the most professional exposure, and the most liberal research capabilities.

---

27  Adizes, I. *Industrial Democracy: Yugoslav Style.* New York Free Press, 1971. Reprinted by Adizes Institute..

*I've noticed that with computer professionals, they switch companies at the drop of a hat if they're offered better computers elsewhere. The same is true of academics. Their loyalty is to their field of knowledge, not to the organization that employs them.*

Exactly. Each component of capi reflects a different self-interest. If you want to solve a pre-problem, what do you have to do? Think about the common interest and how to create a win-win climate. Think about why the people you need should come and solve the problem together.

> If people share a problem they should share a solution too.

> A person should not be part of the solution if he isn't part of the problem; and if he is part of the problem, he better be part of the solution.

The mistake you might make is to call a meeting and say, "Ladies and gentlemen, we have a problem and *my* solution is…" They're going to think, "If it is your solution then it is your problem. What do you want from us?" If people share a problem they should share a solution too.

What you should do is lay the groundwork for the discussion. Approach each member of the group whose cooperation you need individually, and convince them that they have a problem that is your problem too. Then call a meeting and say, "We have a problem. We have common interests to solve this problem. We're in this boat together! Agree?" Let each person express himself until a climate of common interest to solve the problem emerges. Then start looking for a common solution. You might say, "I have a *suggestion* for a solution, but I'd like to hear what you think so we can arrive at *our* solution."[28] It is not a compromise. It is a consensus.

*Several years ago, when Miguel de la Madrid was running for president of Mexico, he had a slogan, "La solucion somos todos," which means "The solution is all of us." According to your theory, if the solution is in the hands of all the Mexican people, then the problem is of all the Mexican people too.*

---

28  There is a seven-day course at the Adizes Institute—E2 Training—which teaches detailed protocols for leading such a discussion to arrive at common solution that all support.

Which includes Mr. de la Madrid and his government, as they were part of the problem too. (I bet he did not see it that way though.) The people alone are not the problem and the government alone is not the solution. Both have to accept responsibility for being the problem and for finding the solution.

Managers sometimes ask their employees, "Are you part of the solution or part of the problem?" This is an artificial distinction. A person should not be part of the solution if he isn't part of the problem; and if he is part of the problem, he better be part of the solution.

*Give me a business example.*

Take a company with low productivity. Is that something that is desirable to fix?

*Sure.*

Okay, is it within management's square of responsibility to increase productivity?

*Sure!*

Now let me ask you: Is it a problem or a pre-problem?

> Productivity is not going to increase until management and labor learn to work together.

*It's a problem for management if management has all the authority, power, and influence needed to increase productivity. But management does not have all the necessary managerial energy to solve the problem. There are unions and non-union workers that wield power and influence. All that management has is authority and some authorized power, but not enough to solve the problem. It's a pre-problem.*

Right, and if it's a pre-problem, authority needs to coalesce with power and influence. That means productivity is not going to increase until management and labor learn to work together.

Productivity is not a technological problem. It is a political-philosophical problem reflecting political values. The United States possesses excellent technology, thus a lack of technology is not what is causing low productivity. American workers, as individuals, are no less dedicated than the Japanese. The evidence is seen in how well they work under Japanese management. Productivity is a political problem between two power centers: management and labor. Do you know one of the reasons Japan and Germany shine economically? They buy technology from the United States, then their management and labor cooperate and use it to outshine American performance. American manufacturing is steeped in the concept of adversarial relations between firms and within the firm. Pluralism is breaking down businesses, even families. We are carrying individualism too far. We prefer to fight one another rather than unite against foreign competition. It makes sense to have competition in the marketplace, but we have brought it into the company too.

*Are you saying you like capitalism in the marketplace and socialism in the company?*

> Capitalism in the marketplace and socialism in the company.

America negates the rights of labor in decision making, just as the Communists negated the rights of private ownership in the creation of value. This is a major mistake. Russia departed from Communist ideology and legitimized private ownership, a revolution in Russian thinking. We need a similar revolution in ours. We need to legitimize the right of labor to manage and accept responsibility with (not against) management.

> Low productivity is a pre-problem, not a problem.

Low productivity is a pre-problem, not a problem. We are in denial by saying management should solve it. Management can't solve it alone! You have to call a meeting when you have a pre-problem. You have to ask yourself how you can present it as a shared problem with labor and create a climate in which we can arrive at a joint solution.

*What if you can get rid of some people and then seize power? Wouldn't that convert a pre-problem into a problem?*

The problem might not warrant such a sacrifice. Firing and replacing people is an expensive maneuver. It costs you about a year's salary for every person that is replaced in the organization. It takes about six months to train a new employee and the person who was fired was probably not productive for the last six months during which they worked. Moreover, replacing people does not always work. You might choose the wrong person. It is expensive and very destructive to fire people. Better to develop teamwork.

## The Pre-Pre-Problem

What happens when the dart falls into the influence circle? It's my responsibility, but I have neither authority nor power, only influence.

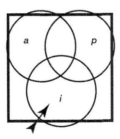

This happens in many organizations. The people above you have the authority, the people below you have the power, and you are in the middle. You have only influence to carry out your responsibility.

> *Thank God I at least have influence, but it sounds like good cause for tension and high blood pressure.*

Some people simply relax and say, "The hell with it. It's not my responsibility. If I don't have the authority or power, I can't be responsible." So they shrink the area for which they feel responsible. That may be the strategy if you do not have influence, and in many organizations, there are things for which nobody takes responsibility. Consequently, the organization is ineffective and the clients suffer. But if you have influence, you cannot and should not shirk responsibility. You should use it.

> *Assuming I want to do the job, what do I have to do?*

You have to use your influence. I call this situation a pre-pre-problem. In this situation you have to convince the person with authority to call a meeting of those with power. The total group can then coalesce to have the capi needed to solve the problem for which you are responsible.

> *This seems very difficult.*

Not once you learn the necessary skills.[29] You have to communicate to your bosses in their own language. The way you communicate with a (P) is different from the way you communicate with an (A), an (E), or an (I). Each of them speaks a different language.

I got an insight about this by watching my children. They were in the kitchen talking. Maybe five and six years old. I was eavesdropping on their conversation. One said to his brother, "They said no," meaning that we the parents refused some demand he made. The brother asked: "Who said no, Mama or Papa?"

That makes a difference. Different styles give different meanings to the same words. For instance, big (A)s, whether Bureaucrats or Administrators, usually do not like to talk about opportunities. For them, an opportunity is a problem. They always think about the repercussions of suggested ideas.

Arsonists or Entrepreneurs usually hate to talk about problems. "I pay you to solve problems," they say. They prefer to talk about opportunities, and an opportunity for an (E) is a problem for an (A). That's why they usually don't understand each other well.

> The words *opportunity* and *problem* truly mean the same thing.

As we already said, In Chinese, both words have the same character: *wēijī*, 危机. If you solve the problem, as a result you become stronger and better. You learned, so it was really an opportunity. On the other hand, if you miss an opportunity by doing nothing while your competitor exploits it, that could be a problem for you.

That's why I translate the Chinese word into English as oppor-threat. It describes a situation that could be an opportunity or a threat. It is whatever you make of it. You decide whether it is an opportunity or a problem. Oppor-threat is a neutral word while problem and opportunity are charged with emotion.

*Good. I am in charge. What it is depends on what I think.*

Here's another example about differences in style. When (E)s disagree with ideas, they're usually very vocal about it. They continuously talk and think out loud. Because of this, they dislike being alone. They're so talkative and creative you can hardly finish telling them a joke. If you start one, it will remind them of a different one.

---

29  The Adizes Institute has a course that teaches these skills, or you can read my book *Leading the Leaders*, op. cit.

They'll even interrupt your punch line. They're very expressive. If they disagree, they make themselves heard. For them, silence means agreement. The Jewish people, who are known for their strong (E) traits, have a Hebrew expression: *Shtika ke hodaya*, "Silence is agreement."

With (A)s, it's the opposite. They are quiet when they disagree. Look at the Scandinavians or British. When they disagree, they just freeze and look at you!

> *I can see now how that can cause tremendous miscommunication. An (E) trying to convince an (A) about some new idea. The (E) talks, talks, talks, and the (A) doesn't say a word. When the (E) leaves, she'll think, "Fantastic! He's sold." Meanwhile the (A) is thinking, "She's crazy. She's going to destroy the company. The idea will never work."*
>
> *Sometime later, the (E) will ask the (A), "What happened with the idea we agreed about?" The (A) is surprised: "Agreed about? I thought the idea would have been a disaster."*
>
> *"But you didn't say a word," says the (E), who now has one more reason not to trust the (A).*

Let me give you a third example of how different (PAEI) styles may speak the same language, but their words have different meanings.

When you suggest to an (A) that he approve a decision about some change that has not been tried before, he is inclined to say no because he sees many problems with implementation. When you try again and explain more, he still says no. You keep explaining, and finally, when he is sure he fully understands it—and that happens only when he realizes that there is no risk involved—he will say yes.

> *So?*

This means that for (A)s, "no" does not mean no, it means maybe. You have to continue interpreting the "no" as "maybe" until they realize there is no risk, at least for them. For (A)s, "yes" means yes. For them, to say yes is like giving birth. They really suffer to say yes, but once they do, you can depend on it.

> *What about (E)s?*

For Creative Contributors or Arsonists, it is just the opposite: yes means maybe. If you ask an (E) whether he can do something, and it looks interesting, he may say, "Why not?" But this attitude does not last. He may change his mind, especially if it is not his idea. When you are ready to act he might say, "No! I disagree."

For (E)s, "yes" means maybe and "no" is definite. If he says no and you assume the matter is still open for discussion, you'll be in trouble when you bring it up again.

(A)s have difficulty saying yes; (E)s have difficulty saying no.

A "no" from an (A) means "maybe, tell me more," and a "yes" is definite and finite. For an (E) it is the opposite. A "yes" means "why not" and a "no" is definite and final.

That's why (A)s and (E)s misunderstand each other. (A)s hear "yes" from (E)s and move ahead. Then the (E)s change their mind, driving the (A)s crazy: "You said yes." The (E)s answer, "Well, I was just thinking out loud."

> *I saw this happen when I was working with a CEO in Australia. He was one of the biggest (E)s I've ever worked with. When talking to his vice president of manufacturing, he asked, "Why don't we have a manufacturing facility in Brisbane?"*
>
> *His vice president asked, "Well, should we have one?" The CEO said, "Yeah, why don't we?"*
>
> *So the vice president of manufacturing, who had a (PAei) style as we would expect, started planning to build the facility. Two months later, the CEO was very upset: "Why in hell are we building a factory in Brisbane?"*
>
> *"You said we needed it," the vice president said.*
>
> *"I was just asking you why we don't have one. I didn't tell you to start building one!"*

Yes, people often don't know whether (E)ntrepreneurs are thinking out loud or deciding. Sometimes when subordinates believe the (E)s are deciding, they discover it wasn't a decision and get blamed for acting on thoughts. The next time the (E) says something with the same tone of voice, the employees remember the last episode and don't act. The (E) then becomes upset because his staff didn't do what was expected of them. The employees feel there is no way they can win. No matter what they do, they're going to be humiliated for something. (E)ntrepreneurs always act disappointed and disillusioned.

It's the same in reverse. It drives (E)s mad to hear "no" from (A)s: "How can you say no? I haven't finished speaking and you're already saying no." But the (A) didn't mean "no," he meant "maybe, tell me more."

Now, for whom is "yes" really yes and "no" really no? There is no confusion.

*The (P)s.*

They don't understand what's going on when people question their yes or no. To them it's very simple and obvious. They are the black-and-white people. No gray area for them. They hate maybes: "Why can't people just communicate?" they ask.

Finally, for whom do "yes" and "no" mean maybe?

*The (I)s. It's not surprising that (I)s and (P)s dislike each other.*

A chart of these tendencies would look like this.

| said \ meant | (P) | (A) | (E) | (I) |
|---|---|---|---|---|
| yes | yes | yes | maybe | maybe |
| no | no | maybe | no | maybe |

If you want to solve a problem when you have only influence, you have to know the different meanings people attach to the same words. If you don't, you'll miscommunicate. The rule is don't treat them as if they were you.

> **The rule is don't treat them as if they were you.**

Usually we speak to others as if we were speaking to ourselves, so an (E) for instance will speak to others as if they are (E)s too and be upset when they don't understand her. The trick is to communicate with language they understand.

*This has been a long conversation. Would you please summarize for me?*

In order to implement a decision, the decision must be well defined. Why, what, how, by when, and who must be established. Then you must have the authority, power, and influence to carry it through.

Depending on whether you have capi; just authority, influence, or power; or a combination of the components of authorance, you have to develop a strategy for implementation. Are you starting with a problem, pre-problem, or pre-pre-problem? If it is a pre-pre-problem you have to use influence by persuading in the style the listener understands. If you have only authority it is a pre-problem. You have to know how to create a win-win climate by searching for the common interest. Then you will arrive at a conclusion that all can support. If you have capi, it's your problem and you have to learn how to use capi, not abuse it; if you use only the power component of capi, it will eventually backfire.

If you have capi, you can be a technician. Supposedly you have the capability to implement the decision. You have the authority to decide, the knowledge to influence, and the power to enforce. You do not have to convince anyone, just order and inspect. If you have only authority, you have to be a politician. You have to create a win-win climate in which everyone is in this together. If you have only influence, you have to be like a streetwise psychologist, sensitive to people and their stylistic differences. You have to know how to communicate with people in a language they understand.

*It means that a good manager, leader, or parent should be a technician, politician, and a psychologist, right?*

Yes. You need all three. Too many people say, "I love to manage. It's people I can't stand," or "I hate politics." All they want to do is make good decisions, but they do not want to worry about "selling" their decisions. They don't wish to deal with people's unique interests and communication styles. They feel ill at ease when they have to solicit other people's cooperation. I have news for them—bad news. There are only a few cases in which a manager has capi and can afford the luxury of being a technician. Most of the time, a person does not have full capi over all of his responsibility, and thus, needs to coalesce it.

Efficiency of implementation depends on how much capi can be coalesced for the task. How much cooperation can be secured for accomplishing the responsibility, from people necessary for the implementation. For that, a person must be a technician, politician, and psychologist.

## 184 – MASTERING CHANGE

Let's add what we've discussed to our diagram before we move on.

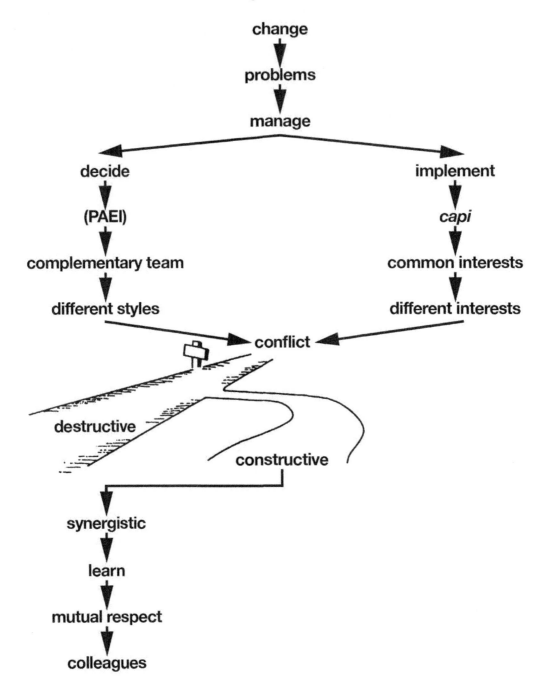

# CONVERSATION 10
# What Makes the Wheels Turn

Just to be sure we understand each other, would you like to summarize what we've discussed so far?

*So far we've said that:*

*Life is change.*

*Everything alive is a system composed of subsystems.*

*When there is change the subsystems do not change synchronously. That creates gaps that are manifested in what we call "problems." We have to decide what to do about problems and not to decide is to decide.*

*Decisions have to be implemented or it is as good as if there was no decision made.*

*Deciding and implementing decisions is what management is all about, whether we call it management or leadership or governing or parenting. It is all one and the same. We need to manage change.*

*To manage anything, we must make good decisions and implement them using minimal energy and resources.*

*How well we manage, lead, or govern depends on how good our decisions are and how efficiently we implement them.*

*A good decision requires that four roles, or imperatives, be fulfilled: (P), to (P)rovide the needed service; (A), to (A)dminister for efficient service;*

(E), the (E)ntrepreneurial role, to position for the changing future; and (I), to (I)ntegrate the organization.

These roles are necessary and sufficient to make organizations effective and efficient in the short and long term.

An organization that is both effective and efficient in the short and long term is healthy. But that is not enough. The system must have also interdependency based on common interests.

The purpose of management, leadership, government, or parenting is to see that the (PAEI) roles are performed, and that there is common interest, that the system is healthy. If the system is a business, a byproduct of being healthy is being profitable in the short and long term. If it is a country, it will have a sustainable society and economy. If we are talking about a family, being healthy will result in a well-integrated, functioning family.

Since no individual can be a perfect (PAEI), we need a complementary team.

> An organization that is both effective and efficient in the short and long term is healthy.

In a complementary team there will necessarily be conflict because it is composed of differences in style.

To make the conflict constructive, we need to learn from each other's disagreements. For this to occur we need mutual respect.

We can predict whether a decision will be a good one if we know whether it was devised by a complementary (PAEI) team that operated with mutual respect.

To implement decisions, we need capi: coalesced authority, power, and influence. We need to build a coalition of the people necessary to implement the decision. Implementation is always faster if propelled by integrated self-interests.

Implementation is always faster if propelled by...

*Integrated self-interests?*

Try again, please.

*By common interests? But what is the difference? Is common interest not the same as integrated self-interest?*

No. Integrated self-interests are short-term oriented. Common interests have a bigger picture, a higher purpose. It is much tougher to get common interests without a higher purpose.

*That makes sense.*

Who should be the people involved in decision making?

*First, those who have the authority to approve a decision. Second, those who will carry out the decision in the field; they have the power. Third, the people with the technical and professional knowledge needed; those with influence. We need to create common interests among them if we want to have the decision effectively implemented.*

Excellent summary.

*This is all well and good, but something has been bothering me since our last conversation. How did the myth of the perfect (PAEI) manager come about in management theory? It seems like a fundamental error.*

The mistake lies in the way management theory is researched. The best characteristics of many different people are chosen through research to create a model. But such a model is really just a fanciful collage that does not and cannot exist. We are all human beings with strengths and weaknesses. None of us is perfect. I attribute that error to the manner by which research is conducted. Moreover, management theory was first developed in the United States where the culture is individualistic. Naturally, they personalized the whole process of management into one individual, the Leader.

*Okay, the perfect (PAEI) leader does not exist, but are we not trying to develop one?*

Are you referring to business school graduates who believe they have all the answers? I have criticized business schools for this failure at the International Academy of Management.[30] The problem is that we train individuals. They are not trained to seek input from those who complement them and could help them make good decisions. They receive no training in

---

30 "Contemporary General Management Education: A critique." Speech delivered at the meeting of the International Academy of Management, Atlanta, Georgia, September 27, 2013. Transcript available at http://www.ichakadizes.com/contemporary-general-management-education-a-critique/

uniting people with different interests, even though they need the cooperation of those people to carry out decisions. The implementation process is also a source of conflict. We need to examine that as well.

*Let us go there now.*

We've said that in order to implement decisions efficiently we need a commonality of interests between the necessary parties involved in implementation: a win-win climate, whether it is achieved by integrating self-interests or identifying common interests derived from a higher purpose.

> Stylistic differences can be synergistic when mutual respect creates a learning environment.

*I can see that in a marriage. The spouses might start with a common interest of building a family, but over time they develop different needs and start to go their separate ways.*

The same happens in business. After some time the different partners have different interests: One has children who want to join the business, the other wants to retire and sell his shares. In this case, change means a change of interests.

*What do we do? What requires a mere contribution from you may require a total commitment from me. I may not want to do what is in your interest. I am the pig in your earlier story.*

That is how conflict can become destructive. Those who have the authority to decide can be undermined by those with power. They can make a sham out of decisions by simply not implementing them properly. They can undermine decisions to protect their interests. In the same way, those with authority may make decisions that are clearly in their own interest at the expense of the interests of those with power.

Whenever there are diverse interests among those who are needed to implement a decision, the political process of securing implementation can be lengthy and expensive. It may demand a lot of managerial energy.

*So there are actually two sources of conflict: One is miscommunication—we interpret the same words or body language differently, we process information and make decisions differently—and the other is divergent interests, which lead to lack of cooperation.*

Right. Either we don't understand each other because we have different styles and/or we have conflicting interests.

> *We solved the problem of conflicts that stem from differences in decision-making styles: Stylistic differences can be synergistic when mutual respect creates a learning environment. But how do we make conflict constructive when we're working with divergent interests?*

First, accept reality. Only when you accept that there is conflict can you harness it. Notice I said you have to harness conflict, not resolve it. Don't try to fight or eliminate conflict, make it functional. Make it work for you.

> *But you just said that having a win-win climate all the time is utopian.*

Yes. The people involved in implementation realize that a win-win climate does not occur in the short term, but they see that it will exist in the long term. This sort of long-term belief is the basis of many good marriages. When there is long-term commitment, one partner will give in today and the other will give in another time. It evens out eventually.

> *You mean you have to start with commitment? It still sounds utopian. If I acquiesce in order to overcome a short-term conflict of interests, I must trust that the other party will reciprocate in the future. I must trust that my short-term sacrifice will be good for me in the long term. If I don't trust the people with whom I have a conflict, why should I believe they will cooperate over the long term? If I don't believe they'll cooperate later, why should I cooperate now?*

Obviously, you won't give in at all unless you believe the favor will be returned. Thus, to implement decisions, mutual respect is not enough. We must also have mutual trust. We have to trust that over the long term we will both benefit. Only then will we be willing to cooperate in the short term in spite of the short-term conflicts of interest.

For decision making we need colleagues—not necessarily people who agree with us, but people whose disagreement we learn from. As we said earlier, a colleague is someone with whom you are in confrontation all the time, but you welcome it because you learn from it.

For implementation, on the other hand, we need friends. A friend is someone who shares our interests. He will not stab you in the back because stabbing you will hurt him as much as you. You share interests, and because you share interests implementation is swift.

In Hebrew the word for friend is *haver*, which comes from the root meaning to be connected: HVR. Since you are connected, what happens to you happens to your friend as well. Francis Bacon said a friend is a person who halves your sorrow and doubles your happiness, through empathy and shared interests.

You should surround yourself at work with people who are your colleagues and, at the same time, are your friends. They disagree with you and you learn from those disagreements, but they share your interests so those disagreements benefit both of you. That is how a marriage should be too. Although your spouse does not always agree with you, there is total agreement on one thing: The interests of the family are common.

> *I think I can predict whether that decision in the envelope will be implemented!*

> *First, did those needed for implementation participate? Could we get the people needed for capi together?*

What then?

> *Do they trust each other?*

If you want to implement decisions efficiently, you must make sure that all the people you need for implementation have common interest in implementing the decision, if not in the short term, then in the long term. There must be a win-win climate, a symbiotic relationship such as the one friends have over time. That is why friends are proud of how long they have been friends. Their mutual trust has overcome many tests and conflicts.

> *I see: Since, at least in the short term, there is probably going to be a conflict of interests, there must be mutual trust that in the long term things will work out and interests will be mutually satisfied.*

Right. Say I invite you to dinner. I pay for it. You win, I lose. But what will happen next time we go out to dinner? Who pays now? You see, in the short term there is a conflict of interests, but in the long term it gets compensated. For that to happen you must have faith that your sacrifice will be reciprocated.

In English we say life is give and take. In other languages, though, like Arabic, Turkish, and even modern Greek, it is said differently: life is take and give. There is a difference. In give and take there is trust. You give and trust that it will come back, and later you will take. When you say life is take and give it means that there is no trust. You want to take first to be sure you do not lose, and only then do you give.

In those societies where they say life is take and give there is no trust. What made America successful is its culture of trust. (You will see later why trust and respect are important factors for economic success.)

For a symbiotic, friendly, win-win climate, you must have mutual trust. The way to transform potentially destructive conflict into constructive conflict is to create a nurturing, symbiotic environment. Symbiotic means the parties perceive that a proposed change will eventually work for the benefit of all involved.

If there is mutual trust, you and I will perceive the mutual benefit of change and allow it to happen. Without mutual trust, there will be lots of resistance.

*I know what four questions I should ask before opening the envelope.*

What are they?

*Were the four (PAEI) roles performed? Was there a complementary team?*

*Second, was there mutual respect in making the decision?*

*Third, did the team have capi?*

*Fourth, did they trust each other?*

The principle is good, and the questions are right, but there is more to it. It is not easy to have a complementary team of (PAEI) styles and, at the same time, have capi. To discuss how to make that happen let us go back to the beginning of our conversations.

*Oh no. Why is life so complicated?*

Life is not complicated. It is very complicated to make things simple.

## The Importance of Love and the Sequence of Organizational Therapy

We said change is here to stay and has been here forever. Change generates problems because change causes disintegration (subsystems do not change together). If all problems are caused by disintegration, we already have discovered the therapy...

*Integration.*

Right. Integration is a function of Mutual Trust and Respect, and the highest degree of integration is love.

*You mean to say there cannot be love without Mutual Trust and Respect?*

Yes, I do.

*But why is love the ultimate integration?*

For two people to benefit from one another, one has to give and the other has to reciprocate. With mutual trust, there can be a lag in the exchange. In a loving relationship there is no lag time between giving and getting paid back: The giving is the taking.

For example, when you take your kids to the circus, do you take them because you trust they will pay you back when you are old and feeble? Or do you do it for the pleasure of seeing them giggle, laugh, clap, and rejoice? Love is when you don't keep an account of what you do for the person you love, when you give because the giving itself enriches you—the more you give the richer you are. In the history of mankind there are those who could give totally, endlessly, engulfed in total love: the Buddha, Moses, Jesus Christ...

*Mother Teresa?*

Or volunteers who help people with AIDS, or who help the homeless, or a diligent worker, or a truly dedicated employee or manager. They are all givers and the more they give, the more they love, and the closer they get to the biggest giver of them all—God. We all have the potential to give. We are all made in God's image by allowing ourselves to love and give. The ultimate trust is trusting the universe, God—whether we think of it as the God of the Jews, Hindus, or Christians, or the tao—a higher consciousness.

Giving to others for the purpose of enriching ourselves happens when we love as a parent loves the children he takes to the circus. Without love we'll feel miserable sitting at the circus. We'll get upset when we see these kids clapping their little hands about something we think is quite frivolous while we left all that work undone at the office.

When a manager is given an organization to lead, she should create and nurture a win-win climate, a symbiotic environment based on Mutual Trust and Respect, and if she can, do so to the degree that it approaches love.

Leaders should have a common purpose in creating this environment, nurturing the spiritual core of the organization. Love your fellow workers. Love your clients. Love the product you are selling. The more love in the system the more Mutual Trust and Respect, the more integration, the easier is to change, and thus the easier is to succeed in a changing environment. What do you think made Steve Jobs so successful? He was in love with the product, with the design, with its functionality. He was passionately in love, and the customers reciprocated, voting with their dollars.

Here's the way it would look on our master diagram.

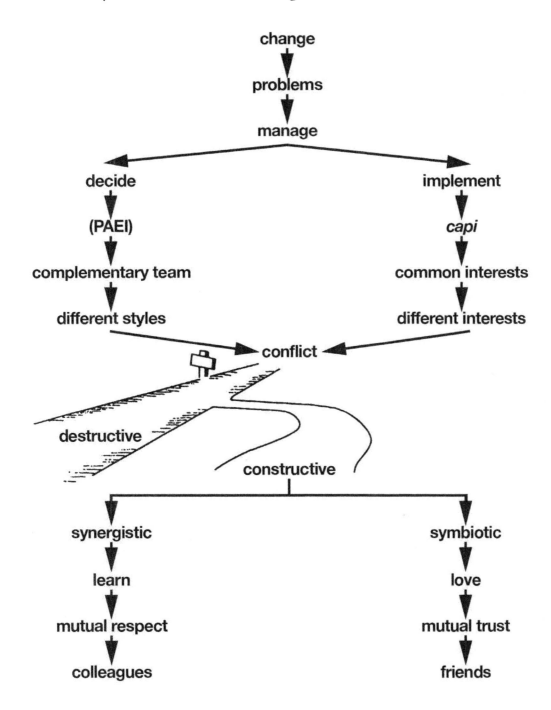

Now, you try to put it all together.

> *Conflict is a byproduct of change. It can be destructive or constructive depending on whether Mutual Trust and Respect exist.*
>
> *Mutual respect is necessary so conflicts of styles can be constructive, so we can learn from each other's differences and make better decisions.*
>
> *Mutual trust is necessary so we can perceive that a win-win climate will exist in the future. Then the people involved will cooperate in implementing decisions in the present.*
>
> *When all of the above occurs, we have constructive, not destructive, conflict.*
>
> *I want to repeat: I know what questions to ask before opening the envelope. Did the team analyzing the problem have capi, were all the (PAEI) styles represented, and was there Mutual Trust and Respect in reaching the diagnosis and the solution?*

Yes, you understand it well.

During the French Revolution the slogan was *liberté, égalité, fraternité*. It fits well into our diagram. *Liberté* is on the left side, the freedom to speak, which is the foundation of respect. *Egalité* fits on the right side with common interests. *Fraternité* should be in the middle—it is love. Love is there when there is Mutual Trust and Respect, when we are both friends and colleagues, when we are free to speak, teach other, enrich each other with our differences and still have common interests.

Look at the top of the diagram. The *c* of capi integrates *api* the way (I) integrates (P), (A), and (E). For love we bring *c* and (I) together. We are different in style and interests, but we are together, not in spite of our differences but because of them. We make things grow by cooperatively interacting and share the gains of that interaction.

> *Common interests sounds like socialism and diversity of styles sounds like democracy. Jointly it looks to me like your theory fits well with a socio-democratic agenda.*

It does. I made a presentation to that effect to the General Secretary of the World Wide Secretariat of Social Democratic parties in the world.

*Tell me now, what is more important, trust or respect?*

Think about it. Can you trust people you don't respect?

*Yes, I can. Someone may not be as intelligent as I would like him to be, but I also know he wouldn't deliberately hurt me.*

Can you respect people you don't trust?

*Only with great difficulty. If I don't trust the people, I probably won't listen to them either.*

Exactly. Trust has to be established before respect can be established. That's why we usually say "trust and respect" rather than "respect and trust." Interestingly enough, I've noted that there is no happenstance in how people use words. Folk expressions are full of wisdom!

*Your claim that trust has to precede respect has interesting repercussions. Can you give me an example?*

> Trust has to be established before respect can be established.

Look at what happened to the Soviet Union. Mikhail Gorbachev was pushing for glasnost and perestroika—that was how he was going to change the Soviet Union. Glasnost is on the left of our chart. It is to have political freedom, to have the right to dissent. Would you agree that freedom of speech is based on mutual respect? Perestroika was to restructure economic interests, and interests are related to trust. He started with glasnost first, with freedom of speech, with mutual respect. That was a mistake because glasnost undermines political strength, which is necessary to carry through economic reforms. He started with respect rather than with trust.

I wrote him a paper when *TIME* magazine named him man of the year, warning him that the changes he wanted to carry out would cause destructive conflict, which is what happened.

*The Chinese are doing it the right way, then.*

I believe so. So is Nursulan Nazarbayev, the president of Kazakhstan. He is restructuring the economy while maintaining political power. Eventually he will have to release political power too or there will be unrest, so Nazarbayev started the transfer of political power in 2015 with the hundred steps program. In China, the signs of unrest have been present for years—Tiananmen Square is one example.

The two sides of the equation, the two sides of our map, have to be synchronized, but in the right sequence.[31] Trust, then respect.

*Does this sequence apply to personal life too?*

It is true in a marriage as well. There is no respect unless there is trust first.

*I wonder, exactly how do you manage an organization with Mutual Trust and Respect? Most aren't managed that way, so your theory applies to only a handful of organizations in which trust and respect are an integral part of the culture.*

> Don't just rely on MT&R, develop it.

> The more change the more threat there is to a culture of Mutual Trust and Respect.

I have not stopped with the theory of Mutual Trust and Respect, I have worked out a process to change organizations so that they can produce the trust and respect they need. So they don't just rely on MT&R, but develop it. It doesn't happen just by talking about it. It takes commitment and hard work. Furthermore, when you develop such an organization, it doesn't maintain that trust and respect for long unless you keep repeating the process that nurtures the desired culture. Every system tends toward entropy unless you put energy into it. The more change the more threat there is to a culture of Mutual Trust and Respect.

*How do you convert an organization with no Mutual Trust and Respect into one that has both?*

After fifty years of working with my Associates at the Institute, in thousands of companies of different sizes, in a variety of industries, in over fifty countries, I found out that there are four factors that produce Mutual Trust and Respect. These apply to any organization. We are now testing it in family therapy and on a macro level within a country.

*What are those four factors?*

MT&R is a function of having common vision and values, a functional and diversified (PAEI) structure, a collaborative decision-making process, and mature people who command and grant MT&R.

---

31  In the first edition of this book (1991) I wrote: "If [the Soviet Union doesn't] change self-interests into common interests, political freedom may be used to express the different self-interests, and the USSR could disintegrate."

*It makes sense that we would need common vision and values, but why is structure so important?*

Organizational structure determines the distribution of responsibility, authority, and rewards. This distribution determines the differentiation of self-interests. Also, different tasks attract different kinds of people.

We have already established that we need all (PAEI) roles to be performed in an organization. We have established that there is no single individual who can simultaneously perform all four roles, thus, a complementary team is needed. For a complementary team we need a complementary structure. A functional structure should provide space for (P) activity separate from (E) activity, etc. We need (P) departments, (A) departments, (E) departments, and (I) departments.

*Can you give me an example?*

> For a complementary team we need a complementary structure.

Sure. The (P) role is usually performed by operations, sales, or manufacturing. (E) is performed by R&D, engineering and marketing. (A) is accounting, quality control, audits, human resources administration. (I) is performed by human resources development.

We already discussed how the roles are incompatible and endanger one another. Thus, in a well-structured company you should not have one VP for sales and marketing. That would be mixing (P) and (E) and, predictably, if you do so (E) will suffer. Short term, which is what (P) focuses on, will squeeze attention from the long term, which is (E)'s focus. Such companies have a marketing department but it is not performing the marketing function. It really does sales support but calls itself marketing. This is a very complex subject and if you want to know more please read my book *Managing Corporate Lifecycles*.

*What about the other factors?*

Structure alone is not enough. Since people have different styles, they must learn how to communicate with each other. A correct process of collaborative, participatory decision making is necessary.[32]

---

32 The Adizes Institute's E2 course teaches students how to communicate in a collaborative way with different styles in order to minimize miscommunication.

But having common vision and values, a correctly structured organization, and the right tools to communicate with different styles still isn't enough. Some people have a chip on their shoulders and neither command nor grant respect or trust. They had a distrusting, disrespectful attitude before they joined the organization, so changing the organization will have no immediate effect on them. If they cannot change you might have to change them.

If you want to change an organization's behavior, first you must develop a common vision and values that all decision makers in the company share. Then you need to treat its structure, the decision-making process, and finally the people themselves.

Start with the collaborative process. Change how people decide. Then, using the new process, change the distribution of responsibility, authority, power, influence, and reward structures. As you change the structure and processes, people's behavior will change. They will become more open and participative, and Mutual Trust and Respect will grow.[33] Those who can't change will probably leave the organization.

*This sounds either too complicated or too simple.*

It's neither. It's a process that doesn't exploit trust and respect. Instead, it develops a system that creates and nurtures trust and respect.

Too many consultants preach trust and respect but don't know how to create it. They raise hopes, which, when not satisfied, just make people skeptical of management theory and of consultants. It's not surprising that business schools have been accused of being irrelevant and that consulting is considered the second-oldest profession.

I experimented over many years with organizational cultures that suffered from mistrust and disrespect, and developed this methodology to change a culture to one that is governed by trust and respect. It required developing the right structure, process, and people with common vision and values in the right sequence.

People often make a key mistake when trying to change an organizational culture. They ignore structure and process and focus exclusively on people. If there is no teamwork, they fire the people and replace them with others who are thought to have respect and trust. But this doesn't necessarily work.

---

33  The Adizes Graduate School grants doctorates in Organizational Transformation where this program of organizational therapy is taught.

With the wrong structure and process, even well-meaning people start behaving in a destructive and disrespectful manner. The environment causes people to change their behavior, regardless of how well meaning they are.

*Can this system of change you have developed be learned?*

Sure. The Adizes Graduate School offers a doctorate in this methodology. It involves learning and then doing an internship under supervision. The total program takes three years.

> When you pray, you accept your vulnerability.

*This has been a rich conversation—I have enough food for thought to last me a while. You even made me want to go back to school. Or go and pray.*

When you pray, you accept your vulnerability. You accept that you are part of a bigger system of consciousness, that your deeds matter because you belong, and you affect the totality just as that totality affects you. Prayer can be reading a chapter of the Bible, or a verse, but it doesn't have to be only the Bible or a prayer book. Do not (A) your prayer; (I) it. You can pray by whistling, or meditating, or breathing, or practicing what you love, whatever way you feel (I)ntegrated with the totality you belong to.

# CONVERSATION 11
# How to Communicate with People Whose Style Is Different

*Where did we leave off last time?*

As you recall, to manage anything well, we have to make good decisions and then implement them with as little internal disintegration as possible. When we're not managing well, we are either making bad decisions or implementing them in a more prolonged, painful, or expensive way than necessary.

*Right*

So far we have said that conflict is natural because we need a complementary team to make good decisions and a commonality of interests to implement those decisions. Both create conflicts: conflicts of styles and conflicts of interests. To make these conflicts functional, not destructive we need…

*A culture of Mutual Trust and Respect.*

Do you recall the four factors necessary for MT&R from our previous conversation?

*Common vision and values, a collaborative decision-making process, a diversified (PAEI) organizational structure, and mature people who command and grant trust and respect.*

One way to easily remember those four factors is to think of cooking a gourmet dish. For that you need fresh, high-quality ingredients. That is the people factor. They are a critical ingredient, your raw material. Then you need a recipe. You can destroy the best ingredients if you do not have a recipe that shows you how to cook them together. That means a collaborative decision-making process. Next you need a good oven and cooking utensils. That is the structure. Last, you need to decide what kind of meal you want to cook; for example, is it a Mexican or Italian meal? You need to have common vision and values.

We can also classify the variables in (PAEI) terms. What do you think common vision and values are?

> *(E)*

Diversified structure?

> *(A)*

Collaborative decision making?

> *(P)*

And the people factor?

> *(I)*

We have not yet discussed how to develop a common vision and values—we just do not have all the time needed for these discussions—but I have made a video on the subject.[34]

We briefly touched on the subject of structure when I explained why you should not have one VP for sales and marketing, or for production and engineering. For more on structure you can read *Managing Corporate Lifecycles* or watch a video of mine about the subject.[35]

Later we'll discuss what kind of people grant and command MT&R. As to the collaborative decision-making process, it has three parts. To begin, we must learn how to have an effective dialogue, how to communicate with a person in a style he can understand, and that is the subject of this conversation. The second part is how to handle different perceptions, and the third part is how to manage meetings, which we will cover in future conversations.

> *Great, I am ready.*

---

[34] TopLeaf video series, "How to Define an Organization's Mission." Available from www.adizes.com
[35] TopLeaf video series, "Is Your Company Structured Right?" Available from www.adizes.com. Also see Adizes, *Management/Mismanagement Styles*, *The Ideal Executive*, and *Leading the Leaders*, all op. cit.

We determined that one source of miscommunication lies in individuals' styles of demonstrating agreement or disagreement. For example, when (E)ntrepreneurs disagree with an idea they will usually be very expressive about it. They're also expressive when they agree with an idea.

*Is that why I don't know whether they're agreeing or disagreeing half the time? They speak so animatedly, that it seems as if they're always disagreeing.*

That energy can upset us. We might even feel we have to disagree with them, now that they have raised their voice at us. When (A)s disagree, however, they are very calm. They just look at you, lower their chin, and freeze. That can cause miscommunication because (E)s interpret the silence as agreement when (A)s are actually disagreeing.

We also discussed how the words "yes" and "no" can have different meanings depending on the speaker. You can't define the words according to your own understanding. You have to look at who is speaking, rather than listening with your own bias.

*What do you mean by listening with your own bias?*

In all the world's major religions there is something called the Golden Rule.

*"Do unto others as you would have them do unto you."*

This is the wrong approach to management communication. If you communicate with others as you want them to communicate with you, what mistake will you make?

*If you are an (E)ntrepreneur, you'll communicate to others as if they are (E)s.*

This idea isn't anything new. If you go to the bank to apply for a loan, you're not going to wear loud or shabby clothing, are you? You'll probably dress conservatively, sit quietly, and answer the banker's questions politely. You are attempting to be responsive to her style. You are trying to act like a banker.[36]

Before you talk to people, you have to ask yourself, "Whom am I talking to?" When people talk to you, you have to ask yourself, "Who is talking to me?" Then you can correctly interpret what they are saying and can communicate to them in a way they can understand.

---

36 The Adizes Institute has a test, the Management Styles Indicator (MSI), to analyze the style of a person, what he would like his style to be, and what style is required by his responsibility. Available at www.adizes.com/msi-resources

## 204 – MASTERING CHANGE

*This is interesting, but how does it relate to management?*

One aspect of management or leadership is the selling of ideas. If you can't communicate and convince, you cannot lead. All sales people will tell you that you must know your clients. You have to focus on communicating to your clients so they will understand you even though each of them speaks what sounds like a different language.

Let's try to systematize this with a diagram that describes decision-making styles as they impact communication.

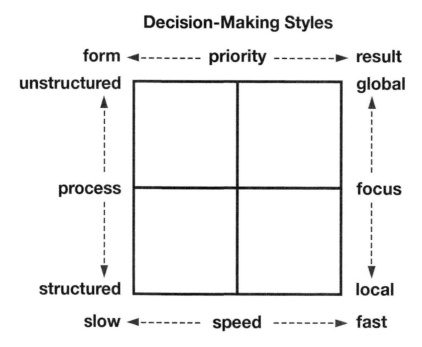

In the upper part, you have priorities. On the right side is result orientation—the *what* and *why*—versus process orientation—the *how* and *who*. Some people are results oriented, while others pay more attention to the process of producing results.

The horizontal line at the bottom of the diagram indicates the speed at which people make decisions. On the left side the decision making is slow, and on the right side it is fast.

*What does all this mean?*

It means that some people make decisions slowly. There's a joke about bureaucrats: You shouldn't tell a bureaucrat a joke on Friday because he might laugh in church on Sunday. This is not true for (E)ntrepreneurs, who react very quickly. They will interrupt your joke because it reminded them of another joke.

*What do the vertical lines stand for?*

On the right side we have focus: global at the top, local at the bottom. This dimension corresponds to the window analogy we talked about before. One person may see the view while somebody else sees only the dirty frame. Some people have a global view, while others pay attention to the details. The last variable is the process by which people make decisions. Some process information in an unstructured way, others in structured manner.

*What do those terms mean in this case?*

In an unstructured process, a person may start talking about Y, which reminds him of Z. Then he goes to Q, then to B, then to C, and finally, to X. He goes back and forth, because he is thinking in a holistic way; everything is related to everything else. In structured processes, however, people are linear. They don't like to start talking about B until they fully understand A.

If we look at the chart, we'll see that the four styles—(P)roducer, (A)dministrator, (E)ntrepreneur, and (I)ntegrator—will fit into the four boxes. Who has the global, fast-moving, unstructured style of decision making?

*The (E)ntrepreneurial types.*

Who is fast, structured, and focused on details and results?

*The (P)s.*

They are like railroad engineers: They say, "Show me the tracks and get out of the way." In the workplace, they are the ones most likely to say, "What do we need to do? Let's go and do it. We have a business to run. Talk less, do more."

*That makes sense.*

Who has the structured, slow-moving style focused on process and details?

*The (A)dministrators.*

Now read the (I) style from the chart.

*They are process-oriented, slow, and unstructured; that is why they can be so politically astute. They have a global view. They can change and adapt.*

If we look at this diagram and the different styles of different people, we can see why they might miscommunicate. The (E)ntrepreneurial types will be most in conflict with the types diagonal to them, the (A)dministrators. Mixing these two together is like mixing oil and water. It is going to be very difficult.

*Can you give me some examples of these conflicts?*

The (E)ntrepreneurs process information very quickly. They usually start thinking with very little stimulus. When an (E) goes to a meeting with an (A)dministrator, he has already started thinking in the corridor. By the time he hits the (A)dministrator's office, he's already moving at 150 miles an hour. He hits the (A) like a ton of bricks. (A)s are slow, not because they are stupid, but because they are thinking about all the repercussions of what the (E)s are saying. It takes them time to process each idea. When they get hit by the ideas of the (E)ntrepreneurs, it's like an avalanche. For any single (E) idea there are at least ten repercussions that matter to (A)s. The (A)dministrators can't handle the load or the speed, and soon stop thinking and listening all together. They just let ideas pass them by, accusing the (E)s of being full of hot air. The (A)s might start hoping the (E)s leave soon so they can get back to work.

*Meanwhile, the silence of the (A)dministrators is misconstrued by (E)s as agreement.*

Right, and imagine the misunderstanding that ensues. (E)s don't like to make appointments. The moment they have an idea they want to deal with it, and they might show up unannounced at the (A)s' office. The (A)dministrators, however, hate surprises. The (A)s have everything organized—their desk, their files, their day, their vacation, their year, their life—and here comes an unguided missile messing up their life.

*Moreover, (E)ntrepreneurs rarely have the patience to talk about boring problems of implementation, the* how *dimension. They spend most of their time talking about why something needs to be done. (E)s see the whole landscape from above, and not necessarily any of the details.*

The Native Americans have totemic symbols for people that describe their styles.[37] When a warrior was called Big Eagle, this was a way of describing what we are calling an (E) style. He soared through the sky with a spectacular view of the horizon, but his feet were not on the ground. He lacked a full sense of reality.

---

37  H. Storm. *Seven Arrows*. New York: Harper & Row, 1972.

The Native Americans would have called the (A) style a buffalo—very slow and heavy, but once it decides to charge, watch out! The buffalo doesn't change direction easily. It would probably run you over first. Now, just imagine an eagle and a buffalo trying to charge together. It would be very difficult, wouldn't it?

*What happens when (A)s try to talk to (E)s?*

(A)s call ahead and schedule appointments which (E)s usually change or miss. When they finally meet, (A)s discuss so many details that it deeply annoys the (E)s. If you ask (A)dministrators about a problem, they usually start by explaining the past. They tell you how the problem evolved, as if you wouldn't understand the problem without knowing its history. (A)s always seem to start with Adam and Eve. After two hours, they're only up to the Renaissance. You have to meet for another four hours before finally hearing about the present time.

(E)s and (P)s, on the other hand, have the attention span of a squirrel. Finally the (E)s will say enough history, what's the solution? The (A)s, with a two-thousand-year view of the problem, will claim that it will take how long to solve it?

*Another two thousand years!*

It's called analysis paralysis. Bureaucrats suffer from it.

The (E)s have a totally different time frame. They don't like looking at the past. For (E)ntrepreneurs, the past is dead. They are looking to the future. They're eagles flying high in the sky, looking beyond the horizon. They see opportunities, and they have difficulty communicating what they see because although they can sense it, the details are not yet clear. If you ask them to describe it in detail, they will still describe it in generalities.

Furthermore, (E)s dislike talking about problems. Their answer to a problem is, "It's your responsibility." (E)s focus on opportunities while, for an (A), those opportunities are problems.

*Aren't (E)s concerned with why problems exist?*

No. They prefer to focus on opportunities. Problems drain them of energy.

*What about the solution?*

When you ask (E)s for a solution, they usually get upset. They feel the opportunities they foresee should have been dealt with already. That's why it's usually uncomfortable working with (E)s; they get upset easily. What they don't realize is that they're flying at high altitude. The (A) is not moving. He has more and more questions and doubts that rain on (E)'s parade.

The (E)s will usually run out of the room in the middle of the discussion. They just can't stand all the details. The (A)s feel ignored, abused, and abandoned. They feel they are working for sea gulls, which appear from above, let out a shriek, drop a shot on your boat, and disappear.

*What about the other extreme, the case of (P)s communicating with (I)s?*

Task-oriented, fast-moving (P)s are usually not very personal or sensitive. This upsets the (I)ntegrators, who want to slow down and pay attention to people. They will usually accuse the (P)s of being hatchet men, insensitive and macho. The (P)s, on the other hand, think (I)s are too weak and too slow.

> We should be even more conscious of how we deal with subordinates because we usually take lightly those we believe we can control.

*It doesn't sound as though these two get along any better than the (A)s and the (E)s.*

They don't, and they don't necessarily like each other, either. Each thinks the other is insensitive: (P)s think (I)s are insensitive to what the organization needs, while (I)s think the (P)s are insensitive to how people feel. That can create hard feelings and a lack of mutual respect between the two types.

*What about the (E)s and (P)s?*

(P)s and (E) also do not understand each other well. (E) might think aloud something that a (P) will interpret as a decision and start moving to implement although no decision was made. Those (P)s—who would be called rodents in the Native American totem—are so close to the ground they can't see beyond their whiskers. They don't understand what the (E) is talking about. They don't share the vision.

*I understand the nature of these conflicts, but what do we do about them?*

What you need is to be able to sell your ideas to people who are different from you.

*Great how?*

Many books have been written about how to lead employees from the top down. What is needed is bottom-up leadership. We are not talking about communicating only with a boss. The Adizes Methodology pertains to communicating with peers and employees as well. In fact, when communicating with employees the methodology is more difficult to use because we usually ignore an employee's style. That is a mistake. We need staff cooperation in collaborative decision making no less than we need the boss's cooperation. We should be even more conscious of how we deal with subordinates because we usually take lightly those we believe we can control. Some people make this mistake with their spouse or children, treating them with less respect than they would grant a stranger.

Start thinking about how to communicate with people in general. Think of people as if each one were your boss. This means you will have to sell your ideas without using authority or power, just your influence.

> *How do I do that? You say I should try to talk to people in their own language, but first I have to know who they are. How can I find out whether people are (P)s, (A)s, (E)s, or (I)s before I talk to them?*

We have a test, the Management Style Indicator, available from the Adizes Institute, but you can't refuse to talk to people until they submit to psychological tests.

> *But if you don't know someone very well or have never met her before, what do you do?*

Ask her what job she performs. If people are in marketing, expect them to be (E)ntrepreneurial. If they are in sales, they may be more of the (P)roducer type. If they're in accounting, they may have an (A)dministrative orientation. Look at their jobs; try to assess their behavior, then verify your assessment. Ask them how they like their jobs, what they like and do not like. Look at their offices. Look at their desk, clothes, posture, and energy. Be sensitive to them. It's not as important to quantify personality traits as it is to be conscious of whether they understand you or not. Then adapt your style so that you can communicate clearly.

> To make a decision, all the (PAEI) roles must be performed, so people naturally move to perform a missing role.

> Simplify life so that we can deal with its complexities.

Also, watch for this phenomenon: If two (E)s get together the one who is a stronger (E) might take on the (P) style as well, while the other (E) might assume the (A) and (I) styles.

> *Why?*

To make a decision, all the (PAEI) roles must be performed, so people naturally move to perform a missing role, although it is not their natural strength. Natural inclinations are only a starting point. The environment, the nature of the task, and the other people involved have a large impact on what style a person exhibits. So don't be so fast to brand people. Observe them, listen and feel, and use the tools from these conversations plus your own intuition.

*This is complicated.*

Right. Life is not simple. All we are trying to do in these conversations is simplify life so that we can deal with its complexities. For example, to assess someone's style in a job interview I use the following system: I tell the candidate to ask me ten questions. I tell them that I will answer them all to her satisfaction. To be sure she asks everything she needs to know, if I offer her the job she has to decide on the spot whether to accept or to reject my offer. As she asks her questions I can analyze whether the question is (P), (A), (E), or (I) question. For instance, if she asks about the goals of your company, what do you think her style is?

*That is (E).*

If she asks, "What exactly am I supposed to do?"

*That is a (P) question.*

If she asks about salary and fringe benefits?

*(A).*

The questions reveal the person's needs and thus her personality style. It is not a precise, scientific system, but as a rule of thumb it works.

*Once you've figured out someone's style, what do you do with that information? What would you do when talking to a (P), for example?*

(P)s are quick decision makers. They behave as if they don't have a lot of time. They're usually under pressure to deal with a crisis, so they must focus on results.

Let me ask you a question: If your boss were a (P) and you said, "I need three hours to discuss a problem with you." What would he say?

*"Three hours? Sure, how about in ten years? Maybe by then I'll be able to find my desk!"*

How much time can you request realistically?

*Five or ten minutes, maybe fifteen at the very most.*

When talking with (P)s try to be short. Start with the end of your argument, with your conclusion. Give a (P) the bottom line, because that's all he has time for. You can supply the support materials and answer any questions later.

*What do you do if the person is a Lone Ranger, not just a (P)roducer?*

Tell him it's a crisis. For the Lone Ranger that's a legitimate reason to give you time. You should say, "We have a crisis. We must deal with it immediately. I'm already applying the solution. I just need your approval."

*Why would that work?*

If you don't say you're under time pressure or that you're in the middle of implementing a solution, what will the Lone Ranger say?

*"Put it on my desk."*

> The (A) will be precisely wrong. She runs a well-controlled disaster.

Then the problem will sit there with a hundred other problems, while you're stuck with no solution. Lone Rangers aren't going to delegate to you, so you have to take initiative yourself. You have to legitimate what you do. With Lone Rangers the problem must be a crisis, there must be time pressure, and you must take initiative to solve it, or it will not be dealt with in a reasonable amount of time.

Now, will the same approach work with (A)dministrators? If you call an (A) and say, "We have a crisis and I'm already implementing the solution, I just need your blessing," what do you think would happen?

*You'd be fired.*

An (A) would say, "Who gave you the right to start implementing a solution? How dare you proceed with implementation without getting approval?" The (A) will be precisely wrong. She runs a well-controlled disaster. Don't you take initiative until you get the (A)'s approval, even if the company is sinking.

If you are a (P) working for a Bureaucrat, you've probably made this mistake. You've probably had a crisis and solved it. When you went to your boss to get his blessing, you expected praise but you got quite a surprise instead. The fact is, you applied a (P) solution, and the (A) didn't appreciate it at all.

*What is the correct procedure with (A)s?*

(A)dministrators, or Bureaucrats, depending on how extreme their style is, are more interested in how than what. Their style is slow and structured, with a focus on process. You have to fit your style to their style, so you must pay close attention to form above function. The first thing you must do is schedule an appointment. (A)s don't appreciate surprises. If you do pop in unexpectedly, they won't listen to you for the first half hour. They're upset because you caught them unprepared or because you came unprepared. Tell them in advance what the meeting is about so that they can get ready for you. Next, you have to use what I call a coefficient of error.

> *What's that?*

(E)s and (P)s move quickly; (A)s and (I)s move slowly. They have different concepts of time. For instance, my style is (E), and I have found that my coefficient of error is six. This means that if I tell my staff they can do something in one hour, it will really take six hours. If I tell them we can do it in a week how long will it actually take?

> *Six weeks.*

You see, for me as an eagle flying in the sky, one beat of my wings takes me a long distance with relative ease. However, those down on the ground have to run up and down hills and canyons to travel the same distance. Following my small movements from below is extremely difficult. But being an eagle up in the air, I might ignore the difference, which would cause an error in my expectations.

So before an (E) calls an (A) and says, "I need to meet with you for half an hour," the (E) should think about his coefficient of error. If it is six, like mine, the (E) should say, "I need a half-hour meeting with you, but knowing me we had better schedule three hours." What the (A) doesn't want is to schedule a half-hour meeting that ends up taking three hours. The (E) must ask for three hours and tell the (A) what the agenda will be. No surprises.

Next, if you are an (E) or (P) talking to an (A) or (I), I suggest you learn to slow down.

> *Slow down?*

(E)s constantly run out of breath. Their mind moves faster than their lips. In Mexico they say the first one who stops talking to take a breath loses the argument.

> *I have noticed in countries with an (E) culture it seems as though everyone talks at the same time. How do you suggest learning to slow down?*

Say you are an (E) or a (P) dealing with an (A). You arranged for a three-hour meeting and told the (A) what you'd be discussing. Start by slowing down as you walk to the meeting. Take a deep breath. When you arrive, you should have slowed down to the (A)'s speed. For every one of your ideas, the (A) will think of many, many repercussions. The (A) needs time to process your information. If you don't slow down in the corridor, do it during the first few minutes of the session.

In modern society, the (E) style that causes us to rush and the (P) pressures to perform cause people to run around breathless. Slow down! Start a meeting with a relaxation response: close your eyes and breathe deeply. Relax for a few seconds. This idea comes from Dr. Herbert Benson of the Harvard Medical School.[38]

*I know his work. But he recommends the relaxation response to avoid the undesirable effects of stress.*

Stress and good decision making don't get along. The more relaxed you are the better your decision will be because you'll be more aware of what your body is telling you.

*What my body is telling me?*

> Stress and good decision making don't get along.
>
> Think and analyze, but in the end, listen to your intuition by listening to your body.

A body is a data warehouse where you store your experiences. Don't we say, "I have a gut feeling," or "This problem is giving me a headache," or "This situation is making me tense?" Don't you ache after a stressful meeting? Your body was storing the experience. Next time, when you have a similar problem, your body will react to the experience with a gut feeling, a headache, or tension. Your body is communicating your past experiences. Pay attention to your body, respect it, and trust it. You have made a good decision only when your body feels relaxed. If you are tense, if it doesn't "smell good," if it "feels rotten," even if all the numbers and experts indicate that you should do something, what should you do?

*Don't do it.*

Think and analyze, but in the end, listen to your intuition by listening to your body. You can also communicate better by watching the body language of the people you are talking to. Watch their eyes, eyebrows, and hand movements, and synchronize what they say with how they say it. You can't do that if you are preoccupied with your own pains.

If the parties in a meeting are relaxed, they communicate and understand each other better than if they are in pain; so slow down to get a fast result!

*I understand, although I believe I am going to look weird next time I start a meeting with "Ladies and gentlemen, please take a deep breath and relax!"*

---

38  Herbert Benson. *Relaxation Response.* New York: William Morrow, 1975.

You will get a weird reaction the first time around. Next time, they will ask for it. Try it.

*What else should I remember when communicating with (A)s?*

Go to the agenda and start with the first item, and watch the (A)'s eyes. This is very important. The moment her eyes go wandering, the (A) is thinking about the repercussions of your idea. Stop talking. I know this is very difficult for an (E), but you must wait for the (A) to finish processing the information. Wait for the (A) to return from her wanderings.

*What should I do in the meantime? Just sit there?*

If you are an (E), you usually have many other ideas you want to present. While the (A) is thinking, you could make a list of those ideas. You should always have a pad of paper and a pen while in a meeting. If you don't write those ideas down, you'll worry that you might forget them later, causing you to keep talking when you should be quiet. If you know that you can find those ideas any time, you won't feel so hard-pressed to say everything at once and send the poor (A) into a daze.

*When the (A) comes back from her deep thoughts, won't she have questions?*

The questions will most likely be about implementation. An (E) will probably get upset and think, "I can't believe this. I am trying to make millions of dollars and this person is bugging me about insignificant details." (E)s often think (A)s are denying heavenly light because they can't find a candle.

> (E)s often think (A)s are denying heavenly light because they can't find a candle.

> You have to understand together the *what* and *why* before addressing the *how*.

*Yes, this can drive (E)s insane.*

First, don't get upset. Do not resist a stylistic difference, instead learn to recognize it and accept it. Then you can deal with it. What you should do is acknowledge the question. Maybe you could write it on a flip chart, so the (A) can see that you are not ignoring the question. Say, "After we finish the report we'll address all the questions in detail. If you have any more questions, please write them down." This way you are acknowledging the (A)'s concerns, yet you don't get sidetracked. Acknowledge all the questions but don't discuss them in that moment. Once you have finished presenting the big picture, summarize and say, "Now let's look at the questions." In other words, you have to understand together the *what* and *why* before addressing the *how*.

As you discuss the questions, you might find that the (A) was right to raise them. Some questions about implementation can justifiably negate your wonderful idea. But you should not discuss the *how* until you have jointly understood the *what* and the *why*. You can't start with *what not* until you jointly understand *what yes*. You can't all talk about cost until you all understand the value. Cost does not exist in a vacuum, it is relative to value.

> You can't talk about the cost until you all understand the value.

*How long should you stay in a meeting with an (A)?*

Stay only the length of time you agreed upon. Don't say, "Ten more minutes." First, there is a good chance it's not going to be just ten minutes but more like half an hour. By that time the (A) will be furious. He has a schedule to live by. If you cannot finish in ten minutes, you will have to rush, and the worst mistakes in judgment are usually made in the last ten minutes of an extended meeting when people rush and are stressed.

*But the (E) won't like this procedure. Asking them to stop on time is like asking a fish to fly.*

Some fish do fly, and some birds dive under water. I'm not asking you to do what you like to do, but what you need to do. Do you think the bird goes under water for fun? It's going to feed. Being a leader requires selling ideas to others. You know how difficult it is to sell your own ideas to yourself; imagine how much more difficult it is to sell them to others.

> The worst mistakes in judgment are usually made in the last ten minutes of an extended meeting.

*Are there other considerations when you deal with an (A)?*

Yes, many. This conversation is just a start. For instance, to (E)s numbers don't have to be exact; they're only a way to express a degree of magnitude. An (E) might say, "We sold a million," when the fact is we sold somewhere between half a million and one and a half million. But for (A)s, 999,999 is not a million. That's why (A)s usually don't trust (E)s, and often (E)s get accused of lying. (E)s must be careful not to confuse ideas with facts because (A)s take people literally. When (A)s catch you in a mistake, no matter how small, they no longer trust anything you say.

*Enough about (A)s. I don't really like them anyway.*

Watch your attitude. They'll keep you out of trouble. The bigger the (E) is in your (PAEI) code, the more (A) you should seek out. Success is a complementary team based on mutual respect. That means accepting each other's styles as legitimate.

*You're right. I have to remember that this is work, not a social club. Now, how do you handle (E)s?*

> (E)s must be careful not to confuse ideas with facts.

We already know (E)s resist any idea unless it is theirs. Before meeting with an (E), you have to think about how to make your idea appear to be the (E)'s idea. Can you walk in and say to an (E), "Here is problem X, the solution should be Y. I've worked it out to the last detail, I'm just asking for your approval." That's how you succeeded with the (A) style. Is (E) going to like that?

*No. In fact, the (E) would probably say you have the wrong problem and wrong solution.*

Looking for a hole in your reasoning, the (E) will attack the diagnosis. The (E) will try to find out what's wrong in an effort to put her own stamp on the solution. Finalized plans, in which there is nothing left for the (E) to contribute, will not be acceptable.

For an (E), the (A) approach means you are taking charge and leaving her behind. You're ignoring her by not consulting with her. She feels disrespected, and will find a way to put you in your place sooner or later. If you ignore her, she is going to make you notice her, and notice her in a big way.

*Then how should I approach (E)s?*

Don't ever go to them with a "final" solution to a problem. Don't ever expect them to simply agree with you. You must leave the whole issue open ended, using phrases like: "May I suggest... I've been thinking... It appears that... What do you think?" Let them put their stamp on your idea. You should treat all (E) people like this, not only your (E) boss. I'm also talking about dealing with employees who are (E)s. They'll hate you telling them what to do, how to do it, and when you want it done. Why? Because you're not letting them use their brain. The (E)s want to contribute and you won't let them use their creativity. Talk to them in their own language. Ask them what they think, what they suggest, how they can help improve this. Enlist them so that they will own the idea.

*How do you deal with (I)s? What are (I)ntegrators or, in extreme cases, Super Followers or Soaped Fish, looking for?*

Why don't you try to answer that?

*They're looking for agreement and political consensus.*

If you tell an (I), "The problem is this and the solution is that. We want your approval," what will he say?

*"It's not time yet. We're not ready. Have you talked to Rudy? Have you talked to Paul? Have you talked to Denise?"*

> Different people motivate, organize, and discipline differently. You must pay attention to the differences.

An (I)ntegrator is going to ask questions to assess the political climate—the degree of consensus already available. So, before you go to the (I)ntegrator you have to get all the necessary people to buy into your idea. You have to talk to Rudy and Paul and Denise to find out where they stand. You have to (I)ntegrate them first. Then say to the (I)ntegrator, "We have a problem. All of us have discussed it. We agree on the solution, and we want your approval." The (I) will immediately ask, "What about Joe?" If you didn't talk to Joe, who is apparently important on the political map, the (I)ntegrator will say, "I don't think we're ready yet." But if you can say, "We talked to Joe and he is totally behind it," (I)ntegrator will say, "What are we waiting for? Let's go!"

Before giving their blessing, (I)ntegrators will go down the list of important people to make sure everyone is behind an idea. They understand capi intuitively.

*What happens if I misread the person I'm talking to?*

Your strategy will backfire. Just imagine you're an (I) talking to an (E) boss, and you treat him as another (I). All your life you have tried to resolve conflicts and be sensitive to people. You talk to all the people affected by the problem or the solution. You resolve all the conflicts and integrate everyone. Then you go to your (E) boss and say, "We had this problem. We all met and agreed what the problem is, and we all agreed on the solution. We just want your agreement on it." What do you think? How will the (E) boss react?

*She would probably sweat, thinking, "My God! There's been a coup d'état behind my back. No one told me about the problem, they just got together and caucused against me. They have a solution and now they are backing me into a corner to approve it." The (E) will look for the first opportunity to fire the (I).*

Traditional management theory virtually ignores differences in style. Different people motivate, organize, and discipline differently. You must pay attention to the differences. You must deal with people according to their styles. (P)s plan differently from (A)s, (E)s, or (I)s. Everyone has a different way of looking at the world, and that's why everyone wants to be treated differently. This has implications for designing reward systems, hiring and promoting people, evaluating performances, how we treat our children, and how we should treat our spouse. It impacts how we should treat each other, period.[39]

Differences in communication styles have implications for advertising as well. One way to look at market segmentation is through demographics: education, sex, geographical location, and so forth. Another way to look at it, I suggest, is through personality traits. This (PAEI) methodology has been used by many advertising agencies to appeal to different people in different ways. Take a car, for example. The (P)roducing types look for the functionality of a product, so advertising directed at (P)s should focus on gas mileage, legroom, trunk space, and seating capacity.

Advertising aimed at (A)s should stress the warranty, repair record, and resale value, but for (E)s, facts like resale value and gas mileage are boring. (E)s probably look at what the car symbolizes. Sex appeal attracts the (E)'s attention, why else would anyone pay a hundred thousand dollars for a Ferrari? It's very difficult to sit inside one, and you can't drive 150 miles an hour in the city, but the idea of a sexy car and what it communicates to others is its main appeal for an (E). The car is a means to achieve the goals of the (E)'s fruitful imagination, not just a means of transportation as it is for a (P) or a good return on investment like it is for an (A). That's why when selling to (E)s, the colors, music, and images are very important. Sometimes it's difficult even to identify the product. The total image is being sold.

> *This explains something: Creative directors in advertising agencies are usually (E)s so they create advertisements they like. If they present such ideas to the vice presidents of an aging organization who are (A)s, they'll be kicked out mid-presentation.*

Smart account executives in advertising have to know how to differentiate between clients and customers, the end users.

*What about selling to (I)s?*

---

39  A detailed elaboration on this subject can be found in Adizes, *Leading the Leaders*, op. cit. For Adizes applications to marriage, see Ichak Kalderon Adizes, Ruth and Yecheztkel Madanes: *The Power of Opposites*, to be published in 2016.

To (I)s you're selling the affiliation. The advertisements for Rolex watches are a good example. The ad refers constantly to the fact that world leaders wear the watches. The message is that if you want to be identified with these people, you should wear the same watch. It's a symbol of belonging.

*Interesting that (I) type of advertising comes from Switzerland. If Switzerland had no (I) and (A) it would not survive, with Italians, French and Germans all in one country.*

Good advertising campaigns have messages hitting all four (PAEI) market segments, or four separate campaigns aimed at the different segments.

*Would you summarize all this?*

To communicate successfully requires skill because different people understand the same words differently. They also have different needs to be satisfied. You must pay attention to those styles and needs if you want to sell your ideas.

*Wait a minute! There's a complication here. Nobody is ever a perfect or exclusive type. We behave differently under different conditions or when interacting with different people. It seems as if we have multiple (PAEI) styles, not one. What then?*

> Whenever people are tired or upset they usually start behaving in their own style and ignore the style of the people they're talking to.

You must be sensitive. Try one approach, and if you are not being understood, try another approach. You should always keep your eye on the people to whom you are selling ideas, and adapt and change your style until your audience fully understands. Every leader must speak the four (PAEI) "languages" to some degree if he wants to communicate well. That's why good managers must have well-rounded styles, and why traveling abroad and getting to know different cultures is an important part of a person's education.

*Now I feel as though I can never relax. I'll have to watch the person I'm speaking to and how I'm speaking. This makes me tense.*

Luckily, you don't have to do it all the time—only when there is conflict or when you don't easily understand another person.

*The problem is that is when I'm least able to watch my style and adapt it to the other person.*

Yes. Whenever people are tired or upset they usually start behaving in their own style and ignore the style of the people they're talking to.

*So when people attend important meetings it's extremely important that they be relaxed and well rested?*

Some people even meditate and fast before crucial meetings.

*Are you serious?*

There are also times when people should stop a meeting altogether and reschedule it.

*When?*

When you're heading toward a breakdown. Let's say you're very familiar with the workings of a certain machine, such as your car. You know the normal humming sound the engine makes, and if someone unfamiliar with your car asks what that noise is, you can say, oh, it's normal. Once you know what a normal noise is, you can identify noises that aren't normal and could indicate a breakdown. What should you do when you hear such noises?

*Stop the engine immediately.*

Absolutely. The same is true in personal relationships. Sometimes a conflict is normal and nothing to worry about. It may even be music to your ears because you know you are both learning. It's pain with gain! But when you hear abnormal noise, you intervene.

*How do you know what is normal and abnormal in conflicts?*

Each of the (PAEI) styles has a typical abnormal noise, called backup behavior. It appears when people aren't listening to or learning from each other anymore. It usually starts when people feel intimidated and fear they are losing control.

*I bet it begins when they start losing trust and respect.*

Yes, and the danger is that if they don't stop the discussion it will be like a machine breaking down. It will keep sputtering until major, and sometimes irreparable, damage is done. What is breaking down is Mutual Trust and Respect.

*What are those typical backup behavior patterns?*

When (P)s feel they are losing control, they become little dictators. They proclaim, "That's it. I've heard enough! Here is what we're going to do and that's it!"

(A)s usually freeze. They become very quiet. Their jaws lock. They don't look at you, but through you. They ignore you and pursue their own agenda. In Hebrew there is a military expression that describes this behavior: the dogs are barking; the convoy keeps moving.

*What is backup behavior for (I)s?*

They yield. "Oh, that's what you mean? No problem. Fine. Don't worry."

*You are right. When my wife, who is an (I), says never mind, I'd better start to mind. There is trouble brewing in my marriage.*

(I)s sway with the wind, especially when it's blowing hard, but they do not mean it. Like the tree that bends in the wind but straightens itself back up when the wind stops, so does the (I). He seems to agree, only later you find out that nothing really has changed.

The most dangerous backup behavior is that of (E)s.

*I know: They attack. They go for the throat. They cut you to pieces and destroy your self-respect by publicly demeaning you. That is my boss.*

Then they forget the whole thing. They kill you, and the next morning act as if nothing happened.

*But (A)s never forget. They keep a detailed diary in their minds, and sometimes on paper.*

This sort of conflict occurs in many marriages. (E)s marry (A)s because they are complementary. Traditionally the (E) is the male and the (A) is the female. He attacks her, and she withstands it silently while mentally cataloging it. Years later, when she wants a divorce, he falls to pieces because he doesn't have a clue what happened or why. Then she reminds him what happened on that infamous afternoon ten years ago. He is shocked because he has very little memory of the fight. He hardly remembers what he had for breakfast, much less what happened ten years ago. But (A)s do not forget and do not forgive easily.

*You just explained something very painful for me. A big (E) easily reverts to backup behavior and shows displeasure easily. The other person, an (A), closes down because she feels threatened. When (A)s do that the (E) feels ignored, which is the worst thing that can happen to an (E), and gets furious. That causes him to escalate his attack, and the more he attacks, the more she closes down. He is falling apart while she freezes her emotions.*

Right! She is in as much pain as you, only she shows it differently.

*What should we do?*

> Talent alone does not make for success. To produce results, the more talent you have, the more self-discipline you must have.

Whoever is more in control of his or her emotions, even by a little bit, has to stop the discussion the instant backup behavior is sensed. You should not resume the discussion too soon, either. What did you do with the machine that sounded as if it were breaking down? You stopped it. Should you just start it up again?

*No. You should check the source of the breakdown first.*

The same holds for personal conflict. After you have stopped the discussion and cooled off, you should find out what caused the other party to feel threatened. Clear up that issue before continuing the discussion.

When you notice backup behavior in a heated business meeting, say something like, "Let's discuss it tomorrow. I hear you and I want to give you the full attention you deserve. I am too emotional right now." Refuse to continue the discussion. (P)s and (E)s will get upset and insist the problem be resolved. They hate pain and want to get it over with. When they hear abnormal noise, they don't slow the machine down, they speed it up. Don't get sucked in. Stop the discussion. The next day start off by asking, "What happened yesterday that upset you?" Try to find out what it was. Only when that issue is resolved should you restart the machine and go back to discussing the issue you were dealing with.

*This requires a lot of self-discipline.*

Right. Talent alone does not make for success. To produce results, the more talent you have, the more self-discipline you must have or you will burn out in no time.

*And self-discipline alone is barren.*

Absolutely. You need both talent and self-discipline. Analyze the people who have been successful in any field—sports, arts, business, politics—and you will find equal amounts of talent and self-discipline.

# CONVERSATION 12
# Perceiving Reality

So far we've said that different people not only behave differently, they think differently. If you want to sell your ideas to people, you have to think as they do and communicate in a language they understand.

> If you want to sell your ideas to people, you have to think as they do and communicate in a language they understand.

> You don't learn only from teachers or books. You can learn from rocks, flowers, and children.

People process information and reach conclusions at different speeds. People have different priorities in decision making. Even the same words have different meanings to different people. There is another source of miscommunication we need to address as well, one that stems from differences in perceptions.

*Before we move on, may I first ask how you learned what you are teaching me now?*

That's a good question. You don't learn only from teachers or books. You can learn from rocks, flowers, and children also. I learned about perceptions from my kids when they were toddlers. The oldest Topaz, was in his highchair banging his spoon and splattering food all over the place when he suddenly pointed at something and shouted, "Mine!"

I was puzzled as to why my son was developing "capitalistic tendencies" so early in life. Why was he so materialistic, so possessive? What was going on with his upbringing? Why wasn't his first word *love* or *give*?

Later my second son, Shoham, did the same thing at about the same age. I learned that children all over the world shout "Mine!" at about the same age, in all countries and in all languages. I wondered why.

After working for years in changing organizational cultures, I realized grown-ups shout "Mine!" all the time too. After years of observation, I had the following illumination. A situation can be perceived in three different ways, or in any combination of the three. If you look at this diagram, you'll see three circles labeled *is*, *want*, and *should*.

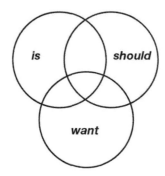

The first perception of reality is the *is*. It's the present reality. It's right now. For instance, you are listening to me right now, however, maybe it crossed your mind that you should be working. Some little voice in the back of your mind is telling you what you should be doing, rather than what you are doing. That *should* is the second perception.

The third perception is what you *want* to be doing. While you are listening to me and thinking you should be in the office, you really *want* to be with your kids.

*This sounds like a lot of internal conflict.*

It is what you are doing versus what you believe you should be doing versus what you want to be doing—and that causes emotional pain.

Let's explore some intersections of these perceptions: What happens when *should* overlaps *is* without *want*?

*I do what I should do although I do not want to do it.*

Right. Like taking medicine or going on a diet.

Now, how about the intersection where *is* overlaps *want* without *should*?

> *That is drinking or smoking. I do what I want although I realize I should not do it.*

How about *should* overlapping *want* but not *is*?

> *Oh, I know that one. It is when I get upset with my teenage daughter: "I want you home by midnight. You should be home by midnight the latest. I am worried sick. Why are you not home by midnight?"*

"Mine!" is where the three circles overlap: What *is* happening *should* be happening, and you *want* it to happen. When children shout "Mine!" they're not being possessive. What they're really saying is: "I want that" and since children don't know the difference between *want*, *should*, and *is*, what they're really saying is: "Since I *want* it, it *should* be, and it *is*."

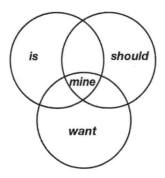

In the first five or six years of their lives, children cry a lot because they're learning to differentiate between the three perceptions. If you tell toddlers, "Don't touch the oven; it is hot," what do they do the moment you turn your back?

> **If we succeed in learning to appreciate the *is*, we enjoy the best time of our life.**

*Touch the oven!*

They get burned and cry. They are starting to learn the difference between *want* and *is*.

If you tell children, "It is ten o'clock; you should go to sleep because you have school tomorrow," what do they say? "I don't *want* to go to sleep." They are learning to differentiate between *want* and *should*, and to act according to *should* and not exclusively according to *want*.

When we grow up and experience a mid-life crisis, we realize that the *should* and the *want* are not that crucial. What is very relevant is the *is*. We learn to live with reality. If we succeed in learning to appreciate the *is*, we enjoy the best time of our life. We finally learn what we like and still have time to enjoy it. We put aside the *shoulds* and *wants*. We like the *is*, and enjoy the now.

> Mature love is present when we accept and love our partner in *spite of*.

*But the best is to be in the state of "mine," right?*

Yes, and a way to see *mine* as happiness is when we are in love or, rather, infatuated. We say to the person, "You are *mine*." What we are really saying is, "What you *are*, what you *should* be, and what I *want* you to be are one and the same. You are perfect." But I don't call that true love. I call that "puppy love" or "temporary madness."

*Temporary madness?*

Yes, because after we get married we discover that what *is*, *should not* be, and what *should* be, we don't necessarily *want*, and what we *want*, *isn't*. In mature love we move from the overlapping core of teenage love to mature love, which means accepting reality and imperfection.

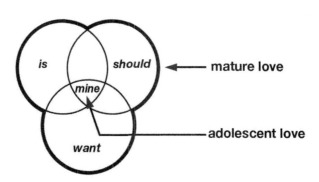

The French differentiate between loving and liking this way: You like *because of*; you love in *spite of*.

*Mine* does not equal love. It equals immature love. Mature love is present when we accept and love our partner in *spite of*.

The love of others starts with the love of oneself which means accepting your own imperfections first. You have to forgive yourself before you can forgive others. Thus, love grows from the inside out, not from the outside in. No one can give it to you. You give it to yourself first before giving it to others.

> You have to forgive yourself before you can forgive others.

In India people often don't marry out of love. They do not expect the three circles to overlap as in "Mine!" They marry out of commitment, not out of infatuation. In these societies love develops. The spiritual leader Master Chariji says love is a choice we make. It is like a muscle. The more you "exercise" it, the more you experience it.

In the West, with our romantic expectations, we expect "Mine!" to be continuous. When we don't continually experience it, we get upset, we experience pain driven by unfulfilled expectations, and we ask for a divorce. In one of his lectures Rabbi Kushner, the author of *When Bad Things Happen to Good People*, tells the story of a modern couple who asked him to officiate at their wedding. They wanted to change the vows: Instead of saying "until death do us part," they wanted to say something like "for as long as we love each other." In this case, was there a commitment to nurture love, or an expectation to benefit from love regardless?

*How, specifically, does this relate to management or leadership?*

People confuse *is*, *want*, and *should* in all spheres of life. Look at some of our political writings: "All men *are* created equal." Aren't we confusing *is* with *want* and *should*? Are people born equal, *should* they be born equal, or do we *want* them to be born equal? Another example: "America is the leader of the free world." *Is* it? *Should* it be? Or do we *want* it to be?

*But why this confusion?*

People with different (PAEI) styles perceive reality differently. For instance, which tendency do (E)ntrepreneurial types exhibit: *want*, *should*, or *is*?

*They come from want.*

They confuse *want* with what *is*: "Since I *want* it, it *is*." That's why typical (E)s will say, "We *sold* a million dollars' worth of goods," but when the (A)s ask where the contract is, (E)s might answer, "Well, the client is meeting next week to decide." You see the (E) said "sold" as if it *is*, while in reality it was still in the realm of *want* and *should*. An (E) might say, "We are the leaders of our industry." People are surprised. He continues, "You will see, we will be." He confused the *want* of the future with the *is* of the present.

*This reminds me of a manager who said at a meeting, "We are the best company in the industry." When she was challenged, she said, "Well, we have all the ingredients to be the best."*

If you study history you will find many examples of wars conducted with this confusion. Many people have died because a leader was a dictatorial (E) who operated exclusively on the *want* perception, ignoring *is* and subordinating the *should* to serve the *want* exclusively.

*Do you have an example?*

Hitler, towards the end of World War II, was conducting the war on the map of Europe using his fingers to measure distances, ignoring reality, and executing messengers who communicated the bad news of that reality.

*Who perceives that since something should be, it is, disregarding the* want?

(A)s. If you ask an (A), "Do we have a solution to this problem?" He might say, "Yes, we do! We spent a million dollars on it, didn't we?" You might challenge that statement by saying, "I know we *should* have a solution because we spent a million dollars, but that's not the question. *Do* we have a solution?" When do we *have* a solution? Only if it *is* working.

Now tell me, which type perceives that what *is*, is? To hell with the *wants* and *shoulds*, they say.

*The (P)s.*

Yes, and who is continuously dancing around so that you can't figure out if they are talking about what they believe *is*, what they *want*, or what they believe *should* be?

*The (I)s.*

(I)s are capable of understanding the differences because they don't really have an exclusive process by which they come to reality. At the same time, they do not reveal their thoughts, since they want to read yours first.

*That can create a lot of confusion.*

The confusion stems from the fact that different people perceive the world differently, as we've discussed several times already. An (E) comes to a meeting and says, "We sold (*is*) a million dollars."

The (A) responds, "Where *is* the contract?"

The (E) says, "We *are* going to get the contract next week after they decide."

"No chance they will sign the contract" says the (A). "We *are* far too expensive. We are not competitive." (*should* = *is*)

"Yes, but we *should* have the contract soon," responds (E). "I love our product. How can they resist buying it?" (*want* = *should be*)

Perhaps the (I) intervenes and says, "Now let's talk this over. What is the problem?"

Meanwhile (P) just wants to finish the meeting, get back to work, and avoid this interpersonal nonsense. "Listen guys! Do we have a contract or don't we?" (*is* = *is*)

> People continually confuse *is*, *want*, and *should*. When we only look at value, it is not a *should*, it is a *want*.

How does understanding these differences in perception help you with collaborative decision making?

Whenever I conduct meetings with companies that I'm coaching to Prime, I insist that the words *is*, *want*, and *should* be used in the (P) sense. So if people say, "We *are* the leaders of the industry," they had better be speaking in (P) language. If they are not the leaders, I expect people in a meeting to say, "We *want* to be the leader of the industry, but we *are* not yet. What we *should* do in order to become the leader is..."

Do you see how I'm using the words now? If you sit in a meeting and listen carefully to the way people talk, you'll find they continually confuse *is*, *want*, and *should*. Instead of saying, "I *want* to do something," which might be uncomfortable to say, they say, "We *should* do that." I reserve the word *should* only for those situations where the value is higher than the cost. When we only look at value, it is not a *should*, it is a *want*.

*Is there a particular sequence for using the three perceptions in leading change? Which one should we use first?*

It's like having three different colored lenses for your camera: the sequence in which you put them on determines the color of the picture you get. The usual mistake in planning is to start with *want*. It is assumed that planning can't be successful without dreaming. As George Bernard Shaw said, "The reasonable man adapts himself to the world; the unreasonable one persists in trying to adapt the world to himself. Therefore all progress depends on the unreasonable man."

But if you start with unreasonable dreaming, insisting on something that *does* not and *cannot* ever work, it can become a nightmare. Somebody has to wake up and say, what *is* the reality? Planning should start with what *is*. It is like a medical diagnosis, which has to precede prescription. Once you have analyzed what *is* going on, you move on to what you *want* to do, from which you derive what you *should* do.

> The way to make change is to first accept reality.

The sequence for planning then should be: what *is* the situation; in light of that, what do we *want* it to be; and in light of constraints on the *want*, what *should* we do. Then go do it to create the new *is*. Avoid the childish trap of "since I *want* it, it *should* be, and it *is* going to be." Arsonists can be "spoiled brats." That's how (E)s sometimes destroy what they've built. They stay attached to their big enterprise and the dream it represents. They refuse to recognize what *is*, clinging to the *want* perception exclusively. They're not willing to budge, and as they refuse to recognize that their dream *is* not working, piece by piece they lose what they worked so hard to build.

The way to make change is to first accept reality. The way to move on is to accept where you are. As long as you fight your present state, you won't have the energy to move toward the future. Once you accept reality, all your energy is available to make change. Thus, managing the change sequence, organizational therapy, must start with *is*.

The sequence for changing a situation should be: *is*⟶*want*⟶*should*⟶new *is*.

If you confuse the sequences, you're a fanatic. The philosopher George Santayana said that a fanatic, having misunderstood what the reality is, doubles, triples, and quadruples his efforts. That's how he gets stuck deeper and deeper in the sand.

No change is possible without accepting reality first. For instance, you are not going to lose weight until you admit you're overweight.

> *From what I understand of Arsonists they have a hard time accepting reality.*

They do. Arsonists cling to dreams even after they become nightmares. Often, they wait and rely on miracles. The founding Prime Minister of Israel, Ben Gurion, when asked how Israel was going to survive an attack by the neighboring Arab nations, said: "Those that do not believe in miracles are not realists."

> *But you told me Arsonists change direction all the time, remember? The big wheel turns back and forth while the little wheels get ground to dust. Now you tell me they do not change.*

> Arsonists cling to dreams even after they become nightmares.

The globe is not flat. Is it? If you keep going right you will end up on the left. The same is true for love versus hate, hot versus cold. If you have a fever, you feel cold. If you love someone very, very much, you have the beginnings of resentment. The same holds true with change versus stability. Have you looked at wheels turning very fast? They appear to stay in one place. The more it changes the more it is the same.

Nothing can be more permanent than a continuous temporary. (E)s change everything except change itself. The more things change, at a certain point, they don't change. (E)s believe they make strategic decisions while, at best, their decisions have only a tactical impact. Too much change has the impact of no change. It is a continuous mess.

Arsonists might make many, many changes, except to the dream itself. So, although there are many changes, nothing really changes.

# CONVERSATION 13
# Quality of People

*Could you please summarize what we've covered?*

Let's do it together.

In order to manage we need to decide and implement. It's impossible for one person to make good decisions all the time. We need to consult with others. We need a complementary team, composed of different people with different styles. Naturally, this generates conflict.

When time comes to implement the decision we need common interests of those whose cooperation we need for the implementation to be successful. That also creates conflict of interests.

But we make it work by creating a climate of Mutual Trust and Respect, so we can learn from each other. We talked about creating common vision and values, the right (PAEI) structure, and the kind of communication needed for collaborative decision making. But we also need the right kind of people, who command and grant trust and respect. We have to create a group of colleagues.

We look for someone who will complement our argument by pointing out the weaknesses. By incorporating criticism, the argument grows stronger.

*That is, as long as there is mutual respect.*

Absolutely. Conflict does not destroy a marriage. Conflict is to be expected because we each fell in love with and married someone who was different from us. What destroys a marriage is not what we fight about, but *how* we fight.

A study conducted at Yale University followed a select group of married couples over many years. The purpose was to find the personality traits that predict which couples will stay together. What they found is very interesting. There are no personality traits that predict who will stay married. Instead, they found that what predicts the survivability of marriages is not the differences in personalities, but how the couples handle the differences. I believe mutual respect is the factor that determines how the differences are handled.

Marriage counselors are reporting something else very interesting. The reasons people divorce are the same reasons they marry. We are attracted by our differences, not similarities. Since we know we are not perfect individually, we usually choose a mate who is strong in areas where we are weak. This is wonderful before we get married, but what might happen later? The differences that were so attractive before become a source of difficulty later. People who cannot handle those differences end up divorcing or suffering a lot.

A marriage may also have conflict in capi. Conflicting interests are brought about by dual careers. What is good for one might hurt the interests of the other. Couples should not dream about a utopian marriage in which there is no conflict. Expect conflict and learn how to harness it, rather than running away from it or getting depressed about it.

> *Can conflict be constructive in a marriage?*

Sure. For example, in some marriages, conflict is a source of bonding. Some couples grow closer after their conflict than they were before. Other couples grow further apart with each fight. What is the difference? It is not the content of the conflict, but how they handle it.

You have probably had a fight with your spouse or someone else close to you. Years later, you don't remember the details of the fight, but you never forgot how it was fought. You still get a bad taste in your mouth remembering it. What you will never forget is whether you can trust and respect that person.

It is Mutual Trust and Respect that make conflict constructive or destructive. I have advice for you: Any time you disagree with someone, watch closely how you disagree more than what you disagree about.

> *I must respect people in spite of their being different in style and judgment.*

As Otto von Bismarck said, "Respectfully even to the gallows."

> *I must develop a system that nurtures mutual trust in spite of the conflict of interests.*

Leadership excellence can be achieved in an organization of colleagues who communicate well, and who are also friends and thus cooperate. They have Mutual Trust and Respect for each other, so they have both synergistic and symbiotic relationships.

*I can see the banner covering the building: "Managerial excellence through teamwork: cooperation, communication, and Mutual Trust and Respect."*

Not bad!

*But how do we know whether we have that communication, cooperation, respect, and trust?*

You can see it in body language. When a decision is made in a climate of mutual respect, people turn to each other. They congregate and make decisions together. They face each other. Once they agree on a decision, if they also trust each other they can afford to turn their backs to each other while implementing the decision.

In a climate without MT&R, body language is just the opposite. Because people don't respect each other's opinions, they will most likely turn their backs to each other during decision making. When they set out to implement the decision, because they don't trust each other, they will face each other and inspect each other.

Tell me which way you face during decision making and implementation, and I will tell you how well managed your organization is.

*Is there another way to tell how well managed an organization is?*

Yes. Making a decision together, rather than individually, takes more time. In organizations managed with mutual respect, it takes longer to make a decision because people make it together. But implementation is swift because people trust each other to perform the assigned tasks. They aren't back-seat drivers, and there are no arguments. Disagreements were dealt with proactively in making the decision.

In a badly managed organization, where there is no trust and respect, people make decisions very fast because they make them individually. But implementing takes forever, because of the back-seat driving and continuous second guessing—because there is no trust.

Well-managed organizations manage the "long short" way, while badly managed organizations take the "short long" way.

> *This helps me understand the Japanese approach to management as compared to the American approach. In the United States, decisions are made quickly but implementation is slow. In Japan, it takes a long time to make decisions, but implementation is fast.*

A German manager once asked me why a Japanese competitor was so fast with innovations, when the German company had the same R&D budget. I replied, "They are faster because they are slower." He thought I was trying to be funny.

The Japanese practice a lot of mutual respect. One characteristic of Japanese culture is that losing face is shameful. One may even be driven to commit hara-kiri because of it. And to cause someone else to lose face is even worse.

> *What about mutual trust?*

Japanese companies are committed to the employee for the long term and expect the same commitment in return. This mutual commitment creates a climate of mutual trust. It is this trust that nourishes a win-win climate and encourages cooperation.

> *Unfortunately, it's not always that way in America. Sometimes management takes care of itself first and the employees later, if at all. When a company is in trouble, management uses its golden parachutes and fires the workers. Then Americans are surprised that unions don't necessarily want to cooperate with management. Why should they?*

When you trust and respect, you care; and when you care, you listen; and when you listen, you learn. The end result is a symbiotic synergistic relationship.

Some relationships are only synergistic without being symbiotic. Democracy, capitalism, a market economy—these systems are designed for growth. They are synergistic but not symbiotic; the rich might get richer while the poor get poorer. Conversely, the socialist system tries to coalesce interests—the proletariat, intelligentsia, farmers—into a classless society. Communists tried to create a symbiotic society, but it wasn't synergistic. As British Prime Minister Winston Churchill observed, "Capitalism is an unequal distribution of wealth. Communism is an equal distribution of poverty."

> *So what do we need? Both systems?*

Yes. A true social democratic system that is both synergistic and symbiotic. In other words, one that prospers and grows while protecting the common interest of the total society. The short description of this hybrid system will be adversarial relations outside the company—market economy, capitalism in market forces—and socialism, caring for each other, inside the company. This includes the community because the people working in the company belong to that community.

## The Common Denominator of Success

The success of any system—whether it is micro or macro, whether it is a single human being, a family, an organization, or a society—can be predicted by one and only one factor: the ratio of external integration to internal disintegration.

$$\text{Success} = f \left\{ \frac{\text{External Integration}}{\text{Internal DISintegration}} \right\}$$

External integration is the amount of resources an organization invests in identifying and satisfying client needs, and finding changing opportunities that the company's capabilities can satisfy profitably. Strategic planning and marketing perform this role.

If you take all books on marketing or strategic planning and summarize them, then summarize the summaries, at the end the kernel of knowledge is this: how to match opportunities to capabilities successfully. It involves, for instance, market segmentation and product differentiation, among other things.

Internal disintegration is how much managerial energy is wasted inside the organization, and is a function of Mutual Trust and Respect. If there is little or no Mutual Trust and Respect, the energy spent on internal disintegration will be very high. It is wasted on rumors, accusations, judging each other, and destructive conflicts.

The laws of physics tell us that energy at any point in time is fixed. There is no perpetual endless energy. What I have discovered in my work is that this fixed energy is allocated in a predictable way: First it goes to handle internal disintegration, then what is left, if any, goes to external integration.

*Can you give me an example please?*

Assume you visit a friend who is in a hospital. He was in a car accident. The doctor might ask you to limit your visit to no longer than five minutes. Why? Because your friend has no energy for you. He needs all his energy to heal himself. Sick people sleep a lot because they need the energy to get better. Imagine you are very ill, and someone wants to discuss with you a strategic plan on how to penetrate, say, the New York market. You will probably tell her to come back later. Why? You have no energy to deal with the subject.

> *The secret to finding another person is finding yourself first.*

Since human energy, at any point, is fixed, the amount of energy available for external integration depends on how much energy is spent on internal disintegration. The formula applies to individuals, to family life, to companies, and to countries.

If people suffer from low self-esteem, low self-respect, and low self-trust, they'll be riddled with inner conflicts. They may be good looking, smart, and rich, yet they will be unable to have a successful relationship or career. Most of their psychological energy is spent dealing with problems that stem from their low self-respect and self-trust.

When human beings lack self-respect and self-trust, most of their energy is spent between their ears. They are worried about what people think of them. They are trying to find out who they are and what they should do. Little energy is left over to deal with the outside world. Before they can meet someone else and develop a relationship, they must first learn to trust and respect themselves. The secret to finding another person is finding yourself first.

You probably know of some physically attractive people who have little or no success with the opposite sex. At the same time, you probably know people who are not especially attractive but who are very much in demand. What is happening? The first type exudes no energy. Lacking self-trust and respect, these people project indecisiveness and rejection. The other type, who do respect and trust themselves, have all their energy available to focus on their partners. They are attractive because they exude energy.

The condition for loving others is loving yourself first, but that does not mean being selfish. It means having mind, body, emotions, and spirit all in synchronicity, and having trust and respect for those four aspects of one's self when they are in conflict.

Respecting your own vulnerability and weakness, and trusting that you will eventually find the right solution is the secret of success. Success is not the destination, but the condition of your journey. Self-respect and self-trust means having faith in yourself—a precondition for having faith in others. There is no faith unless you love yourself, and to love yourself means to accept your inner conflicts and integrate your mind, body, emotions, and spirit into a whole. It is this peacefulness and self-acceptance that make people attractive and beautiful from the inside out.

People who are in inner conflict are tense and spread pain around them. They are neither good spouses nor good leaders. Having a facelift, driving fancy cars, or indulging in other forms of conspicuous consumption will make them physically attractive, but only for a short while at best. Physical beauty is skin deep, as they say

Educating our children means instilling trust and respect. Self-trust and self-respect. Respect for the body and for the emotions. Respect for parents, elders, teachers, the society we live in, and, yes, respect for the flag.

It is more important to educate children to "be" rather than to "know." What children know will often become obsolete in a very short time. Who they are will last a lifetime.

> *You know, I think the (A)s took over educational institutions. They measure know-how ad nauseam with standardized testing. It is an efficient education, but I doubt its effectiveness. It teaches you to know but does not teach you to be.*

I agree, but let's continue to the next level of analysis. Let's assume that we have people who are centered, who have self-respect and self-trust. They have energy to deal with the outside world, except that they have a disastrous family situation devoid of respect and trust. They have problems with their parents or spouses or children. Where is their energy spent now?

Research shows that executives who go through a divorce are practically useless to the corporation for about two years. They can't succeed during that time, not because they are objectively bad, but because at that point in time their energy is going somewhere else. For them, success is to survive the upheaval with the fewest scars possible. Perhaps one source for the slow decline of productivity in the United States is the breakdown of the American family. One thing is certain: Low American productivity is not caused by a lack of technology or financial resources.

Let's look at the next level now: people who know who they are, who they are not, and have a supportive, respectful, and trusting family. All their energy is available to deal with their career, but their organizations have no culture of Mutual Trust and Respect. Marketing is fighting sales; production is fighting engineering; accounting is fighting everyone. When the client arrives, what can this person say? "Come back tomorrow, I am exhausted today."

Now, let's assume we have an organization with common vision and values, and the right structure, process, and people. It has developed and nurtured Mutual Trust and Respect, but it operates in a society riddled with corruption and hatred between religions, nationalities, and races. Now what? Can it compete well internationally? Where is the energy of that country going? How much energy is there left if the unions fight management, the military fights the government, and the government fights the people? Without respect and trust, where is the money going? To Switzerland! The country might be rich in resources, but it cannot succeed because its relationships are bankrupt.

> If we are strong inside, we can deal with any outside problem and handle it as an opportunity.

Compare the successful economies of Japan and Switzerland, nations with few physical resources, to some of the developing nations rich in oil, gas, diamonds, and other resources. The developing nations can't use their resources constructively because of their internal conflicts. Colonial powers exploited them, and the native governments often behave the same way after independence. The colonial powers brought the missing elements of (A) and (E) to the colonies. In order to dominate, colonizers would often dis(I)ntegrate a colony by turning one religious or ethnic group against the other. When the colonialists left, they took away the (E) and left behind a huge (A) and a broken (I), thereby causing low (P). This is the inheritance of many Third World countries.

The tragedy of colonialism is not what the colonists took out of the colonies, but the culture and system they left behind or reinforced—a culture of elitism, exploitation, control, and bureaucracy. Third World countries now need to bring the weakened (I) component of their culture together. Peace first. Peace among Muslims and Hindus. Peace in Angola, and in South Africa. Only after (I) grows will the next job be to debureaucratize the government, i.e., reduce (A). Only then can these countries build (E)ntrepreneurship and, as (E) increases, (P) will start growing.

> *For success, a culture of MT&R is critical and indispensable for sustainable economic growth.*

Absolutely. What you have is the result of who you are, while who you are is not the result of what you have.

What all the above examples illustrate is that success comes from within. Too many companies worry exclusively about strategic planning and about how to beat their competitors. They are like the universe: expanding in the margins while collapsing at the core.

Success comes from the inside. If we are strong inside, we can deal with any outside problem and handle it as an opportunity. If we are weak inside, then every outside opportunity will be perceived as a problem.

The problem with America is America, not global competition. It is the American system that has less Mutual Trust and Respect than, say, the Japanese. Who are the Americans beating? Societies with even less Mutual Trust and Respect than the American system. True, we have to take into account other factors such as size and resources, but just imagine how much more these countries could be doing if they could capitalize on Mutual Trust and Respect.

In a recent lecture in Johannesburg, I said that South Africa is at a major intersection in its history. It can become either the Switzerland or the Balkans of Africa. It will depend on whether it can develop a culture of Mutual Trust and Respect.

*So the way to improve the performance of a company, a country, or a person is not by changing strategy, but by changing the internal environment?*

Right. Once you change the internal environment, the right strategy and direction will emerge more easily. Without a healthy internal environment, even the best strategy will have great difficulty being implemented.

*But if that's true, some countries could be very successful.*

Sure. Take Israel, for example. It has people from more than seventy different countries who have come together after being separated for two thousand years. It is a true United Nations. These differences create a tremendous amount of energy, which, if channeled with Mutual Trust and Respect, could make Israel an enormous success.

*What stands in its way?*

Historically, Jewish people were prohibited from having a country of their own and from doing manual labor. They were therefore unable to develop strong (P) and (A) traits, and developed strong (E) and (I) qualities instead. For (E)s, respect is a challenge. (E)s are usually quite arrogant and feel they know better than others. Trust is also a problem for (E)s. They have strong tendencies toward paranoia. Furthermore, for Jews, especially after thousands of years of persecution culminating in the Holocaust, trust does not come easily.

Increasing the level of respect and trust in Israel would take more than just talking. In light of the Jewish historical experience, realistically speaking, Israel can't take chances and act as if it trusts the world. It is thus in trouble, although it seems to be doing well economically.

Using the same tools of analysis, there will be no peace in the Middle East until MT&R is established.

*What about Europe?*

Europe as a European Union could have been a giant. It is rich with cultural diversity, a market economy, and open borders. It could have become a serious contender for world leadership if it overcame its history of disrespect and mistrust.

*But that did not happen.*

In spite of common market, it is without common fiscal and monetary policy. The system has too much (A).

*Looking at our chart, I notice something that you haven't explained yet. Why is the road to destructive conflict a straight highway, while the path to constructive conflict appears to be a complicated route?*

# QUALITY OF PEOPLE – 243

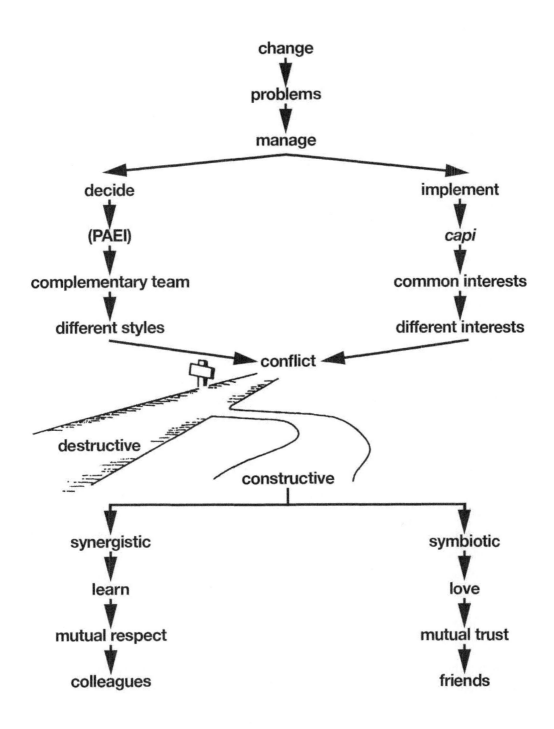

The road to destructive conflict is easy because there is nothing you need to do to make conflict destructive. It is destructive by itself because of change. As we discussed earlier, if you leave a machine unused and unattended for a while, it won't start. "But I didn't do anything to it," you might complain. That's right, and that's why it won't work.

Time is change, and unattended change is destructive by its own nature. This is the principle of entropy, in which every system naturally tends toward chaos. To make change constructive, you have to work on it.

*But why the complicated exit to constructive conflict? Why is the exit sign in small letters?*

So that only people who drive slowly and carefully can see the sign pointing to the exit.

*Why must they drive slowly?*

Have you ever noticed how people in conflict behave? They are in pain. And what do they do when they feel pain?

*They speed up.*

Yes! They speed straight down the highway of destructive conflict. They raise their voices, talk faster, call other people names, or even storm out of the room. What's happening? They can't take the pain. Those who relax, slow down, and keep a cool head have a chance to resolve the conflict, or at least a chance to understand it. They're the ones who can see the sign and take the constructive road.

*How do you slow down?*

The tougher the situation is, the more relaxed everyone needs to be. I have found by working with senior executives around the world that the most successful ones are those I call "duck managers." A duck appears calm as it floats along on top of the water, but under the water its feet are paddling as fast as they can. Likewise, a good manager can be relaxed in spite of the conflict. He doesn't lose his head or objectivity about a subject, and never deals with conflict in a destructive, disrespectful way.

*You mean a good leader is a person who knows how to disagree without being disagreeable?*

That's right. Think Yiddish, act British. Or, to quote an English proverb, use soft words and hard arguments. This principle applies to everyone—not only to managers, but to spouses, children, and parents as well. Some people do the opposite and agree disagreeably. Even if you reach an agreement with them, you don't want to repeat the experience. It was too painful.

*Yes, I know. Arguing with emotional people is exhausting.*

That is true in international relations too. How we handle our enemy is extremely important. Never show disrespect to your enemy. You will never find peace that way. Even wars have to be handled respectfully. You must communicate trustworthiness or the end of one war will simply sow the seeds for the next one. The resentments Germany harbored after World War I sowed the seeds of World War II. After World War II, however, the United States wisely proposed the Marshall Plan to Europe, and the United States reconstructed Germany. If it had not done so, Germany would not be part of NATO today.

You must always leave a way for your opponent not to lose face, or the next time you will face a far more determined enemy. During the Yom Kippur War in 1973, it is reported that then-Secretary of State Henry Kissinger prevented the Israelis from advancing too far into Egypt, claiming that Egypt must not be crushed or Israel would never find peace.

A system must be based on trust and respect and should control any attempts to destroy that base.

*How about anti-democratic parties within a democracy?*

In my judgment, democratic societies act properly when they ban parties that are anti-democratic and have no respect for the democratic process. Otherwise, totalitarian political parties can gain power democratically and then abolish the democratic system, as the Nazi party did. This should not be allowed. The philosopher Herbert Marcuse expressed this well when he wrote, "There can be no tolerance toward systems that renounce tolerance."

*The political application of Mutual Trust and Respect is very interesting, but right now my problems are with management. Tell me more about the kinds of people needed to make conflict constructive.*

# The People Factor: Identifying Leaders

To make conflict constructive, one of the factors we must focus on is the people; we must have people who command, and grant, respect and trust.

Staff people (as opposed to line managers, who have to produce the results for which the company exists), have a functional responsibility in marketing, data processing, or accounting. You may be able to put up with their individual style as long as they know their professional field. But once people become line managers, who they are is more important than what they know. If they don't know something, they can hire whomever they need to advise them. A very successful corporate president once told me, "I have three doctorates although I never finished high school." I asked him how that was possible. "Easy," he said, "I hired them." Know-how is easy to get; you can hire good people. To be is much more difficult. Being trusted and respected is critical for being a leader.

*But what do you do with people who do not grant or command respect and trust?*

Recommend them to your competitors. That will undermine those companies more than your most competitive products. Sow dissension within your competition. Let them start fighting and wasting energy while you surround yourself with people who command and grant respect and trust, and emerge victorious.

*What about people who have only one of these characteristics? For instance, what if they command respect but don't grant it?*

That's not good in the long term. People who give respect but don't command it aren't good even in the short term. If the people aren't trustworthy, I don't care how much they know, they cannot succeed as leaders, managers, or parents. Period.

Tell me how much respect you command and grant, how trusting and trustworthy you are, and I'll tell you whether you're a good leader, a good parent, or a good spouse. In short, I'll tell you what kind of a human being you are.

*So being the right kind of human being is part of managing well?*

That is the essence of it all. A good manager (or parent, or spouse, or political leader) is not valued for what he knows but for who he is. It is easier to hire someone who is and teach him to know, than it is to hire someone who knows and teach him to be.

If we were to randomly read some resumes, we would find that what people write about themselves is (P) and (A) oriented: what they have done, what degrees they've earned, and what titles they've held. It doesn't tell us much about who they are as human beings. Are they respected? Do they disagree in a way that is enriching to others? Do they even know how to disagree? The resume does not say whether they are trustworthy. Maybe they're human sharks who attack the moment they smell blood. Maybe they'll knife you if you turn your back on them. This information doesn't appear on a resume, but it's the most important thing managers need to know about a person they are going to hire.

*How do you decide whom to hire then?*

Call former employers to find out whether your applicants are trustworthy and respected. Ask how they contributed and how they handled disagreements. You want to know what kind of people they are.

*Isn't it difficult to get that kind of information?*

Yes. In the United States there are laws that make this information difficult to obtain. Nevertheless, you should look for leaders. Remember, the difference between managers, mismanagers, and leaders can be expressed by the (PAEI) code. Mismanagers have one or more blanks in the code. Any single blank makes them mismanagers. Managers have a complete code but have low (I). For example, big (P)s with small (aei)s are normal managers. They are (P)roducers. They'll be good first-line supervisors but won't go beyond that unless they are flexible and willing to learn and change. To be a leader you must have high (I) plus one or more of the other roles.

In a complementary team, people have to link up. People with blanks in their code cannot link up with people who excel in that missing role. What's more, people who are not well rounded will have considerable difficulty changing and growing.

Leaders—who by our definition should have high (I)—are aware of their strengths and weaknesses. When you interview someone for a job, one of the first questions should be, "What are your strengths and what are your weaknesses?" The person who says "I don't have any weaknesses" or "my weaknesses are my strengths" shouldn't be hired. People who don't know their weaknesses don't know who they are. I would be afraid of working with them or for them.

*Why would they be a problem?*

To command and grant respect, you have to know who you are. Only by knowing who you are will you be able to identify what other styles you need to build a complementary team.

*I can identify the styles of those around me, yet I'm having difficulty identifying my own style in (PAEI) terms.*

This is common. My friend, Professor Sam Culbert of the John E. Anderson Graduate School of Management at UCLA, says it takes two to know one. No one knows himself in a vacuum. We see ourselves through the eyes of others. We know ourselves through the impact we have on others. Logically, if we know the managerial style of others, it makes sense that others will know our own style. They respond to or cope with our style. That's why Lone

Rangers develop gofers, Bureaucrats have yes-yes clerks, and Arsonists prefer subordinates who behave like claques.

If you want to know who you are, watch the impact you have on others. Be sensitive to how people react to you. Watch how your subordinates and peers behave. Be open to receiving feedback.

Many years ago I was lecturing in Mexico. I lectured in English and was assisted by a simultaneous translator. I grew tired of the translation because the audience was reacting to the material a minute later—my lecture was out of sync. So I asked the audience whether they would prefer if I spoke in Ladino, the fifteenth-century language I used with my family, a mixture of Spanish, Italian, and Portuguese. The audience agreed.

It was quite arrogant on my part to lecture twentieth-century material in an archaic language, but I tried, and something very interesting happened. When I asked the audience, in fifteenth-century Spanish, "Did you hear me?" they winced as if I had said something very strange. I asked in English, "What did I say?" Someone answered, "You asked us if we felt you. The verb to hear in modern Spanish is *escuchar* and you were using the word *sentir*, which means to feel."

At that moment, I had an illumination. Five hundred years ago, the senses of hearing, feeling, and listening could all be expressed in one word: *sentir*. It really means to sense. Even today, in modern Spanish, when somebody is hard of hearing, people say he is *mal de sentido*, literally "hard of feeling."

What has happened over the last five hundred years? In Spanish, we now have several words instead of one from the past. It means some people can hear without listening, and some people listen but don't feel what you say. They can repeat every word, even analyze them, but they don't feel what you say. Five hundred years ago, since *sentir* was only one word, it meant that people heard, listened, and felt what they heard. They were more in touch with each other.

> *Interesting. The same is true in Greek. On the island of Corfu, where they speak a somewhat older dialect of Greek because of its isolation, the words for feel and hear are the same too.*

You want a leader, spouse, or parent who not only hears or only listens to what is being said, but feels what is being said. Our technological and economic development has been accompanied by increasing emotional and social isolation. I find people in developing countries hear and feel what I say better than those in developed countries.

I had another illumination when I was in Chicago one cold winter. I was driving my car in a big snowstorm. Outside it was freezing, but inside the car it was so warm that I removed my jacket. I sat only an inch and a half away from the freezing cold, yet I was very comfortable.

The same phenomenon occurs emotionally in modern life. Technology has trained us to tune out. We box ourselves in. Out there, people are falling apart emotionally, but we stay within our own space and pay no attention to them. We have learned how to separate feeling from hearing from listening. Consider the expression "tune out." We treat people like a radio station we don't want to listen to.

For some people, the time it takes to make the transition from hearing to listening to feeling is quite long. A friend told me that his dog senses instantly how he feels when he gets home from work. As soon as he walks through the door, the dog either jumps on him or, if he is upset, goes to the corner, curls into a ball, and waits. On the other hand, it takes my friend forever to communicate how he feels to his wife. By the time she hears, then listens, then feels, he is even more upset.

Let's summarize: For good leadership we need Mutual Trust and Respect, which means that good leaders are people who command and grant respect. What sort of people are they? First, their style is well rounded. They don't excel in everything, but they're capable of adequately performing all roles. They have strengths and weaknesses, but no blanks in their (PAEI) code.

Second, good leaders know themselves. A way to know yourself is by paying attention to what you do to others. Are you aware of how others respond to you? That will tell you who you are.

Good leaders are people who hear, listen, and feel. They do not just hear without listening or listen without feeling. They are sensitive to the impact they have on others. They are conscious. They are present.

People who don't know themselves are usually the ones who think they know exactly who they are. They live in a vacuum; they don't allow feedback from the outside.

Good leaders accept their strengths and their weaknesses, because the first condition for accepting the weaknesses of others is accepting your own. If you cannot accept yourself, how will you accept others?

*I hear you loud and clear. Mutual Trust and Respect must begin with self-respect and self-trust. These qualities grow from the inside out. To achieve good leadership, first look inward.*

Good leaders can identify in other people the strengths that they lack in themselves. This is very difficult, though. Big (E)s can identify other big (E)s, but they don't know how to identify and evaluate an (A)'s strengths. They don't know what criteria to apply. As a matter of fact, they don't even like (A)s.

That's why good leaders should have a well-rounded style. They are in touch with what they do, have a balanced view of themselves, accept their weaknesses, and can identify the strengths of others in areas where they are weak. Furthermore, they accept others who are better than they are in certain respects, because they accept that they are not good at everything. They can deal with the conflicts that stem from those differences. They are secure enough not to be threatened by disagreements. They can hear, listen, and feel. In essence, they can create a learning environment.

*Can you list the qualities of a good leader?*

Sure. Good leaders are people who:

1) Have a well-rounded, flexible style

2) Know themselves

3) Are aware of their effect on others

4) Have a balanced view of themselves

5) Accept their own weaknesses

6) Can identify strengths in others

7) Accept others who are different

8) Can harness conflict

9) Create a learning environment

*In short, they are mature people.*

Yes, maturity makes good leaders. Maturity comes from experience, and experience comes from making bad judgments and learning from them. The process of maturation is accompanied by pain. It involves losing attachments to your past to make space for new attachments in the future. Not everybody knows how to lose those attachments, how to let go. Winning is easy, losing is difficult. A good leader is one who comes out a winner after he loses. The road to heaven is through hell.

*So you are against the fast track that allows young business school graduates to start at the top of the management pyramid?*

Absolutely. They are frequently propelled to the top by what they know, not by who they are. They don't have the experience that teaches them maturity and humility. Good leaders are humble. They know their weaknesses and seek the assistance of others. In Spanish there are three levels of knowing: 1) to know information; 2) to know how to do something; and 3) to know how to be.

In modern society we overemphasize the knowing of information, the how-to, and almost ignore the critical importance of how to be. Leaders must know how to be if they want to command and grant respect and trust.

*This conversation was good, but heavy.*

There is more to come.

# CONVERSATION 14
# How to Convert Committee Work into Teamwork

Once I was invited to lecture in Canada. The chief executive officer of the host company picked me up at the airport the evening before the lecture, and invited me to a hospitality suite to meet the other executives attending the program. They were playing poker. There were three tables with four executives at each one. They joked and laughed; their energy was high. Hundreds of dollars changed hands. It was well past midnight when they finally stopped playing.

As they were leaving, I noticed something very interesting. At one o'clock in the morning, after playing poker all night, their adrenaline was still flowing. They said, "Great game! Let's get together again soon."

I wondered about what had happened. If I had taken those same executives and put them in a meeting where they would have to make decisions on say, budgeting, they would've been exhausted after two hours, drained of energy. None of them would look forward to the next committee meeting.

Seeing this exhilaration, I wondered about the difference between playing poker and attending a committee meeting.

If the same executives were given a group assignment to make a decision, why wouldn't they behave the same way they did in the poker game? Tell me, what's the difference between playing cards and conducting management by committee meetings?

*They were playing, having fun.*

Fun is the outcome, not the cause.

*They like the challenge in poker.*

They compete in business as well. That's certainly a challenge.

*They all start with an equal chance?*

True, but you could say the same in business as well.

*Rules! The game has explicit rules.*

Right. You wouldn't play poker, or any other game, with people who violate the rules. You wouldn't trust them. All games have rules.

That poker game inspired me to write training programs on participatory management by teamwork, rather than by committee.

> Life is one long game and you'd better learn the rules.

When children make up games, the first thing they do is agree upon the rules. If someone breaks the rules, they stop playing and fight.

Any interdependence in life is governed by rules, we just have to discover them. There is no functional interdependence without rules of conduct, although we do not always understand or have an awareness of these rules. Life, my friend, is one long game, and you'd better learn the rules.

*So where does this take us? Why is knowing the rules and playing by them so important?*

There is no teamwork without Mutual Trust and Respect, and there is no Mutual Trust and Respect without adherence to mutually agreed upon rules of conduct.

*If that's true, then following the appropriate rules will also result in teamwork.*

Now you understand. Here's what I did: I applied (A)dministration to (I)ntegration. First, I realized that anything that fosters disrespect or mistrust must be forbidden, and everything that strengthens trust and respect must be encouraged.

*That is the bottom line of your methodology for managing organizational transformations?*

Yes, there must be rules of conduct that foster respect and trust!

*But what does respect mean? How do you generate respect by making rules?*

I found the answer in the work of philosopher Immanuel Kant. He said that respect is the acceptance of the sovereignty of the other party.

*What does sovereignty mean in this case?*

Think of what it means in international relations.

*Sovereignty means that a nation has the legitimate freedom to do what it wants regarding its own internal matters.*

Right, and if a nation makes a decision about its internal matters that we don't like, we can't send our army to force that nation to change its decision. That would violate its sovereignty.

The same applies to interpersonal relations. The day I say, "How dare you think or say that?" I have sent out my metaphorical army to force you to change your mind. I accept your sovereignty to think and speak as you choose because you have the legitimate freedom to form and express your own opinions. If I protest the expression of your opinions or insist that you change them, it is disrespectful because I am violating your sovereignty.

*Mutual respect means, then, that we accept each other's sovereignty to think and express ourselves differently?*

Right.

*How about mutual trust?*

That is a bit more complicated to explain, but let's do it. We said from the beginning of our conversations that change is part of life, right?

*Right.*

In English we say that life is give and take.

*Yes.*

Why don't we say that life is take and give, like in Turkish or Arabic?

*Because when you give first, you trust it will be reciprocated.*

This is important because in the short term there is no win-win, no commonality of interests. Someone wins and someone loses. However, if it is reciprocated, it eventually balances out.

A person will give if he trusts that it will be reciprocated.

Cultures that say take and give have little trust. They are riddled with conflicts. For trust there must be faith.

> *Could you give me some rules that you have tested to guide me through this maze?*

I've developed rules that I tested in many companies in different cultures around the world. I found that people could change their behavior without *talking* about Mutual Trust and Respect, if the structure of the organization was right. Good fences make good neighbors. Where people had common vision and values, and followed the rules of conduct of MT&R in their discussions, guess what? People started *acting* with MT&R; it developed naturally.

You are free to think whatever you want. What I care about is how you behave.

> *That seems so artificial. That would not be honest or genuine. You are preaching manipulation.*

Some people say, "Prove to me that there is God, then I will believe." Other people say, "I believe there is God. Let us find Him." The first group will never find God.

> *Why not?*

For the skeptic there are no answers. For the believers there are no questions. If you believe that there is God you will find God in the smile of a child, in the summer breeze, in a sunset, everywhere you look. If you believe there is no God no proof will suffice to convince you.

We first believe, *then* we go and search for information to support our belief. So start believing in Mutual Trust and Respect. Assume the other person is trustworthy and that there is something to learn from him. Then check the evidence.

Behave as if you trust and can learn from the other person. If the person deserves your trust and your respect, it will grow. If you start with disrespect and mistrust you will never have the chance to develop trust and respect. You will not give other people the chance to prove you wrong.

> *But that means I have to take chances.*

Yes. Start with small doses.

> *This discussion represents a real paradigm shifting in my thinking. What are the rules of conduct?*

They are very simple, but their simplicity makes them powerful. I warn you not to discount their power just because they are simple.

*Why are you warning me?*

Because some people have been conditioned by the academic world to think that if something isn't complicated, it's too simple to be worth anything. In fact, just the opposite is true. I've spent years trying to simplify things, and believe me, it's hard work.

*So tell me, what are those simple but powerful rules you've learned.*

An entire course at the Adizes Institute trains students how to apply the full spectrum of rules, but I'll give you a sample. One rule deals with the starting time of meetings. Meetings don't usually start right on time. The few people who show up on time feel foolish. Important people will probably be late, and the more important they are, the later they believe they can arrive. You can often analyze the whole organizational hierarchy by the order in which people arrive for a meeting. The boss arrives last, and if anyone arrives later than that, it's offensive.

The first rule in this Adizes Methodology is that meetings start on time. This shows respect for everyone attending.

*But what if it's impossible for someone to be on time?*

That's okay. People may be up to ten minutes late as long as they pay an agreed-upon penalty for every minute of tardiness. Latecomers pay their penalty and sit down. Paying the fine indicates that they realize they've broken the rules. It is a symbolic act, not a financial punishment. No explanation for tardiness is necessary and regardless of how legitimate the excuse is, payment is expected nevertheless. As a matter of fact, the penalty should elicit laughter. In many companies, instead of paying money, people have to do push-ups. They can choose to do real push-ups or executive push-ups.

*What are those?*

You bend your knees up and down, up and down. It is funny. Can you see the president of a company doing that? I have Prime Ministers doing that. People laugh. Clap hands. The person doing the knee ups and downs laughs too. It develops camaraderie. And people do not come late if they can help it.

We also end meetings on time, respecting that people might have other assignments.

*I remember why: When meetings get prolonged, (P) pressure emerges and bad judgments are made.*

True. Ending on time also shows that you recognize and respect that the other person has other commitments.

Another rule deals with who speaks in meetings. When people speak about a deep emotional problem or something they've created, they usually keep thinking about what they've said long after they've stopped talking. They're listening to their own mental "tape," checking whether they've said what they wanted to say. When that happens, their eyes usually start wandering. The danger is that somebody else might start talking, but to whom are they listening?

*Obviously to themselves.*

That's why it is very difficult to communicate, especially with creative (E)s. The slightest provocation starts them thinking so intensely that they don't hear others. That's why they're often accused of being arrogant and disrespectful. It isn't out of disrespect that they don't listen; it's because they have so many of their own ideas to consider.

In committee meetings, rather than teamwork sessions as the Adizes Methodology prescribes, when a person finishes speaking, the chairman usually passes the right to speak to somebody else. This procedure is a big mistake. Especially with (E)s, because they are not listening to others and they can dominate the meeting taking most of the floor time. So in Adizes the rule is that no one can interrupt a person who is speaking until that person passes the right to speak to the next person.

*How do we know when someone is finished talking?*

You tell me. Who is the only person in the world who knows that you've finished saying what you wanted to say?

*Me!*

Right. Only the people speaking know when they have finished. Here is the second rule of the Adizes Methodology for managing meetings: People may talk for as long as they wish. If they stop talking, think about what they have said, then resume talking, that's okay. No one else may interrupt. When they really feel they've finished talking, they look to their right, which signals to others who wish to talk that they may raise their hand. The person who has just finished speaking calls on the next person to her right who has a hand raised. Notice she doesn't call the person who raised a hand first, but the first person to her right who has a hand raised. Furthermore, the person speaking must call the next person by first name only.

*Why must they use first names only? Why not use the last name or just gesture to the right? Why not just say "pass" or nod, signifying permission to speak? This sounds terribly constraining. I thought you were an (E); now I think you're a closet (A).*

The only way you can evaluate what I am talking about is by experiencing it, not by analyzing it. Please understand: I have worked out the minutest details of how to convert an organization's culture from one that lacks trust and respect to one that has trust and respect. Theory is nothing until it is tested.

This rule about addressing others by first name only was developed for many reasons. When you are emotionally involved with an issue, you might forget the name of the person to whom you are speaking. It may take a few seconds before you can remember it. For instance, it takes me ten seconds to remember my son's name when I want to address him when I am upset with him.

If you do remember a name, that's a sign that you have finished processing information and are ready to listen to others. If you have difficulty remembering, you haven't really finished thinking. Don't rush it. Go back and think about the issue again. Think about what you have said, restate it, and correct it as many times as necessary, until you're certain you have said what you wanted to say.

When you come back from your deep thoughts, turn to your right, and if you can instantly recall the first name of the person on your right with a hand raised, you have finished thinking and talking.

*Why can't I use his last name?*

There is a good reason for that. Remember when you were a child and your mother or father got upset with you? They would call you by your full name: "Jonathan Smith, it's time for you go to bed." That's how they made it formal. On the other hand, it's harder to be upset when you use a person's first name. This is your insurance policy against the group becoming upset over a subject. If everyone has to call each other by first names, that will lower the level of frustration and hostility. Somebody might be very upset, and speak and speak and speak. When the time comes to pass the permission, that person will usually take a deep breath and calmly say, "Joe." He will not be able to say "JOE!" in an aggressive way. The last name can be expressed in an aggressive way, as was done by our parents, but not the first name. That's the rule for keeping the climate friendly. Furthermore, people love to hear their first name mentioned. It reinforces a supportive climate, no matter how painful the discussion.

*Why not pass to the first person who raises a hand?*

Because then the (E)s will dominate the meeting. (P)s or (E)s will raise their hands first even though they haven't finished thinking about what they want to say. They will do that just to get the floor. They're going to present half-baked ideas. People in the meeting will start behaving aggressively as they compete for airtime. By calling the first person on the right who has a hand raised, you create a situation in which others will simply have to wait.

*Why is waiting so good? That's exactly why I hate meetings. They take forever.*

In Hebrew, the words tolerance, patience, and pain all come from the same root, SVL. That made me think: What we want in teamwork is mutual respect, but there is no mutual respect without mutual tolerance, right?

*Right.*

I can't say, "I respect your opinions, but I don't tolerate them." That doesn't work. There is no respect without tolerance, and there is no tolerance without patience. I can't say, I tolerate your different opinions, but I have no patience to hear them. The only way you can tolerate someone's opinion is to have the patience to hear what she has to say. Now, tolerating different opinions and developing the patience to hear them is painful.

*I can see why so many people show disrespect in committee meetings. They cannot take the pain of being tolerant of people who disagree with them and have no patience to listen to the end of their argument.*

What do people do when they have different opinions and there is little tolerance? They raise their voices and speak quickly. Do you know what they're exhibiting? Pain! They rush through the meeting, trying to escape the pain. They are speeding headlong on the highway to destructive conflict.

Calling on the first raised hand to the right, even though others may have raised their hands first, forces the other people to wait. As they wait, they develop patience, and as they develop patience, they develop tolerance. Slowly, they learn to live with pain.

In my opinion, one of the purposes of management training and development is to increase a person's ability to handle the pain that stems from conflict.

Experienced leaders know how to deal with the pain involved in dealing with people. They're like Teflon: Nothing sticks to them. Less-experienced leaders who can't sustain pain have difficulty managing because they lose their heads at the first twinge of discomfort. They go into backup behavior and misjudge. Experience is important because it helps managers develop the ability to handle interpersonal pain.

In the Adizes Methodology, we train people to become better managers partly by training them to tolerate the pain of listening to people who disagree with them. What happens is very interesting. Here's an example:

Let's say the seventh person down the circle raised a hand first, but the right to speak must be given to the first hand raised to the speaker's right. Let's say the right to speak is passed to several people before it is finally awarded to that seventh person. At first that person was fidgety and anxious to speak, but by the time he is called on, he realizes he has nothing to say, he's changed his mind. While listening to the others, that person learned something. Mutual respect is developing here, because people are learning from each other.

> *You're saying that if we passed the right to speak to the person that raised a hand first, respect wouldn't develop?*

Right. The (E)s and (P)s, who are fast on the draw, would dominate the meeting. The (A)s would take their time to think things over, and the (I)s, who always watch what's going on would never speak. The (E)s would conclude that the (A)s and (I)s have nothing to contribute and would despise them. Instead of mutual respect, mutual disrespect would set in. By being forced to listen to (A)s, the (E)s might realize they aren't the only ones with good ideas.

The best sign that people are learning and that there is mutual respect is when people don't rush to make judgments. After you manage several meetings this way, you'll hear people say, "I have an idea, but I'm not so sure about it. I would like to hear other people's reactions." They have started listening to each other.

> *Would you go over these rules one more time?*

First, whoever speaks may speak for as long as she needs. Nobody may speak or raise a hand while someone else is speaking. People must wait their turn, no rushing, no pressure. When a person finishes talking, and she is the only one who can make that decision, she looks to her right. Whoever wishes to talk should then raise a hand. The person who has finished talking calls on the first person to her right who raised a hand. She must address that next person by first name. The moment she calls the next person's first name, she relinquishes the right to speak. Now only the person called upon may speak.

> *But the person might talk forever. Some people have something to say, and there are others who have to say something. I could grow old listening to the latter type go on and on.*

If you want to make conversations long, make them short. And if you want to make them short, you had better allow them to be long.

> *There you go again. What happens if people speak out of turn?*

Anyone who interferes with the person who is speaking pays a penalty or does push-ups. The money collected for all violations is given to charity.

People know they're not supposed to violate rules when they see the penalty money pile up in front of them. They wait their turn, and then speak softly. In Hebrew we say "*Divrey hachamim benachat nishmaim*," which means, "the words of wise people are listened to peacefully." In Arabic they say, "*Al agial min alshiatan*," meaning "rushing is from the devil." Stupid people shout and scream at each other.

In meetings that are run according to these rules, you know that no one will interrupt, pressure, or override you. You can think fully about what you want to say. You have the time to check whether you said what you meant to say, and you are always able to finish expressing your thoughts. This enables other people to hear you as well. In turns, we go around the circle until we have finished discussing whatever the issue is.

> *Yes, but what happens if one person speaks about subject X, then another talks about subject Y, and someone else starts with Q? Before you know it, you're talking about fifteen different subjects simultaneously and you have lost the original agenda.*

That's why the chairman of the meeting, called the (I)ntegrator, must see to it that people don't change the agenda. The (I)ntegrator must direct the discussion and interrupt the flow as necessary. By doing this the group will not spread itself out in several different directions. As I said, it takes a seven-day course to learn how to lead meetings correctly.

> *What about the penalties? Do they always work?*

Penalties don't work well with extreme (E)s. They don't work well in countries like Israel and Greece, where (E) is prevalent in the culture. In the United States penalties don't work well in young companies that are very (E)ntrepreneurial.

Big (E)s don't care about money. I've seen more than one case where an (E) would get upset, throw ten dollars on the table and say, "Here is one dollar for violating the rule now, and nine dollars for the next nine times I want to speak. Because I want to speak when I want to."

(E)s don't mind losing a hundred dollars in fines in one session as long as they make their opinion heard. For extreme (E)s, I have a different rule. Any time (E)s violate the rules, they lose their turn to speak. There is no bigger punishment for (E)s than not being allowed to speak. So they quiet down, follow the rules, and participate like any other team member.

*Are there more rules?*

Many, many more.

*Have you tested them?*

I've developed a methodology that has been practiced for more than forty years in thousands of companies around the world. It's been validated in different cultures (fifty-two so far) with different technologies and in companies of different sizes. We have taken companies and converted them from cultures with low Mutual Trust and Respect, cooperation, and communication, to ones with strong Mutual Trust and Respect and strong cooperation and communication. We have converted the energy that was being wasted on internal conflicts to energy that can now be directed externally to deal with competition and to satisfy client needs.

*Does it last?*

It works. But the MT&R culture is not stable. If the companies stop practicing Adizes they will lose the advantage the methodology provides.

*Why would they stop?*

Because change, real change, is painful. Adizes is effective, but not popular, so some companies stop. For instance, if a new CEO comes in who is not trained in the Methodology, he can stop the process, change the structure, and dismantle what was painstakingly built.

The difference between teamwork and committee work is:

| COMMITTEE | TEAM |
|---|---|
| Chair person leads discussion and decides | Integrator leads discussion but does not decide |
| No rules for MT&R | Has rules for MT&R |
| Usually low discipline | High discipline/violations punished |
| All (PAEI) roles not necessarily present | (PAEI) roles assigned |
| Might not have *capi* | Must have *capi* |

Pay attention: MT&R is not created just with the above rules. We need common vision and values. We need a (PAEI) organizational structure. We need a process for running meetings correctly. We need the right people. It is more complex than just turning your head to the right and calling someone by their first name.

*Now please give me the bottom line of your theory. What would you say if you had to say it while standing on one foot?*

Build a climate of Mutual Trust and Respect in your organization by having: 1) common vision and values; 2) a (PAEI) diversified structure; 3) a collaborative communication and decision-making process; and 4) mature people who command and grant respect and trust.

That is the essence. That's how you're going to build a better organization, or country, or whatever it is you're managing, including your marriage, children, community, or your life.

*These were very long conversations. How about summarizing them again?*

Why don't you do it?

# Summary

*Management is the process for solving problems that emerge because of change.*

*Those problems have a predictable pattern: some are normal, some are abnormal. They follow an organization's lifecycle.*[40]

---

40  As described in Adizes, *Managing Corporate Lifecycles*, op. cit.

*In order to manage anything well, we must make effective decisions that will solve these problems and we must be able to implement those decisions efficiently.*

*In order to make effective decisions, a complementary team is necessary. None of us alone can make first-class decisions all the time. Furthermore, in order to implement decisions we need a perceived long-term commonality of interests with the people necessary to implement what has been decided.*

*Having a complementary team and common interests is not easy. There will be conflict. This happens because we miscommunicate when we think, speak, and act differently.*

*Commonality of interests is not a common occurrence either. We don't always have a win-win climate. It is another source of conflict. Conflict is a natural part of the process of managing or living.*

*Because management has to deal with change, no management exists without conflict. Different people think differently about what should be done about change. And different people have different interests that are affected by change. Show me change, and I'll show you conflict. The trick to managing change well is to convert the conflict from being destructive to being constructive.*

*Conflict is constructive, synergistic, when people who have different styles learn from each other's differences. Communication, based on rules of conduct for mutual respect, is necessary for this to happen.*

*If there is a perceived win-win climate, at least in the long run, and if we trust each other that short-term imbalances in interests will even out over time, we will cooperate, and conflicts of interest can be channeled into being constructive too.*

*Therefore, good management is teamwork based on Mutual Trust and Respect, on collaborative cooperation and open communication.*

*For successful teamwork we need rules of conduct in the process of decision making that nourish Mutual Trust and Respect. We also need people who are mature and without any blanks in the (PAEI) code, and leaders must have big (I). We need a correctly structured organization and we need common vision and values.*

*To repeat: Conflict is the reality that accompanies change. We want it to be constructive. For that we need the right culture. For that we need mature people, the right process of decision making, the right organizational structure, and common vision and values.*

*I am especially intrigued by the process of converting the destructive energy created by conflict into constructive energy. The $64,000 question is how do you create such a culture?*

Let us discuss that next.

# HOW TO CONVERT COMMITTEE WORK INTO TEAMWORK

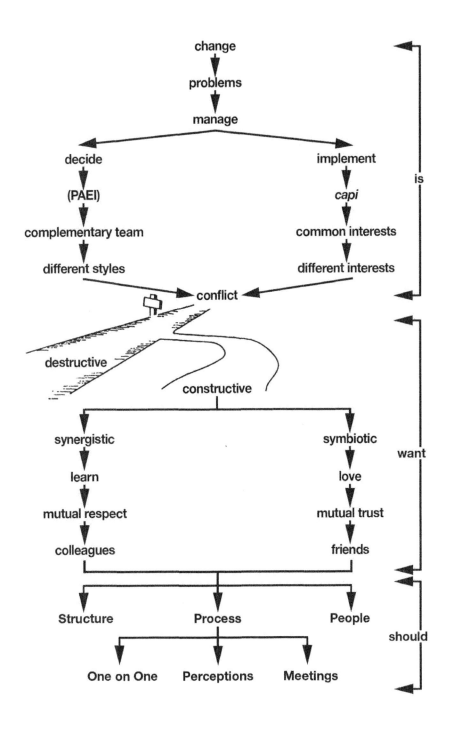

# CONVERSATION 15
# The Adizes Program for Organizational Transformation

## Introduction to Systemic Organizational Therapy (Transformation)

Mutual Trust and Respect can predict whether a company, or for that matter, any system, will be successful, in any way you might want to define success.

*Sounds intriguing.*

$$\text{Success} = f \left\{ \frac{\text{External Integration}}{\text{Internal DISintegration}} \right\}$$

*I remember you did mention this earlier, but please explain it again.*

No system operates in a vacuum. It operates in an environment that interacts with it, impacts it, and is impacted by it.

To be externally integrated means to have a functionally beneficial interdependence. For a company it is measured by market share, by repeated sales.

How does a company integrate externally? It does strategic planning and marketing planning. The common denominator in this effort is to analyze the changing opportunities "out there" and try to match organizational capabilities to those opportunities, preferably better than the competition can.

In personal life, external integration is often called career planning, and the process is the same: What am I good at, what are the opportunities "out there," and how do I match my capabilities to those opportunities?

> **Match capabilities to opportunities, preferably better than the competition can.**

On a macro level, external integration is called economic policy, trade policy, or industrial policy, and is measured by a country's trade balance.

Internal DISintegration is measured by wasted energy. One way to understand it is with an analogy. If you are trained as a mechanical engineer you learn to design a machine with minimal moving parts. The more moving parts, the more chances for wear and tear. Thus, the machine should be designed with maximum pressure and minimum friction. Friction wastes energy that could be used for activating the machine.

We know from physics that at any point in time energy is fixed. What I have discovered is that, within organizations, this fixed energy is allocated in a predictable way. First it is dedicated to dealing with internal disintegration, and the remainder is then dedicated to external integration. Thus, all success is from the inside out, not from the outside in.

Too many companies believe the secret of success is in their strategic planning. Wrong. If they are falling apart internally, no strategic plan will be implemented. At least not quickly.

To minimize internal disintegration we need to build a culture of Mutual Trust and Respect. The Adizes program for organizational transformation is aimed at doing that: It aims to create and nurture a sustainable culture of minimum wasted energy inside the organization, and to build Mutual Trust and Respect.

We have discussed the four factors that determine whether there is Mutual Trust and Respect in a company.

> *They are: common vision and values, a (PAEI) diversified organizational structure, a collaborative decision-making process, and people who command and grant respect and trust.*

> *But how do you go about creating or making those four factors happen in a company, and why do you call it "Systemic Organizational Therapy?"*

It is systemic because it has predictable steps and a prescribed road map describing what to do when, with whom, and how. The Adizes program of eleven workshops, which we call phases, is designed to impact those four factors.

*Do you have proof that it works?*

Yes, I do. Companies produce exceptional financial results. Many of them receive awards for being the most well-managed company in their industry, etc.[41]

We are now starting to run questionnaires to measure morale, but we already have evidence that employee turnover has been reduced. Employees have been offered higher salaries to move to other companies and they have refused.

*What is the program?*

The first workshop is numbered zero because the therapy has not yet started. We just present the theory. We check that the values system, upon which this methodology is based, is acceptable to the company. Do not forget we are "selling" Mutual Trust and Respect. Some leaders do not care about company culture. They want fast results. We direct them to consulting companies that do that—fire, cut costs, etc. That is not what we do.

*Wait, are you against cutting costs?*

Not at all. But we do not cut fat. We convert fat into muscle. Instead of cutting costs, how about increasing revenues?

*Interesting. Go on, please.*

The therapy starts with phase one, called a Syndag™. The group we are working with, up to thirty people, learns how to auto-diagnose the problems of the organization.

*To discuss problems openly is quite a change. Do people open up?*

It is a well-regulated workshop. We teach them rules for how to handle the meeting, how to advance from defreeze to accumulate, deliberate, etc., in a respectful way, so that they learn from each other. They learn rules for Mutual Trust and Respect in this phase. From the beginning they learn the hard rules of who speaks, when, and how, and about coming on time to meetings.

---

[41] See Adizes I., *Conversations with CEOs: Adizes Methodology in Practice*. Santa Barbara, CA: The Adizes Institute Publications, 2015.

We do not talk about Mutual Trust and Respect after phase zero. From then on, all workshops are designed for the participants to learn experientially how to behave in a way that manifests trust and respect.

*And that works?*

Every workshop increases the burden, by introducing increasingly difficult subjects for respect and trust. It is like lifting weights.

In phase one, Syndag, they learn how to discuss and analyze their problems without destructive conflict.

*This is incredible. You mean to tell me you take, say, thirty top executives, put them in a room for three days to discuss company problems, and they do not kill each other? Instead they leave the three-day meeting with consensus on what the problems are, their causes, and what the plan of action should be?*

Yes. It took years to perfect the system. It works.

*I trust you, but to be honest, I would like to see this in action.*

We have records at the Institute of thousands of companies that have done it.

The second phase is to teach them how to solve problems. We pick low-hanging fruit first: simple problems from a subsystem, not systemic problems. For example, we'll address an inventory or collection problem, and teach the group how to compose capi and how to lead the process from accumulation to finalization, at the end of which there is a solution that they promptly implement.

*I see. They are building trust in their own capabilities.*

First they learned how to diagnose, then how to solve subsystem problems. The next phase is how to lead upwards.

*What does that mean?*

There are many, many courses in the world on how to lead subordinates. We focus on how to solve a problem when you are responsible, but the authority is somewhere above you in the organizational hierarchy. This phase teaches people to move problem solving to where the authority is, not where the responsibility is.

# THE ADIZES PROGRAM FOR ORGANIZATIONAL TRANSFORMATION – 273

Phases one, two, and three teach how to analyze and solve problems, coalescing capi downwards, sideways, and upwards. The organization is starting to build confidence. They see results. They can discuss problems without accusing each other, without a witch-hunt. They can solve problems as a team, not through the frustrating process of management by committee.

Now we are ready to address some systemic issues. Overall issues. In phase four we teach and practice how to define a corporate mission that is particular to the organization at that point in time.

> *But all companies have a mission. What is new here?*

Most mission statements I have seen are generic in nature and could apply to any organization at any time. For example, "Our mission is to satisfy our clients and our owners, and be responsible to society," or something similar.

> **We are proud of every client we lose.**

We want to know what the driving force for a particular company is at that specific point in time. It is usually driven by where they are on the lifecycle. The mission is how to move to the next desirable location on the lifecycle, towards Prime.[42]

Phase five is designing the organizational structure of responsibility following the (PAEI) roles. If we are going to have a complementary team we need to have a complementary structure in which the (PAEI) roles can be performed.

Phase six is to change the budgeting system to reflect the new structure.

Phases four, five, and six deal with the organizational architecture. Now that the capi group of the company is aligned with their mission, they have a structure to deliver that mission, and responsibilities and authority have been defined (in phases five and six), we move to transfer the Adizes technology to the company. We train and certify Adizes change leaders in the company, and they then cascade the Adizes program throughout the company. We provide the help desk, the manuals, the training, and professional supervision.

Our goal is to eventually free the client from our intervention. They should know how to maintain the culture of Mutual Trust and Respect, how to make decisions as a team, how to define their mission annually, and how to restructure the company as needed, without outside help.

In other words we are proud of every client we lose.

---

42  See Adizes, *Managing Corporate Lifecycles*, op. cit.

*What? Are you a nonprofit organization?*

We are for-profit, and we are profitable, but that is not our goal. We are like therapists: Our goal is to have the client be healthy. Just imagine a psychologist who is very proud to have a patient for life. Where is the healing?

Once the trained group knows how to diagnose problems and solve problems as a team, now that each person clearly knows his role in the organizational structure and has the authority to dispense his responsibility, the next phase is to teach them how to stretch the organization to peak performance. Now the whole organization cooperates and stretches to be the best it can be.

In phase nine, we teach them, as a team, how to do strategic planning.

*Why is strategic planning so late? Is it not a crucial component of organizational transformation, or what you call therapy?*

What use is it to do strategic planning if there is no Mutual Trust and Respect? If people are fighting and they cannot solve simple problems, how are they going to implement strategic disruptive changes?

We do strategic planning when the culture of cooperation and willingness to change has been established, and the company has stretched to its peak performance. Now strategic plans, strategic changes, have a raison d'être because the company has achieved its peak performance in its present form. Then we can discuss how to disrupt it for even better results.

*In other words, you first plow the land, and bring water and fertilizers, and only then, when the land is ready, do you plant the trees.*

Right on. What use is it to plant outstanding seeds in frozen ground? That is what many consulting firms do. The company is not culturally ready for change but they recommend it anyway.

*What are the remaining phases?*

Phase ten is to create parallel channels of management: top-down is for command and control of the implementation of decisions; bottom-up flow is for deciding what changes to make so the company is constantly changing.

Phase eleven, the last workshop, is to design a reward system that rewards cooperation and peak performance.

*Does the program end here?*

No, the eleven phases are for eleven months of the year. The goal is to do one phase per month, then rest for the month of December. Come January, it starts all over again: new diagnosis, new Syndag, new problem solving, etc.

*So the company is constantly changing. Right?*

Exactly. In delivering those eleven phases the company develops common vision and values, designs and implements an organizational structure that delivers the (PAEI) roles, is correctly decentralized, learns how to make decisions as a team, and, as a result of the program, a culture of MT&R has been established. People change and start behaving with MT&R, and energy that was stuck in internal fights is emancipated to fight competition.

*What about those who do not change, who cannot work in a team?*

They leave, and that is fine. We do not want individual geniuses—arrogant, self-centered, autocratic leaders—anyway.

*This was a tour de force—lots of new information.*

This was just the beginning. Now you should really start studying.

*What book would you recommend I read next?*

First, I would recommend that you read *The Ideal Executive: Why You Cannot Be One and What to Do About It*. Next, read *Managing Corporate Lifecycles: How Organizations Grow, Age, and Die*. Then, if you want to continue your studies, read *Management and Mismanagement Styles,* followed by *Leading the Leaders*.

If you still have interest, the companion book to *Managing Corporate Lifecycles* is *Pursuit of Prime*.

However, this is my strongest recommendation: Whenever you finish reading, read this book again. Having read the end, you will better understand the beginning.

*I will! Thank you for your time.*

Thank you for asking me to share my knowledge. What use is it to have knowledge if it is not shared?

*Goodbye.*

Goodbye, my friend.

# About the Adizes Institute

For the past forty years, the Adizes Institute has been committed to equipping visionary leaders, management teams, and agents of change to become champions of their industries and markets. These leaders have successfully established a collaborative organizational culture by using Adizes' pragmatic tools and concepts to achieve peak performance.

Adizes specializes in guiding leaders of organizations (CEOs, top management teams, boards, owners) to quickly and effectively resolve such issues as:

- Difficulties in executing good decisions.
- Making the transition from entrepreneurship to professional management.
- Difficulties in aligning the structure of the organization to achieve its strategic intent.
- Bureaucratizing—the organization is getting out of touch with its markets and beginning to lose entrepreneurial vitality.
- Conflicts among founders, owners, board members, partners, and family members.
- Internal management team conflicts and "politics" severe enough to inhibit the success of the business.
- Growing pains.
- Culture clashes between companies undergoing mergers or acquisitions.

Adizes also offers comprehensive training and certification for change leaders who wish to incorporate into their practice the Adizes Methodologies for managing change.

Adizes is the primary sponsor of the Adizes Graduate School, a non-profit teaching organization that offers Master's and Ph.D. programs for the Study of Leadership and Change.

For more information about these and other programs, please visit www.adizes.com.

Printed by BoD in Norderstedt, Germany